Voices in the Wind

A Waterton - Glacier Anthology

Edited by

Barbara Grinder
Valerie Haig-Brown and **Kevin Van Tighem**

Waterton Natural History Association

Published in Canada by
The Waterton Natural History Association
Box 145, Waterton Park, Alberta, T0K 2M0

Canadian Cataloguing in Publication Data
Voices in the Wind

ISBN 0-920457-10-X

1. Waterton-Glacier International Peace Park (Alta. and Mont.)
2. Waterton Lakes National Park (Alta.) 3. Glacier National Park (Mont.)
I. Grinder, Barbara, 1940- II. Haig-Brown, Valerie, 1936-
III. Van Tighem, Kevin, 1952- IV. Waterton Natural History Association.
FC3664.W38V64 2000   971.23'4   C00-910281-7
F1079.W3V64 2000

Book Design: Barbara Grinder
Front Cover Photograph: Jim Mepham
Back Cover Photograph: Dave Butler

Printed in Canada by Friesens Book Division

Contents

Preface

This is a book about a very special place that I have come to know and love late in my life, about some of the people who helped shape that place, and some of the people who now write about it. It's a book about southwestern Alberta and north central Montana, the region around the Waterton-Glacier International Peace Park, as well as the parks themselves.

My husband and I moved to Hill Spring, Alberta in November, 1988, on a day so warm and bright we would have a picnic lunch in our new backyard while we moved the furniture in. Chief Mountain was shining in the sun, seeming close enough for an easy stroll. A mild chinook was blowing, a precursor of stronger winds to come. Sparrows were chirping in the cottonwoods and flocks of geese flew overhead on a regular basis.

Hill Spring seemed a pleasant little village, with a strong sense of community and friendly people. It's only a short drive from Waterton, and a slightly longer drive to Glacier National Park in Montana. Three and a half years later those parks would come to be an intimate part of our lives, not just places to visit.

We published the first issue of the *Waterton-Glacier Views* in May 1992, the start of a period when we would alternately boast and curse at having the longest, most beautiful paper route in the world. For three years, from mid-May to mid-September, we made weekly trips from Hill Spring, where I wrote, edited and laid out the paper, to Lethbridge, where the paper was printed, to Fort Macleod, the Crowsnest Pass, Pincher Creek, Waterton, Cardston, Babb, St. Mary, Browning, East Glacier, Essex, West Glacier, Columbia Falls, Kalispell and Bigfork, the places where we distributed the paper and got the stories to fill its pages.

The year we sold the paper, 1995, was also the year Waterton Lakes National Park celebrated its centennial as a protected place. I had met and become friends with Kevin Van Tighem in the course of my work on the *Views*, and somehow we both came up with the idea of commemorating the park's 100th anniversary by putting together a small workshop for people who, like ourselves, write about the natural world. The plan was to hold the workshop in September, when the crowds were gone from the hiking trails, the trees had turned to gold, and the park's wildlife was preparing for winter. We would invite a few of the West's best writers, editors and publishers - from both sides of the border - to be guest speakers, and organize a day of field trips to introduce the participants to the joys of the Peace Park region, as well as the conservation challenges it faces. Participants could thus get tips on how to improve their writing and marketing abilities, and story ideas, so they could put those tips to work and perhaps sell a story that would help them earn back the cost of coming to the workshop in the first place.

The workshop would be a place to network and share ideas on why we write, how we write and what we write about. More importantly, it would be a place where those of us who write about the parks and other protected places could talk openly and honestly about the ways our writing impacted on those places.

Then we presented the plan to the powers that be - fortunately to their approval and support. That first workshop was a success and two more successful events have followed, in 1997 and 1999. This book is an outgrowth of the 1999 workshop. Like the workshop itself, it began as a collaboration between Kevin and myself to celebrate the year 2000, to spotlight the Writers Workshop and raise funds to support it. Valerie Haig-Brown, another writer/editor friend who lives near the park and a participant at all three workshops, agreed to help with the editing. The Waterton Natural History Association agreed to publish the book. And the wonderful writers, photographers and cartoonist whose work graces these pages kindly donated their talents and their material to the project.

All the work that appears on the following pages was produced by people who have participated in the workshops. Some of the material has seen the light of day before, in some version, in newspapers, magazines and books. Some is being published here for the first time. We hope the voices of our contributors enlighten you and touch you, and give you a deeper understanding of this special place we call home.

Barbara Grinder
February 2000

This Place, These People

Wallace Stegner once wrote that he was "shaped by the West," having lived most of his life in it. For Stegner, the vastness and magnificence of the Western landscape were powerful forces which formed his personal interests and imagination, as well as shaped the people around him - the social and cultural milieu of the land in which he was raised.

Though all places can put their mark on the people who relate to them - there are, after all, both city mice and country mice - wild landscapes, like Waterton and Glacier, seem to influence people more than most. In turn people also put their mark on these places.

This mutual relationship between the land and its people is perhaps best evident in the life and writing of Andy Russell, who has lived most of his years in these parts and has shared his vision of wild places and the creatures in them with countless readers.

In "Taking Time to Look" Andy writes about the way the Rocky Mountain landscape formed and the ways it continues to be a formative influence on his relationship with the natural world. Jack Christie and Barbara Stevenson have only recently visited the Peace Park, but have also been affected by what they found. Jack writes about the formation of the Peace Park concept, and Barbara about the parks' status as a World Heritage Site. In "Through the Looking Glass" Barb Grinder tells us a bit about one of the roads she loves to travel.

The people who created the rock art along the Milk River, hundreds, perhaps thousands of years ago, and the people who ran the ranches which were such a significant part of the region's more recent history, were all affected by the geography around them, albeit in different ways. In "Written in Stone" Tom Cameron describes his personal and professional experiences at Writing-on-Stone Provincial Park, about 100 miles east of Waterton - Glacier, but tied to the parks through a shared aboriginal history. Holly Quan tells us about the Bar U Ranch and the people who ran it, and sheds light on the ranching history of the entire region.

Joyce Hildebrand and Joanne Helmer are concerned in their articles with the people who populate the region today, especially the men and women who seek to protect the wonderful, fragile environment of this special place.

Beargrass in Glacier National Park. **Photo by Jim Mepham**

Taking Time to Look

by Andy Russell

Each day in the mountains has its moment of magic. It may come in the evening when the setting sun caresses the tops of the peaks with warm rays of light and colour as though bidding them good night. It might be the opening of the petals of a mountain flower, welcoming the sensuous probings of a furry bumblebee. It may be the sight of a thunderhead's towering column, its mass like carved ivory against the deep blue of the sky as it builds itself on the thermals to a height of miles. It leaves its lasting impression as one stands beside a murmuring river under a canopy of a million stars, the infinite depths of the universe framing the peaks on every side. These are the moments of witchery experienced by those who live with senses tuned, seeing, hearing, smelling and feeling the ever changing expressions of the mountains. One understands then that time alone limits the knowledge to be gained and the discoveries to be made of nature's mysteries.

For to be sure it takes time to develop appreciation, understanding and love. Unfortunately most of us are in too much of a hurry trailing something called security to realize the benefits and gratifications nature bestows on those who side with her. We spread ourselves thin and travel the world's pathways at a frantic pace, yet often we fail to catch up with the happiness so avidly pursued. We encumber ourselves with possessions to the point of paralysis. We create ugly scars by tearing what we want from the good earth. We do not see that the earth would gladly give us much more if only we cared enough to be gentle and to take more time.

To contemplate one of the great peaks of the Rockies and perceive only a massive, shapeless rock is to be blind to the fascinating history that is written in its strata. Two billion years ago the continent of North America was being born. It was a slow and stormy process with the land's general outline taking form in a great ocean's watery womb. The climate fluctuated from one extreme to another. Occasional floods inundated exposed silt flats. Roaring rivers flowed down from the heights of land, tearing loose vast quantities of pulverized rock and building deltas. There was no hint of the Rockies then, only the rough-edged Pre-Cambrian Shield and a few ridges and isolated mountains standing in the faces of the floods. Each of the watery upheavals deposited a layer of silt; ripple marks and mud cracks of some old beaches are still perfectly preserved in the sedimentary rock, hardened by the pressure of its own weight.

Slowly but surely the land began winning the war with the water, lifting and assuming a distinct outline. By observing the signs left in the vast layers of rock we can piece together the story written by nature over the ages. Geologists are not in complete agreement on the age of the Rocky Mountains. But regardless of the length of time taken for them to rise up in jagged outline against the sky, the reason for their appearance is plain enough.

They are the result of a crumpling of the sedimentary layers covering North America, a process known in geological parlance as plate tectonics. An eastward thrust produced an effect comparable to that of pushing piecrust across a rough tabletop. Friction causes the piecrust to wrinkle, bulge and fold back on itself to take a vastly different shape. The earth's crust heaved, folded and faulted itself into ridges and peaks. And lo, we had the Rocky Mountains.

Eighty five million years ago the rock of the Waterton area began faulting; the forces at work gigantic and cataclysmic. Great ridges were pushed up, sections collapsed, and formations even overturned.

The valley of the north fork of the Flathead River in southeast British Columbia shows evidence of such overturned strata in its outcrops. Mighty overthrusts were created when the earth's crust heaved, broke and slid for miles over the surface. One of these stands paramount — the Great Lewis Overthrust, with Chief Mountain projecting above the prairies at its tip, near the international boundary on the east side of Waterton-Glacier International Peace Park. The limestone of this mountain has moved an estimated 22 miles from its original bed. In many places the whole crust is thus lapped, such that if a drill were to pass through the formations of a mountain peak from top to bottom, it might end at precisely the same formation in which it started. Many craggy mountain faces expose in cross section millions of years of earth history.

Between 2.3 billion and 1.9 billion years ago, the only life on earth was aquatic — the simplest and most primitive one-celled variety. But it was abundant life. The lime produced by trillions of these tiny organisms makes up the bulk of the world's limestone, including the great Rocky Mountain limestone formations found today north of Crowsnest Pass. South of the pass in the Waterton area pure limestone formations are rare, for here most of the sedimentary rock is colourful argillite, a slate that sports every hue in the rainbow.

Gradually some living things left the water for the land. Life was becoming more diversified and complex, and almost every creature left signs of its passing. Between the Jurassic Period, 208 million years ago, and the end of the Cretaceous Period, about 66 million years ago, exotic jungles flourished amid steamy swamps in a tropical climate that was incredibly productive. Vegetation was so heavy and lush that vast quantities of it accumulated — the beginnings of our present-day coal deposits. It was the age of the great reptiles, when dinosaurs and other exotic creatures, large and small, abounded in the marshes and jungles. In the only major gap in today's Rockies between the 49th parallel and the Yukon, where the Peace River breaks through in a corridor about five kilometres wide, dinosaur tracks have been found perfectly preserved in the solid rock that was once a mud flat on the edge of a swamp. (Before any real study could be made of their significance, the whole valley was flooded by a power dam constructed across the river. Few people cared then, but some day, when the dam lies obsolete, the Peace may flow free again and the story of the dinosaurs will be revealed once more.)

By the end of the Tertiary Period, roughly two million years ago, North America had won its most recent battle with the sea. The continent had assumed its present shape and fertile grasslands predominated. The big reptiles had disappeared and their numbers been replaced by herds of mammals. These ranged in size from four-toed horses and camels not much larger than jack-rabbits to massive creatures — great hairy mammoths with enormous tusks and, among many others, the brontotherium, an animal constructed along the lines of a rhinoceros with a blunt, forked horn on its nose. There were sloth bears, saber-toothed tigers and giant bison in this colossal circus of strange and mighty animals. All went the way of the dinosaurs. The fleet little horses disappeared, but their larger descendants eventually returned with the Spanish explorers.

Meanwhile, the Rockies had reared their heads to their present height, now craggy and sharp-edged — a vast, tumbled mountain chain flanked by minor ranges all the way across what is now British Columbia to the Pacific coast. The climate continued to cool, heralding the coming of the ice ages.

At least four distinct glacial buildups inundated the Waterton area. Now the mountains stood with only the white crests of their peaks showing above a vast sea of glittering ice. The ice plowed its way southward slowly and relentlessly, smoothing the contours of the country as it went. Ice carved the mountain gorges into U-shaped formations, changing the sharply defined V-shapes of water-eroded valleys.

When the great cold spell ended, about 12,000 years ago, the climate turned milder and the glaciers finally retreated; the work of the ice was revealed. The meltwater lifted the levels of the oceans, flooding the land bridge that joined the continents between Siberia and Alaska and leaving only the tops of the mountains exposed in the Aleutian Island chain. The features of the Rocky Mountains were less harsh and the valleys between them much wider. Today fragmented jewels of ice still hang in the high basins and large glaciers still choke the heads of some of the valleys. The rivers wind down from these in braided channels, and the plow marks of the ice still show as scars on the slopes above the valleys.

On a September day we stand in the timberline basin at the head of the north fork of Kintla Creek in the extreme southeast corner of British Columbia and marvel. For here the country seems to have only recently emerged from the ice, as indeed it has, for the creek still wanders across flat pans of exposed rock unconfined by the channels and canyons that it will cut for itself as time proceeds. In the middle of the valley, amid groves of feathery green alpine larches, stands the Nunatak, a rock edifice 900 feet in height, carved and shaped by the abrasive action of Pleistocene glaciers.

A few hundred yards up the creek lies an exposed limestone reef. It is composed almost entirely of hundreds upon hundreds of stromatolites, dome-like fossilized colonies of blue-green, photosynthesizing bacteria that had been growing in intertidal pools since multi-celled life first emerged. A modern variety still grows in the tide pools of the Great Barrier Reef off the coast of Australia.

This valley is a continuing delight — not only a pristine and remote wilderness, but a track-reader's garden of Eden. One can view the signs left by living things that flourished in the very beginning, the marks of more recent ice and the fresh hoof and paw prints of animals that evolved after the time of the giant bison, sloth bear and mammoth.

I found a stromatolite that had been split lengthwise by frost, lying in the lush green alpine growth, its cabbage-like layers exposed in detail. Within sight, a few yards away in the damp sand by the creek, a big grizzly track showed so fresh that particles of sand along its sharply defined edges were falling into the depression. It was a rare opportunity to observe the evidence of two living things thriving in the same area but separated by millions of years — a link written in stone and sand, illustrating the vastness and insignificance of time. Who are we, that we should be in such a rush?

As though possessed by devils, we pursue those trappings of material wealth we think important. We worry, rip and tear in our frantic accumulation of things. Yet as I stood there pondering the fossil and the bear's paw print I wondered if nature would not contrive, over the millennia, to soften and hide the scars we created, to heal these wounds when man, as unable to cope with change as the mammoth and sloth bear, would disappear. But unlike them, would man be the victim of changes wrought by his own waste?

My companions and I shouldered our packs and headed up toward the top of the pass. As we neared its summit, the unfolding vista of mountains beyond revealed the massive Kinnerly and Kintla peaks to the south, both over 10,000 feet above sea level. Trapped in a hanging basin between lies Kintla Glacier, just a mile or two as the raven flies beyond the international boundary in Glacier National Park, Montana. But our path did not lie in that direction.

Turning, we climbed west up the steep flanks of Goat Ridge. The footing was bad here, with the loose, weathered rock sliding and rolling under our boots at every step. But as we approached the knife-edge of the ridge top, a goat trail materialized out of nowhere, as goat trails are inclined to do in such country. It offered us better footing along the way we wanted to go — toward a secret pass artfully hidden on the spine of the ridge. Years before I had discovered the pass from the far side, by following the other end of the same trail. It led across the coarse scree of Ptarmigan Basin, disappearing as if by magic at the foot of a thousand-foot vertical cliff that seemed absolutely impassable to anything on two legs or four. Yet when I reached the cliff a ledge made its appearance by sheer sorcery, illuminated by the light striking the pitch of the mountain face at precisely the proper angle. The ledge sloped diagonally up the cliff so gently and easily that with a bit of patience and effort one could push a wheelbarrow up to the top of the ridge. There the goat trail takes a step up about three feet and goes through a narrow slice in the solid rock barely wide enough to accommodate a man.

As we reached the ridge this day from the opposite direction, the sun broke through the clouds to light up a vast panorama of peaks in every direction. Behind us lay the tumbled reaches traversed in the last two days, backed by the wild, high mountains of northern Glacier Park. To our left, the steep-pitched flank of little King Edward Glacier clung to the north face of Long Knife Peak, the only remaining piece of old ice left in this stretch of the Rockies south of Mount Assiniboine. To our right and below us, bisected by the ledge, was the Painted Cliff.

Its name is self explanatory, for it is a mass of brilliant colour — contrived by the growth of rock lichen — a multitude of hues ranging from black to brilliant fire orange through red, blue, brown and all shades between. They are not soft pastels for the most part, but gaudy pigments splashed lavishly on the rock face in a design that defies description. It is indeed a rock painting, acres in extent. Let those who think man invented what we call 'modern art' take a look at it, and they will quickly realize that nature has been an impressionist painter for thousands of years.

Lichen multiplies itself by spores only millionths of an inch in diameter. It evolved through a kind of marriage between fungus and algae; the fungus provides a home out of water for the algae, and the algae provide food that the fungus needs to survive. One of the most primitive organisms to be found in the mountains, lichen is the first to appear on barren ground. Slow growing, it may take hundreds of years to spread itself over one square inch of rock surface.

As we paused there, we wondered when it had taken residence in this place and were again confronted by the inconsequence of time as measured by the life span of man. When the ice retreated, leaving the Rockies freshly scoured and sterile, this was a spot where nature's gentle caress first brushed the face of the mountains to restore life among the peaks.

Excerpt from **The Rockies**, *by Andy Russell.*

Andy Russell *is one of Canada's best-known writers on outdoor subjects. His many books include Grizzly Country, Life of a River and Memoirs of a Mountain Man. He has been a trapper, cowboy, trail guide, hunter, film-maker and acclaimed lecturer, and has lived most of his 85 years high on a ridge overlooking Waterton Park. His most recent book, Campfire Stories, was published in 1998. Andy has participated in all three Writers Workshops.*

KEW

One of the questions park naturalists are asked most by visitors from away, is where do the glaciers come from. The Peace Park glacier retreat is a spectacular event that takes place annually, except during leap years when there is no migration, just a lot of rumbling. The glaciers travel down from the polar regions, leaving the north in mid-November, passing through Waterton, and finally reaching Glacier National Park in April. There is no danger to visitors as signs are posted at all glacier crossings. However, grizzlies may hide among the ice, hoping to pounce on unsuspecting people and eat them, to augment their diets when they come out of hibernation.

Donald Kew *grew up in southern Alberta and attended art school in Edmonton. His cartoons and caricatures have been appearing in the Edmonton Sun since 1985, and he produces editorial cartoons for a string of weeklies. He publishes his own tabloid newspaper, the Nisku Wildcatter, and has put out two books of his cartoons and irreverent humor. About 2000 of Don's cartoons were accepted for the Provincial Archives collection and 250 for Canada's National Archives. Don was a participant at the 1997 Writers Workshop.*

World Class Heritage

by Barbara Stevenson

I confess I'm not much of a traveller. Other than the obligatory backpacker's tour of Europe in my youth — and infrequent winter vacations in the Caribbean in the years in between — I stick pretty close to home. This past September, however, I received an offer too good to refuse. The Waterton Glacier International Writers Workshop invited me to be a guest speaker. In return for giving workshop participants some editorial tips on writing for magazines, I would get to visit a World Heritage Site.

Alberta's Waterton Lakes National Park, together with Montana's Glacier National Park, form the world's first International Peace Park. This UNESCO World Heritage Site is visual proof — if any is needed — that there are no borders in nature. The same spectacular mountain ranges grace both sites, the same species make their home within the two parks' boundaries, the same problems confront their superintendents....

Even when the ecosystems are markedly different, the challenges confronting these areas of "unique worldwide value" can be remarkably similar. Industrial activities such as mining and logging are of concern in

World Heritage Sites as far apart as the Amazon rainforest and the Yukon's Nahanni National Park Reserve. Ranchers adjacent to two other sites — Yellowstone National Park in the U.S. and Wood Buffalo National Park in Canada — echo each other's call for the eradication of diseased bison herds within the parks.

Ironically, the fact that many of these world-class natural areas share the same problems could be cause for hope. At Waterton-Glacier International Peace Park, personnel on both sides of the border work together to protect their mutually shared ecosystem. Perhaps, one day, that cooperative approach will be applied to all World Heritage Sites.

Currently, seven of Canada's nine national parks that are within World Heritage Sites report significant impacts from mining on adjacent lands. According to the World Conservation Union, that is a trend that is growing at sites around the world. As one of the countries in the forefront of developing and adopting the World Heritage Convention, wouldn't it be fitting if Canada took the lead in finding ways to design mining projects that didn't imperil the planet's irreplaceable natural heritage? That would be a global initiative truly worthy of a new millennium.

Originally published as the editorial of the winter 2000 issue of Nature Canada, the quarterly publication of the Canadian Nature Federation.

Barbara Stevenson *is the editor of Nature Canada magazine and the director of communications for the Ottawa, Ontario based Canadian Nature Federation. She was formerly the editorial director at Deneau Publishers, a trade book house specializing in contemporary Canadian history and politics.*

"Do not follow where the path may lead.
Go instead where there is no path and leave a trail."
Muriel Strode

Currents of Peace

by Jack Christie

Waterton-Glacier International Peace Park straddles the southwestern corner of Alberta and northern Montana. Here, as they say, the mountains meet the prairie. For the past 67 years, the parks have served as a model of peaceful cooperation. Inspiration comes from Upper Waterton Lake, an elongated, turquoise-hued jewel cradled between the jagged peaks here in the crown of the Rocky Mountains. The 49th parallel runs right through its heart.

A bit of background: Waterton Lakes, which at first was called Kootenay Lakes Forest Park, was established in 1895 as Canada's fourth national park, after Banff, Jasper and Yoho. Glacier National Park, its American counterpart, is nine times as large and was created 15 years later. In 1995, the United Nation's agency UNESCO awarded the International Peace Park World Heritage Site status. That's akin to receiving the Nobel Prize for parks.

The Peace Park designation can be attributed to Rotary International, a community-based service group whose pledge is, " In the name of God we will not take up arms against each other." Rotarians have a long history of involvement with both Waterton Lakes and Glacier national parks. In 1931 Alberta and Montana Rotarians unanimously approved a motion to lobby for the establishment of an International Peace Park at Waterton/

Glacier. Their efforts struck an immediate, deep and responsive chord. In what surely must be record time, legislation approving the creation of the International Peace Park came from both the Canadian parliament and the American Congress the following spring.

These days, Rotary, with the backing of the two parks, is badgering both Canadian and American governments to cease maintaining a 12-metre-wide clearcut that marks the 49th parallel. Letting the swath that ribbons through the park grow back would go a long way toward being a visible example of joint cooperation and to advancing our understanding that nature does not recognize artificial boundaries.

Rotary is also lobbying for a joint interpretive centre to be established at Waterton-Glacier to spread the word of peace. At present, an open-air shelter, the Waterton-Glacier International Peace Park Pavilion, overlooks Upper Waterton Lake. A small obelisk stands beside the entrance, symbolically covered with animal footprints, with the words "May peace prevail on Earth." As you study it, deer graze unconcernedly nearby. Quotes from distinguished North Americans are displayed on the walls. The great Sioux leader Sitting Bull summed it up best when he said "The meat of the buffalo tastes the same on both sides of the border."

Over the past several years, delegations from many countries have come here to observe how these parks serve as a model for peaceful coexistence between neighbours. The Chinese asked for a list of what the parks are doing to get along so well, but no such list exists. Rather, Waterton and Glacier are like a family who share knowledge in an organic rather than an organized way. And while this may appear to be a somewhat haphazard approach, currents of deep peace borne of mutual self-respect flow silently beneath the surface. Now, if we can just green up that clearcut.

'Currents of Peace' was originally broadcast on CBC Radio One, in October 1999. A longer version also appeared in the Georgia Straight.

Jack Christie *began his career in 1975 as a writer-broadcaster with Vancouver Cooperative Radio, He later joined the CBC, where he now contributes a weekly, nationally-syndicated commentary, Beyond the Backyard. In 1986, he started writing an outdoors column for the Georgia Straight and three years later published his first travel guide, Day Trips from Vancouver. He has also written Whistler Outdoors Guide, One-Day Getaways from Vancouver, Day Trips with Kids, and Inside Out British Columbia. Jack participated in the 1999 Workshop.*

Through the Looking Glass

by Barbara Grinder

Though the west side of Glacier National Park gets the most visitors, and is certainly beautiful, I've always favored the east side of the park. I like its melding of prairie and mountain, the many pothole lakes, the incredible array of wildflowers, and its history, that seems to live on in its landscape and its people.

It is true, however, that the communities aren't as upscale as those on the west side, the coffee (with the exception of Richard Mataisz' wonderful brews at Mountain Chief Trading Post) isn't as good, and the roads aren't as easy to drive.

The area's most scenic, most historic, and most controversial byway has to be the Looking Glass Road. Officially known as Highway 49, it skirts the eastern front of the mountains just outside the boundaries of Glacier National Park, between East Glacier and Kiowa Junction. Its southern end affords magnificent vistas of the Two Medicine area, with mirror images of snow-capped peaks reflected in still waters. Its northern end curves around so much topography and is so crooked, that you can almost see yourself going, when you're still coming.

Mirror image, along the Looking Glass Road.   **Photo by Barb Grinder**

Historically, the journey traces the ancient North Trail, used by aboriginal people to travel up and down the 'backbone of the world.' In places, you can still discern the ruts worn into the ground by dog travois crossing the ancient grasses.

More recently, the Looking Glass Road has been the subject of a wrangle between local businesses, the State of Montana, and the U.S. government to keep the road open and maintained. The federal government built the road and was given authority over it in the late twenties; a jurisdiction later repealed. In the last decades, the road has been left to local governments to care for. One year, it remained closed completely because so many repairs were needed, it was unsafe.

Though beautiful, it's a scary road to travel. No shoulders, a deep abyss on the west side, unstable hillsides that wash onto the road on the east; wonderful things to see, but no safe places to pull over and see them. If you've a tendency to car sickness or you don't like heights - avoid it. If you worry about getting stuck in out-of-the-way locations - avoid it. If you come in the off-season - you have to avoid it because it's closed. But take a drive on the Looking Glass Road if you like adventure, beautiful scenery and a chance to imagine yourself following the moccasin steps of an earlier people.

A longer version of this article appeared in the Waterton Glacier Views.

Written in Stone

by Tom Cameron

Perhaps it's for the best that Writing-On-Stone remains largely unknown. This might be the only way to maintain the intrinsic value of this almost magical place in Alberta's Milk River Valley.

Writing-on-Stone Provincial Park protects the largest concentration of rock art on the northwest Great Plains. It offers an opportunity to experience a sacred site in almost pristine condition, thanks to its long-way-from-anywhere location. The merits of the park result from the unique combination of cultural, ecological and recreational values. The rock art itself and the ecology of the Milk River Valley are truly remarkable. A walk on the interpretive trails and a visit to the reconstructed North West Mounted Police Post are rewarding. The rodeo grounds in the park are part of the local tradition. Writing-on-Stone is a sacred place of international significance and as important to the understanding of human history and culture as the oracular spring at Delphi or the Rosetta Stone.

As the crow flies, the park is about 160 kilometres from Waterton Lakes National Park. The Sweetgrass Hills, just south of Writing-On-Stone, are halfway between the front range of the Rocky Mountains and the Cypress Hills that straddle the Alberta-Saskatchewan border. Here the Milk River Valley is incised into a treeless plain. Coming over the lip of the valley the visitor finds a surprise of scrolling river and terraces, sandstone cliffs and hoodoos, and the dense tree and shrub communities of prairie streams. Just to the north lies the Milk River Ridge, separating the Milk River, in the Mississippi watershed, from the Saskatchewan River which flows to Hudson Bay.

If you plan to make the journey, be sure to commit several days for your visit and give the place time to work its magic. Visit the park once, then return again to experience the landscape in all its seasons. Researchers and others familiar with the rock art often comment on how the images appear and disappear with the changing light and weather.

I've been personally and professionally involved with Writing-On-Stone for a couple of decades and have come to know the full range of images that are scratched, carved, pecked, and painted on its rock faces. On a personal level, I remember lazy summer days in the park, walking the trails and tubing down the surprisingly swift river, seeing wonderful vistas and wildlife along the way. On one family camping trip we had a series of high adventures with quicksand, hypothermia, and rattlesnake encounters. We hiked south through Police Coulee to Signature Rock, where we scrambled out of the ravine to view the forested Sweetgrass Hills stretching across the horizon.

Once when I was working in the park, I drove with Rod Keith to the border-crossing town of Coutts, where we were to stay for the night. We were feeling our way south and west along backcountry roads and I was a little nervous about straying into the States by accident. Rod kept saying we were a long way from the Sweetgrass Hills and I kept saying I could see forests, then trees, then individual lodgepole pines, as we got closer and closer to the Hills. It was only when I pointed to a truck with Montana plates and a ranch house flying the Stars and Stripes, that Rod conceded we had strayed too far south.

I usually stayed in the town of Milk River when I was working in the park, but others preferred Coutts and the El Coyote Motel. The El Coyote was an old clapboard hotel that had seen better days. Its pub was a one-of-a kind museum of western memorabilia, with a simulated coal mine room, glass cases of artifacts, and an oscillating fan that at the end of its sweep would lift the tail of the stuffed fox on the wall. When I went to bed I made sure the window opened easily and I seriously considered knotting the sheets together and tying them onto the bedpost. That place was a firetrap. Years later I heard it had burned to the ground.

When I first joined Alberta Provincial Parks in the mid seventies, I was involved in the administration of research and collection permits and became immersed in the archaeological work at the park. Jim Keyser had just been contracted to do the first comprehensive inventory and recording of the rock art, tracing images onto polyethylene sheets. I later coordinated the photographic reduction of these unwieldy full size tracings to Mylar copies. We produced these as page-size prints so the recordings could be more easily studied by researchers and the general public. In 1979, I presented a paper on Writing-On-Stone to an international rock art symposium in Italy. It was exciting to be with the Alberta government in that time of big budgets and it's noteworthy that the resource inventory work done in those years serves as the basis for the current expansion of the protected areas system.

What can be said about the rock art itself? Is it art or narrative? Is it symbolic or realistic?

It's generally agreed that some of the more recent panels are narrative or biographical in nature. They tell stories of battles, horse-stealing raids and other feats of bravery. The earlier works are more ceremonial in content and style and have been associated with vision questing and the attainment of totems or power. Michael Klassen makes the case that the Blackfoot people probably had a continuous relationship with the site and says changes in the content and style of the rock art are related to the change from a pedestrian to an equestrian-based society. P.S. Barry proposes that mystical themes, symbolism and the artistic conventions of shamanism are key to understanding the images. Luc Bouchet-Bert claims the petroglyphs marked the boundary of the Blackfoot and served to deter trespassers. There are even extraterrestrial interpretations of the images. But as George Melnyk writes in *The Literary History of Alberta*, whatever interpretation we put on these images, the site and the environment are an integral part of the text.

It is perhaps surprising that bighorn sheep and grizzly bear are represented in the rock art at Writing-On-Stone. But we know that grizzlies originally roamed the plains before that habitat was invaded by the coming of the white man, and that both animals figured prominently in the culture and livelihood of the aboriginal people who lived here.

Jack Brink, of the Archaeological Survey of Alberta at the Provincial Museum in Edmonton, has long been associated with the interpretation of the rock art and archaeology of Writing-On-Stone. I visited him again recently and we discussed ways to record and protect the rock art, something that's currently much on his mind. The art is gradually disappearing as the rock weathers and Jack was excited about some new techniques for its preservation that would be both safe and non-intrusive. Ian Campbell at the University of Alberta has been studying methods of rock structure stabilization that are being field tested at Writing-On-Stone. Laser images, focused down to the individual grains of sand, could help us measure the rate of weathering.

A new silica solution called Conservare OH, seems able to penetrate the rock and strengthen the surface layer. Jack likens it to a Gore-Tex jacket, that breathes and is permeable to moisture from within, while keeping the effects of surface weathering to a minimum. But scientists must first know if the compound will affect the appearance of the rock and the ochre and charcoal surface pigments, and determine whether it will affect naturally-occurring rock lichen, or limit the use of sophisticated dating techniques, before it can actually be used.

For me, Writing-On-Stone has become a lodestar and a constant factor in my life. When I asked Jack about his personal beliefs, he told me he was a hard-core scientist and not a particularly spiritual person. He thinks most things are explainable if you study them enough. "But," he said, "Writing-On-Stone is the one place in the world that can make my hair stand on end. It's a magical and powerful landscape."

Tom Cameron is a conservation biologist managing a land trust program with the Alberta Sport, Recreation, Parks and Wildlife Foundation. For the last couple of years he has represented the Foundation as a member of the Prairie Conservation Forum, by means of which he has re-established connections with the conservation community in Southern Alberta. He has worked for the Province of Alberta since 1974, as a resource management planner with Alberta Provincial Parks, where he was involved in planning for Cypress Hills, Writing-On-Stone, Beauvais Lake and Kananaskis Provincial Parks. Tom was a participant in the 1997 and 1999 Writers Workshops.

Down on the Old Bar U

by Holly Quan

It's a nice drive from Calgary to the old Bar U Ranch.

First, you head west with the mountains in your face and the city disappearing behind you. Then turn south and roll through the foothills, past pothole lakes, thickets of poplar and pine, and plenty of open pasture. As the road takes you higher into dry, dusty landscape, tree cover becomes sparse and grassland prevails. Slide down through the village of Longview, then cross a bridge over Pekisko Creek and turn in at the brown Parks Canada sign that reads "Bar U Ranch National Historic Site."

You are in the heart of Alberta's ranching country, renowned for range-raised beef of the highest quality. From the 1880s onward there have been many great ranches in this region and the grand-daddy of them all was the Northwest Cattle Company, known widely by its brand: the Bar U.

In 1882, dreams of establishing a ranch fired the mind of one Fred Stinson, a young man from Quebec. Stinson was convinced he could make a fabulous profit raising cattle. Even though he'd never ventured west, he'd heard reports from others who had been to the foothills.

Nor was he alone in his ambitions. To encourage ranching and settlement in the west, the Canadian government in faraway Ottawa instituted a generous land lease policy. For just one cent per acre, a would-be rancher could lease up to 100,000 acres, for 21 years. The single caveat: within the first three years the leased land had to be stocked at the rate of one head for every ten acres.

Stinson convinced Sir Hugh Allan of Montréal to underwrite his proposal for a ranching operation. No stranger to financial risk, Sir Hugh had recently agreed to help finance the Canadian Pacific Railway - the CPR. With Allan's backing, in March 1882 Stinson leased 114,000 acres of rugged foothill country, sight unseen, and named his new enterprise The Northwest Cattle Company. He also registered his brand, a capital "U" with a horizontal bar above. Then he headed west to start his new life as a ranch manager.

His first stop was Chicago, where he bought 21 purebred Shorthorn bulls and hired Herb Millar to accompany the bulls to their new home in the foothills. Millar and his charges traveled by train, then by steamer up the Missouri to Fort Benton, Montana. From there, he drove the bulls north across the border to their new home.

Meanwhile Stinson had arrived in the foothills to find that his holdings included the shallow valley of Pekisko Creek, the Rockies rising ten miles to the west — a perfect spot for his homestead. With the arrival of Millar and the Chicago bulls, the Northwest Cattle Company became a real operation. It was May, 1882.

To give his bulls female companionship, Stinson brought cows from Montana. He also hired Montana cowboys, including George Lane, an excellent manager and leader. By 1885, as lead hand at the Bar U, Lane was boss of Canada's largest-ever roundup, involving over 100 men, 500 horses and 50,000 head of cattle. Among Stinson's employees was Harry Longabaugh, *a.k.a.* the Sundance Kid, who had fled to Canada in 1889 and was hired by the Bar U to break horses.

Early ranching in southwestern Alberta was open range style; cattle roamed freely to graze on the native grasses and were only rounded up for branding and sale once each year. Thus the winter of 1887/88, with extremely cold temperatures and heavy snow, saw thousands of cattle starve and freeze to death. Many large ranches, including the Bar U, suffered substantial losses or went bankrupt. Stinson survived, but from 1888 onward he kept his weanling calves in corrals over the winter. Subsequent winter losses were less than on neighbouring ranches that didn't follow this practice.

By 1890 the Bar U was the third-largest ranch in the Canadian west, complete with its own post office and even a detachment of the North West Mounted Police. Then in 1893, under pressure from prospective farmers, the Canadian government cancelled the ranch leases. Leaseholders were allowed to purchase up to 10 percent of their holdings, so Stinson kept control of over 15,000 acres — still a sizable operation.

But further trouble was brewing back east. Long-standing differences between Stinson and his Montréal backers came to a head in 1901. Hearing rumors of discontent, George Lane — who had left Stinson's operation in 1891 — hurried to the Allan family and offered to buy the ranch. The Allans gave Lane three days to raise $250,000, the largest sale of any kind to that date in the Northwest. Lane and several partners found the cash and bought the Bar U from under Stinson's nose. Stinson, understandably bitter, moved to Mexico where he died in 1912.

George Lane now ran the show, and the glory days of the Bar U Ranch arrived. Lane expanded his operation by leasing land from the CPR. Then came the winter of 1906-07, renowned in Alberta as one of the fiercest on record. By spring Lane had lost 16,000 head.

After the devastating winter, Lane turned his attention to breeding Percheron horses, reasoning that local farmers would require draft animals. In 1909 he imported 72 mares and three stallions from France, at an average cost of $100 each, a fortune at the time. His horses were prizewinners throughout North America and Europe. By 1922 Lane had the world's largest herd of Percherons.

Despite a hard-nosed business attitude, Lane was also a prominent community figure. In the days of the Northwest Cattle Company, Lane and Stinson had been instrumental in establishing the Western Stock Grower's Association, a powerful cattlemen's lobby group that still functions in Alberta today. Lane also played a role in the first Calgary Stampede in 1912, by providing funding to Guy Weadick, an American cowboy and show promoter, for a "rodeo and cowboy extravaganza."

After the first World War, grain and cattle prices slumped, and local farmers were unable to afford the Bar U's prize Percherons. Lane died in 1925, no doubt due in part to financial worries and his hard-driving lifestyle. The Bar U remained leaderless till 1927, when Patrick Burns, perhaps the most famous cattleman in Alberta history, purchased the ranch.

Unlike Stinson and Lane, Pat Burns was not a cowboy, but a businessman and financier whose empire included ranches, farms, and meat-packing plants. His land holdings were so extensive that it was said he could ride from Calgary to the U.S. border without setting foot off his own properties. Burns lived in Calgary and left the management of the Bar U to foreman Herb Millar (the same man who brought Stinson's original 21 bulls from Chicago in 1882). They scaled down the Percheron breeding program that Lane had nurtured, concentrating once again on cattle. The days of open range ranching were long gone; in Burns' time the entire Bar U could operate with a permanent staff of four or five cowhands, thanks to the use of barbed wire fencing.

Pat Burns died in 1937 and his nephew John, along with a board of directors, took over the ranch ownership. The last major cattle drive occurred in 1950, when 2000 head branded with the famous Bar U were driven the 85 miles to Calgary. The proud tradition of this once enormous operation was far from finished though. Later that year Allen Baker bought the property, with 500 head of cattle, and went on to own the Bar U for 27 years, longer than anyone else. Subsequent owners were Lloyd Wambeke and Melvin Nelson, and today, the Canadian people.

In 1991 Parks Canada purchased 370 acres on Pekisko Creek, including the Bar U homestead, for the purpose of creating a National Historic Site. The Bar U is unique among the many huge ranches started in the 1880s, because even the very early structures built by Fred Stinson were in continuous use and are still standing. However, other than the 35 buildings which remain, there are few surviving artifacts. Parks Canada, along with The Friends of the Bar U (a fund-raising and community involvement group) are still scouring the region seeking period equipment, household items, tack and clothing.

The site's interpretive centre, which opened in July 1995, houses exhibits, a theatre, a restaurant, and a bookshop. Until the homestead's structures can be restored, visitors tour the site accompanied by a guide who explains the Bar U's history and the restoration taking place. Ultimately the Bar U National Historic Site will be a living museum with costumed guides, a working blacksmith and cowhands. Already in service is a wagon outfitted with seats and pulled by a team of black Percherons — descendants of George Lane's herd.

The Bar U National Historic Site is a living, touchable link to the visionary Fred Stinson, the tough and hard-driving George Lane, and the savvy businessman Patrick Burns. The fact that the homestead's buildings remain standing is also a tribute to the thrifty and practical nature of the ranchers who lived and worked the Bar U over the years — men who respected the old ways — then, now, and for the future.

'Down on the Old Bar U' originally appeared in the Spring 1999 issue of Old West magazine.

Holly Quan *has been a freelance writer for more than ten years, with interests ranging from food and wine to travel and the relationship of tourism to ecological protection in Banff and the mountain parks. Holly's work has appeared in such publications as Equinox, Reader's Digest, Northwest Traveler, and Canadian Airlines in-flight magazine. Her guide book Adventures in Nature: British Columbia, was published in spring 2000. Holly was a participant at the 1999 Writers Workshop.*

Ranching country, southern Alberta's foothills. **Photo by Barb Grinder**

Against the Grain

by Joyce Hildebrand

It began with an unusual wedding gift from Charlie Russell — a ton of organic fertilizer. But then, Keith and Bev Everts were an unusual couple. Vegetarians turned would-be beef producers, they were working for a rancher in southwestern Alberta through a three-year training program begun at the time of their marriage. They had a small piece of land on the ranch, and they seeded some oats with the wedding gift.

"That was our first exposure to the organic philosophy," says Keith, co-owner with Bev of Stillridge Ranch near Pincher Creek. The fruitfulness of that fertilizer exceeded expectations in many ways. Today Keith is president of Producers of the Diamond Willow Range, a corporation of seven ranching families who are committed to producing and marketing organic beef.

By the early 90s, the Everts family had been ranching sustainably for more than a decade and Keith was full-time managing partner of Ketaorati Ranches, owned by the Norman and Hilah Simmons family. The two families were approached by a group of students from the University of Calgary about participating in an environmental design project. In return for letting the students use the ranches as models of sustainability, the Everts and Simmons would get the results of the students' research into the organic beef market.

Through that market study it became apparent that several ranchers would be needed to supply organic beef to consumers year round. Bev and Keith asked the students to give their presentation on sustainable agriculture to a group of ranchers they thought might be interested in organic beef production. The spark flamed into life and in 1996 the Producers of the Diamond Willow Range was born. Their vision was to raise beef in harmony with the earth, and to increase awareness of the connection between what's on our plates and ecosystem health.

The corporation members agreed their product would be more acceptable to the consumer if it was formally approved by a certifying body, and chose the internationally recognized Organic Crop Improvement Association (OCIA) based in California. To achieve the stringent standards of the OCIA, Diamond Willow beef is produced without pesticides, chemical fertilizers, antibiotics, or growth hormones — all of which are normally used in the production of conventional beef. Genetically modified organisms are also outlawed by the OCIA. In July 1998, after three transitional chemical-free years, the Diamond Willow producers became fully certified.

The Diamond Willow ranchers keep meticulous computerized records so that the beef can be tracked from birth to the retail counter. The OCIA audits each ranch annually. Sick animals that must be treated with antibiotics are taken off the program and sold on the conventional market. To help prevent illness, Diamond Willow producers move their cattle frequently. Immediately after calving, for example, the cow and her calf are moved into a clean pasture on fresh straw to reduce infestation of scours, a calf diarrhoea often treated with antibiotics. If scours does occur and is detected early, it can be treated with a mixture of baking soda and salt.

Diamond Willow cattle spend their last three months in a feedlot owned by one of the members of the corporation. The cattle are kept in separate pens from conventionally-raised animals, and in less crowded conditions to reduce the chance of disease and stress. They are fed organic hormone-free barley, some of which is produced on one of the group's ranches. In conventional production, a growth hormone is normally added to the feed.

Diamond Willow producers don't stop with eliminating chemicals from their operations; like many conventional ranchers they also try to work in harmony with the ecosystem. "Instead of changing a creek for better availability of water," says Keith, "we do a brainstorming session asking how we can use what's there already, while having very low impact." They monitor pastures carefully to ensure continued health of the grassland and move cows regularly so that at least 60 per cent of the grass is left after grazing.

Another benefit of Diamond Willow beef is price stability. The retail price is slightly higher than that of conventional beef due to higher costs: organic beef takes longer to bring to market weight because no growth hormones are used. In addition, the record-keeping and marketing takes extra time; the cattle are processed separately and in lower numbers than other cattle in the feedlot and packing plant; and organic grain production results in somewhat lower yields and higher costs. But by dealing directly with the consumer and basing price on cost of production, the price fluctuations of the conventional market, especially at the producer level, are virtually eliminated.

"We're more than beef," declares a slogan of the Diamond Willow producers, who also advocate a holistic, environmentally sensitive way of life. Environmental education is "as much why we formed the coalition as to market our organic beef," says Bev. Raised in Toronto, she still has strong urban connections and is committed to helping build a much-needed bridge between urbanites and the land, through sustainable agriculture. So far, that bridge has taken the form of media interviews, brochures, videos, and posters in retail outlets.

All members of the coalition volunteer their time for consumer awareness efforts and marketing, amidst the heavy demands of ranch life. They are involved in off-ranch projects, from manure management in the Lethbridge area's "feedlot alley" to grassland projects in Peru.

Most of the members are also involved in the Southern Alberta Land Trust, which is establishing conservation easements on ranchland to prevent further fragmentation of the area through development.

"We have to start learning not to get involved in so many things," laughs Keith, while Bev pulls out a thick binder of minutes recording their long monthly meetings. To ease the burnout that could have set in after the initial excitement of forming the corporation, one of the members, Larry Frith, a local rancher and the chairman of the Waterton Biosphere Reserve Committee, was hired to coordinate the enterprise. The group is determined, however, not to become distanced from the consumer. "We still believe that it's important to maintain a real involvement and be sincerely behind our product," says Bev.

The future of Diamond Willow beef looks bright. In 1997, they produced about 400 animals. By January 2000, that number has almost doubled. Maximum production capability is about 2,000 animals per year. The market for Diamond Willow's product is also growing as awareness of health and environmental issues increases. Phone calls come in weekly from interested retailers, and the group is exploring overseas markets, especially in Japan where there is a strong lobby against genetically modified foods.

Organic ranching won't put the Diamond Willow corporation on the Fortune 500 list, but the Everts don't seem too concerned about that. "It's the lifestyle we've chosen," says Keith. "Our rewards are more than financial." One of those rewards is knowing that they are giving city-dwellers another way to show respect for the land that ultimately belongs to us all.

'Against the Grain' first appeared in the December 1997 issue of Encompass.

Joyce Hildebrand teaches linguistics in Calgary, while pursuing her interests in writing, editing, and environmental issues. She has written for Avenue magazine and has edited numerous books, articles and dissertations. Since 1993, she has worked as a production coordinator, writer, and assistant editor for the Wild Lands Advocate, the Alberta Wilderness Association's newsletter. Her participation in the Waterton-Glacier International Writers Workshop in 1997 led to an association with Encompass magazine, where she now writes "Showcase," a regular column which highlights the works of western Canadian artists and writers who have contributed to the protection of the environment. Joyce was a participant at the 1997 Writers Workshop.

Dedication Personified

by Joanne Helmer

"Hi. My name is Judy, and I'm an environmentalist."

That sombre admission — a variation on the opening statement for meetings of Alcoholics Anonymous — might well be used to introduce Judy Huntley in those corners of society where a genuine commitment to environmental protection is viewed with the same disapproval as a destructive personal addiction. Huntley herself laughs at the thought, but recognizes the similarities.

But she adds, social attitudes are shifting. An incredible change was apparent at a national conference on climate change she attended in 1999. The same older faces who have toiled away on these issues for years are being joined by "bright young people taking environmental studies at university who are knowledgeable, and dedicated, and very angry about the damage we've done to the environment," she said.

When Huntley and husband James Tweedie started their work in the field, environmental studies didn't even exist. Now 53, Huntley recently stepped down after 10 years as co-chair of Alberta's Environmental Network. She has also served as co-chair of the Canadian Environmental Network, and coordinator of the Bert Riggall Foundation, named after an early southern Alberta naturalist who pioneered trails in Waterton and whom Huntley describes as having been both "rejoicing and respectful of the natural world."

She joined the provincial and national organizations to learn how to be more effective at home, and found the work totally absorbing. Their networks link people all over the country so those who work on particular issues, like energy or atmospheric pollution or water or forestry, can get current information and learn how to apply it in their own local situations, Huntley says.

"It's most important when a small local group has to take on a megalith corporation or a provincial government," she says. "They're not totally alone, like a David fighting a Goliath, or isolated and forced to reinvent effective strategies. While there's rarely a chance for the people to meet in person because of costs, networks help their members share knowledge and analyse successes and failures. They ask questions such as 'What worked to stop Amoco from drilling in the Whaleback here and how can people in other parts of the country use that same technique?' "

She says the years of work, which she describes as the equivalent of a PhD in environmental studies, has enriched her life. "I'm now in contact with thousands of people across Canada who are taking significant actions in their lives to give Canada a better future. I know so many people whose lives I can deeply respect."

There's no doubt Huntley would also respect Montana resident, Phil Knight, a representative of the Native Forest Network's Last Refuge Campaign. Knight uses an economic approach to save wilderness, stressing the monetary benefits of working for the environment instead of against it. The municipalities with the healthiest, most diverse economies are those closest to protected areas, Knight says.

"Every county in Montana adjacent to wilderness is growing faster and has more diversity than those which aren't. They're not one-industry boom towns relying on non-renewable resource extraction. They have a chance of surviving economically."

Knight says the Montana counties benefit directly from tourists going through to the wildlands and from people who bring their wealth into the area permanently because of the lifestyle it offers. "Eco-tourism is a booming industry all around the world. We can judge our own future and our prospects for survival from the health of the forests."

Wildlands can provide long term economic sustainability, as well as clean air, clean water, wildlife habitat, and islands of sanity for humans, Knight says, but he adds that it's disappearing quickly. "Half of the world's forests have been lost in the past 200 years and 500 acres of forest around the globe are lost every minute of every day.".

Unfortunately, Knight believes Canada's reputation as the Brazil of the North is warranted, and points out that Brazil loses 12 acres of forest every second, while Canada loses nine acres every second. Already most of the Alberta front of the Rocky Mountains is largely developed for oil and gas exploration. "That kind of development is only beginning in the northern U.S. Rockies and parts of Idaho," Knight explains. "A good portion of roadless wilderness is under temporary protection in Montana and the Last Refuge Campaign wants that protection extended for the next 20 years."

The Last Refuge Campaign is "drawing a line in the sand for wildlife and humans," Knight says. " They're not making any more wilderness."

This article originally appeared as two stories in the Lethbridge Herald, 1999.

Joanne Helmer has worked for the Lethbridge Herald for 26 years, most of that time as an editorial writer, political columnist, book reviewer, and now reporter. Through her work she's been drawn into many environmental debates, especially the decade-long controversy over the Oldman Dam which spawned Jack Glenn's book, Once Upon an Oldman Dam, published by University of B.C. Press in 1999, and a 1993 University of Calgary master's thesis comparing two newspapers' coverage of the issue. Helmer contributed a chapter to the 1995 book Trojan Horse, which details the early years of Ralph Klein's Conservative revolution in Alberta. She was co-host of a half hour political affairs show on Lethbridge cablevision for two years, and has worked for CBC. Joanne participated in the 1997 Writers Workshop.

Remnants of an earlier era.   **Photo by Barb Grinder**

Looking Back

Archaeological evidence shows that mankind has had a presence in the Waterton - Glacier area for more than 10,000 years. Precursors of the Blackfoot, Kootenay, Nez Perce and other native peoples hunted and gathered food, made summer camps, and came here for vision quests and other rituals.

The first white people to visit the area - toward the end of the 18th century - were probably fur traders who left little record of their passing. It was 1858 before Lt. Thomas Blakiston, one of the leaders of the Palliser Expedition, travelled through South Kootenay Pass. Coming upon a lake which he described as "grand and picturesque," he named it after the famed but eccentric British naturalist Charles Waterton.

The history our writers have concerned themselves with here is more recent. Bert Gildart and Heather Pringle tell us two stories about native people of the 20th century. Heather has seen the sacred medicine bundles of the Blackfoot go from being museum exhibits, when she was a young researcher, back to their central place in the steadily revitalized religious life of native people. Her description of a healing ceremony clearly defines the significance of the bundles. Bert describes some of the sad saga of the Blackfoot since the arrival of the white man, seen through the eyes of Mary Ground, who was born as the last of the buffalo disappeared from the plains that border the parks.

No Waterton-Glacier book would be complete without mention of park ranger, trapper and mountain man Joe Cosley. Cosley legends are almost as numerous as the trees on which he carved his name, and many concern his troubles with the law. Writer Bert Gildart had the good fortune to talk to one of the men who knew Cosley, perhaps better than he wanted to, and in a manner Cosley would have preferred to avoid.

Fire and flood are natural phenomena, with significant impacts on people as well as places. Garry Allison has written about two of the biggest conflagrations in Waterton's history, the 1935 fire that burned along the shore of Upper Waterton Lake, and the effects it had on people in the park. At the time, the important role fire plays in species renewal wasn't well known and the fire was seen solely as a negative force. Sixty five years later, we had a better understanding of the critical role both fire and floods have in natural ecosystems. In "When the Waters Rose" Barb Grinder tells us how southern Alberta's June 1995 flood affected both the land and the people who live on it, for better and for worse.

Glacier National Park ranger Joe Heimes.   **Photo by Bert Gildart**

The Capture of Joe Cosley

by Bert Gildart

Early on a spring morning in 1929, Joe Heimes discovered a camp with an illegal cache of furs and, after a hurried trip back to his ranger station to alert others in authority, he returned and settled in behind a large fir tree, determined to wait for the poacher's return.

Six hours later the low clouds that had been hanging over the valley floor began to unleash their load. At times there was rain, other times a mixture of snow and rain. Heimes was getting wet and very cold.

In another two hours Heimes was down to his last cigarette, and even on this miserable day in May the mosquitoes in the back country of Glacier National Park were out in force. He was beginning to get discouraged, afraid the poacher had caught wind of his presence, but Heimes was not one to give up easily. He resolved to wait until dark.

Around dusk his large malamute dog perked up her ears and emitted a low rumbling growl. Clamping a firm hand over its muzzle and unholstering his pistol, Joe began looking around. Suddenly a large rawboned man entered camp, taking strides Heimes recalls as "like Bigfoot." Then the lanky man took off his pack, laid down his rifle and began nursing the still smoldering fire.

"I was half way to him," Heimes says, "before he heard me. Then he looked up and grabbed for his gun. But I had him dead in my sights, and I hollered, 'You lay your hand on that gun and, by God, I'll shoot you right through the guts!'"

The man Heimes had caught that day was no ordinary poacher. His name was Joe Cosley and his history to that time included the distinction of having been appointed a ranger in 1910 when Glacier became a park, being fired several years later for trapping in the park, having a WWI record of killing 60 Germans as a sniper in Canadian forces, and the notoriety of being able to evade both American and Canadian authorities for almost 20 years. "He was," recalled Heimes from his cabin in Lakeside, Montana, "a mountain man who was every bit the equivalent of Kit Carson or Jim Bridger. Luck was all that enabled me to catch him."

Whether it was luck or not is debatable, for Heimes does not appear to have been a man to trifle with. A ranger for 38 years in Glacier National Park, he retired in 1962. In 1990, when he was near 90, his eyes were still piercing, his voice firm and his hands and back strong enough to harvest a cord of wood a day, "Though if you want it," Joe laughed, "it'll cost you $450."

But Heimes still considered the apprehension of Cosley to be luck, and that more luck enabled him to march Cosley out from the backcountry to the eastern mountains from where the celebrated poacher was quickly brought to trial. "Yes sir," recalled Heimes, "Cosley had a streak of bad luck for a while, but only for a short while. Before we were finished, I'd say his shrewdness and luck were back in great abundance."

Heimes caught Cosley on May 8 in the Belly River country of Glacier National Park, a place where winter reluctantly releases its grip on the land. Snow still blanketed the hills and formed white patches across the meadow. "I was preparing for John J. Wes to bring in my spring supplies," recalled Heimes, "and I had to blow a beaver dam which was backing snow melt up the old wagon road. Each year the trail flooded for miles. Wes would come in through Cardston and Mountain View with a Canadian Mounted Police escort in an old wagon.

"Well, at any rate, that's when I saw tracks down there in the snow and the sand, and I could see where someone had been looking around for beaver. My dog and I followed a long way and finally we came to a tarp lying over a pole. Inside, there was a hind quarter of beaver, and a muskrat was stuck between the blankets along with several traps. When I saw that, we went back to the ranger station at Belly River where I called Tom Whitcraft, the ranger then at Waterton Ranger Station. He wasn't there but the Canadians said they'd tell him he was urgently needed and precisely where I could be found. Then, mighty quick, we hiked the three miles back to the poacher's camp and hid behind a tree.

"We waited almost ten full hours before he showed and I caught him. But at the time I wasn't sure who I'd caught. I'd never even seen a picture of him before. But I'd heard a description, so when he gave me a fake name I said, "Well, you sure look like Joe Cosley to me.'

"Glaring back, he said, 'Well, I'm Joe Cosley all right, but you ain't taking me in. Ain't no ranger in this park takin' me in.'

"You know, I might have let him go if he hadn't said that. I didn't want to go to headquarters, anyway. I had a dog team and it meant I might be gone a week. It was too much work. And back in those days poaching wasn't a real serious thing. Generally, we'd just take the furs, unload their gun and let them go. As it was, I spent three days with the man, not to mention what happened after the trial.

"The first night after I caught him we were too far from the station to go back. The woods were thick, and it was almost dark. So we stayed up all night. We just sat there watching each other. And every 15 minutes or so he'd tell me he had to go to the bathroom.

"It was a long night, but finally morning came and Cosley said, 'Well, you might be going but I shore ain't.' I told him then that I'd cut a stick and beat him back to the station, and that just as soon as I finished the smoke he'd given me, we were going. That convinced him, but we hadn't gone over 300 feet when all at once he took off running. Never said 'Goodbye' or nothing.

"Well in '29 I wasn't so bad at running myself, so I took off after him and tackled him. Cosley took a few swings but he wasn't really fighting, just more trying to get away. Finally, he gave up and said, 'OK, I'll go now.' We hadn't gone another 300 feet and I had to make another flying tackle. After I wrestled him to the ground, he said 'OK, I'll go.'

"This happened once more, only this time he was fighting for keeps; I was afraid he'd kill me. Finally, I had the opportunity to take his head and bang it against a tree. Down he went. Then I tied him with the laces of my boots. When Cosley came to, he said, 'I can't go; I'm sick.'

"Well, I knew he was sick, damn sick, and at that point I didn't know what I was going to do. But just then my dog's ears perked up and along came Tom Whitcraft and the Canadian I'd left the message with. Just like the Seventh Cavalry they were, and we walked the rest of the way back to the station. We had no more trouble with Cosley that day.

"Next day Tom said he wanted to go back to Waterton and I said 'The hell with that.' You see Tom was a good looking fellow and a real woman chaser," Heimes said with a twinkle in his eye. "In fact, that's the reason I couldn't get hold of him the first day. He was single then and he'd been chasin' a woman. So I said, 'You're going to let me take this bird over Gable Pass by myself? My God, if Cosley gets away then I'm in trouble and you will be too.' That changed his mind!"

For Heimes, the remainder of the trip to court was without incident. A grueling journey on snowshoes over Gable Pass to East Glacier and then, a day later, a train trip to what is now West Glacier. The trial was held the next day, about two o'clock in the afternoon. Cosley was fined $100, given a suspended jail sentence of 90 days, and released. And that, reflects Heimes, is when Cosley's usual good luck returned.

"What they should have done," said Heimes, "is made him spend at least five days in jail. That would have given us a chance to beat him back to look for all those hides he had cached. As it was I went over to a store in Belton (now West Glacier) and owner Mark Sibley said, 'You know where Cosley is now?' I said 'no,' and that I didn't give a damn, just so long as he stays out of my way, I want to stay out of his way too!

"Mark said, 'Well he's on his way back to Belly River, and he's just left. He's going to try and beat you guys back to his beaver cache.'

"As soon as I heard that, I went to see this fellow up at McDonald Station by name of Clarence Willy. Willy took right off after Cosley and Willy was a good man, a good strong fellow. He followed Cosley 12 to 15 miles but returned late that night and said that Cosley was a little too good a traveler for him.

"Next morning Tom Whitcraft and I took the train back to East Glacier and then drove a Model T by way of Cardston to the Canadian Belly River Station. From there we had to walk, but we weren't too concerned. It was about 30 miles from the town of Belton to Belly River and today that takes a good strong hiker about two days. And that's if he's on good summer-cleared trails!

"But when we got back to his camp all we found were tracks. During the course of the night, that 59-year-old man had snowshoed up McDonald and Mineral Creeks, crossed over Ahern Pass, removed 40 to 50 beaver blankets and somehow disappeared from Belly River country. We couldn't have missed Cosley by more than a few hours. Maybe only minutes. What luck! But to this day, you know I'm not sure whether it was his good luck or my good luck. You see, after that he went north to Canada where I've been told he trapped, wrote old girl friends and became quite a legend.

"But me, I never saw the man again."

* * *

Joe Cosley was born May 24, 1870, aboard the cabin sailboat his French father and Algonquin Indian mother used at the time for commercial fishing in Lake Huron. His early years included homesteading in Ontario, Canada, and moves to various parts of the U.S. southwest. At the age of 25 he was living in Kalispell where he worked as a U.S. Forest Service ranger in what is now Glacier National Park. In 1910 he transferred from the Forest Service to the Park Service and served as a ranger until he was dismissed for his trapping activities. As Joe Heimes said, "Cosley had one set of rules, the Park Service another."

Even in his early years an aura of mystery surrounded Cosley, and people liked to spin yarns about him, some based on the truth, some not. For instance, he had many girl friends, one of whom returned his $1,500 diamond ring. Cosley is reputed to have buried the ring in a tree and then told others of his action. For a while there were diamond ring prospectors peeling away new-growth bark in many areas of the park.

Another legend about Cosley concerns his illegal trapping experiences. Once, when two rangers were attempting to overtake Cosley, they were surprised when he suddenly appeared from the brush and stated that he knew they would be tired, then asked if they would care to join him for supper. He served a delicious French stew. Another time, in what may have been more characteristic fashion, Cosley simply told a ranger that if he ever caught him on the trail again he'd kill him.

Today, Glacier honors the man with a namesake: Cosley Lake is located between Belly River Ranger Station and Stoney Indian Pass, one of the most beautiful areas of Glacier National Park.

Cosley's primary source of income, however, was always trapping, and in this mode he met his demise in September of 1944. At the age of 73, alone in a windswept trapper cabin north of Prince Albert, he died of scurvy. The last entry into his log reads:

"I am growing weaker. I can hardly write. I have reached the end."

* * *

Joe Heimes headed northeast when he was a young man—from California to Shelby, Montana, riding the rails for the sole purpose of seeing the Jack Dempsey-Tommy Gibbons fight. That was in June of 1923 and, at the time, Heimes was 22 years old. He stayed for the fight on July 4, having spent time prior to that talking to the two pugilists. His scrapbook contains posed pictures of both Dempsey and Gibbons, which Joe took himself.

After the fight, Heimes went to Glacier and, as fate would have it, an appropriate job was waiting for just such a man. It was the beginning of a career with the Park Service that lasted until 1962, when he retired as a National Park Service Ranger.

Though never married, Heimes has pictures of a number of women in his scrapbook. His friends say most would ride, walk—even run — to the most remote spots in the park to see him. He died April 8, 1995, and almost until the time of his death, in Montana at the age of 94, his companion was a malamute dog very much like the one he had with him in the Belly River country that eventful day of 1929.

The Great Waterton Fire

by Garry Allison

The year 1935 should have been a quiet one in Waterton. The Prince of Wales Hotel was still closed because of the Great Depression and visitation was down throughout the park. But Relief Program crews had been put to work building highways and the Waterton golf course. And in August fear and excitement came into the lives of the people in the area. Lightning started a huge forest fire along Boundary Creek on the Canada-United States border.

That event left an indelible fear of fire on the Peat boys from Lethbridge. From that day on, George, Cam, and Stafford Peat wouldn't go to Waterton if they thought there was any chance of a forest fire. George, 17 at the time, says their uncle Bert Kelly was conscripted to fight the fire. "Our family was staying with the Kellys at the time of the fire. They had a cabin along Emerald Bay, built by my uncle and Doug Oland, one of the builders of the Prince of Wales Hotel."

"Uncle Bert was commandeered to fight the fire," said George. "They were taking a lot of younger people and I don't know why they didn't get me. I remember all that smoke, and I was scared stiff. Every time we went to Waterton after that, I was afraid we'd be called out to fight forest fires."

Cam Peat says he too was scared to death. Though he was only eight at the time, he still thought he'd be called to battle the blaze. "My mother and dad went out on the Hanson family's boat to the head of the lake where the fire was," Cam says. "They came back covered with soot and ash. When they got off the lake, they headed right back to Lethbridge."

Trained fire crews also came in from Glacier National Park and other areas. The fire, which began August 6, was held in check for a couple of days. Then the infamous Waterton winds swept down the valley and pushed the fire toward the town site. The fire was so intense and moving so fast, at one point they started to evacuate the town. George remembers smoke blackening the sky, obscuring the nearby mountains.

The winds pushing the fire towards the town finally abated and in a short time the flames halted, less than two km from the townsite. The devastation covered more than 800 hectares and burned close to four kilometres along the shoreline. The fire's scar, beginning in the Boundary Creek area, is still visible today and can be seen from boats on the lake. Officials say lightning started the fire.

An army travels on its stomach, and so does a forest fire fighting crew, no matter how remote the location. Frank Goble was one of three cooks feeding the hundreds of men fighting the 1935 fire.

"I cooked for those big crews, over 500 men, which included most every adult male off the Blood Reserve, 150 to 175 of them, all the men from the Relief Camp in this area, as well as anyone they could conscript," says Goble, now in his eighties

There were three cooks, cooking on wood fires. One of the first things Goble did was have a Waterton blacksmith build four huge metal grills to place over the cooking fires. The cooks also bought out Delaney's grocery, emptying it of all canned goods, vegetables and the like. They had to send to Lethbridge for more.

"We set up a camp with a big triangle of planks and sawhorses, and we cooks and our 13 helpers worked behind that," Goble says. "We'd finish supper at 11:30 p.m. and were up preparing breakfast at 1:30 a.m.

I was never so tired in my life. Bacon, eggs, pancakes, coffee, bread, steaks, vegetables, it seemed like they were always on the grill."

Goble remembers the fire crew setting up pumper engines and tanks to move water up Mt. Richards in relays. It took 24 days to get the fire fully controlled. It wasn't out, but it was contained by two bulldozed fireguards to the north and the south, built by American and Canadian firefighters working together.

"Once when the fire was crowning it very nearly burned up a trail crew camped north of Boundary Creek," Goble says. "The fire started to crown, moving backwards. The men immediately left the area, running down through their camp and across the creek. Then they took to the lake. One man couldn't swim but the others helped him. They were picked out of the water by the International launch. When they went back to pick up their gear at the camp everything was burned up."

There were seven men on that crew, Goble remembers, including his brother Clement. "The flames were so hot, that when they lashed out over the lake you could see the steam rising off the water."

'The Great Waterton Fire' was originally published in the Lethbridge Herald.

Garry Allison has worked for the Lethbridge Herald for the past 42 years, starting as a delivery boy and working his way up to one of their most honored reporters. Though he has written about a wide variety of topics, he specializes in articles about history, sports, the outdoors, and aboriginal cultures. He has won awards from the Canadian Rodeo Cowboys Association, Ducks Unlimited and the Alberta Fish and Game Association, and is an honorary member of both the Blood and Peigan Nations. Garry was a participant in the 1997 and 1999 Writers Workshops.

Mary Ground.   **Photo by Bert Gildart**

The Tail of
the Last Buffalo

by Bert Gildart

The year 1882 was a significant one in Montana and southern Alberta. In Montana it was the last year buffalo were seen roaming between the Sweet Grass Hills and the Rockies, and it was the year hunger began stalking the camps of the Blackfeet Indians. Beginning with the winter of 1882, many Montana Indians were forced to eat dogs, horses, soup made from old buffalo bones gathered on the plains, and even grass.

The buffalo had disappeared and subsistence living took its toll. Some say more than 600 Indians died from starvation during those famine years, but the real figure was probably much higher. No one knows the exact number of deaths that occurred on Badger Creek, just south of present-day Browning, but an Indian named Almost-A-Dog is said to have kept a record of each death as it occurred by cutting a notch in a willow stick and the number of those marks reached 555. Between one-fourth and one-sixth of the Blackfeet in Montana perished from starvation. So many victims were buried on the hill south of Badger Creek during 1883, following the disappearance of the bison, that Indians came to refer to the burial site as Ghost Ridge.

In Blackfoot areas of southern Alberta, equally chaotic times were experienced. There, among the suffering, another notable though unrecorded event occurred around 1882 - the birth of Mary Ground, also called Grass Woman. In August of 1982 Mary, now living in Browning, Montana, celebrated her 100th birthday.

More than 100 years old when I interviewed her, Mary had a mind as sound as many half her age. Her recollection of the transitional period, when Indians were forced to join the wider society, was phenomenal, and her life was inspiring. With uncanny ability, she recalled many of her early-day experiences, leaning forward and deftly gesturing with her hands. With moccasin-clad feet, braided hair, a headband and a bright countenance, she was the embodiment of enthusiasm.

Mary's natural father was a trapper of French-Canadian extraction. Her mother was almost pure Indian. But, before she was born, her father deserted her mother, who remarried, this time to a full-blooded Indian.

Several weeks after Mary was born, the new husband noticed the baby's eyes were not changing from blue to brown, and he delivered an ultimatum. "Place that baby in a field of tall grass for the night and, if she survives, we'll keep her." Few infants could have survived such a cold Canadian evening, but little Mary was lucky. Shortly after she was left in the field, she was rescued by an Indian woman who assumed temporary responsibility for her. Four years later her guardian took Mary from the Blood Reserve, south to the Blackfeet Indian Reservation.

"We came over in the dead of winter," recalled Mary. "I was on a travois all wrapped in fur. We left Canada so I could be adopted by the Sherman family."

Mary left Canada about the time an Indian agent named Baldwin ordered members of the Indian Police not to participate in or encourage the Sun Dance, one of the traditional religious ceremonies of the Blackfoot. "It's all like a dream now," said Mary, "but I remember that about 1887 we attended one of the ceremonies. A man's flesh was pierced with skewers and he was suspended by a rope until his weight tore the skin. Then he was freed. Buffalo skulls may have been placed on the man's feet as extra weight to speed the tearing of the skin. I can't be sure about that. I was very young."

When Mary arrived in Browning, Montana there were few opportunities for education. For several years some of the children had been sent across the Rockies to the Catholic School at St. Ignatius Mission. Mary stayed closer to home and became one of the first children to be enrolled in the New Holy Family Mission School, which opened in 1890 on the Two Medicine. There were accommodations for 100 pupils, most of whom boarded at the mission from September through June.

Mary remembered that the agents encouraged schooling, but regulations were strict — at times harsh. Children had to cut their braids and wear white man's clothing or "citizen's dress."

If a child spoke Blackfoot to a friend, "Crack, we got it across the knuckles with a ruler or were placed in a dark closet for hours," Mary recalled. "We couldn't speak our native language," said Mary, "even with our little brothers or sisters."

"Not many people still speak Blackfoot," she said, "but we should practice a few of the common words. You white people have an advantage. You have what is called a dictionary. Our language is handed down."

Paradoxically, Mary's ability to speak Blackfoot was occasionally useful to the school. The most notable occasion followed a murder, when the superintendent of schools required Mary to translate the words of an old Indian involved in the investigation.

"What happened," recalled Mary, "is Frank Double Runner killed the husband of this woman he was in love with. The old full-blood told us that. Then he took that woman with him. The superintendent wanted to ride across the Two Medicine River where Double Runner had set up camp. He wanted to bring him to the tribal police. The superintendent knew Double Runner and thought he could reason with him. But that's not what happened.

"What happened is Frank Double Runner, the number one rifle shooter on the reservation, shot the superintendent's hat off his head. All of us kids and our teachers, too, saw that happen. That sent Superintendent Matson riding back. He was damn glad to get back too. He didn't dare go out anymore. Everyone just stayed in the school, even the tribal policemen and us kids. But pretty soon they heard a shot. He shot that woman. A few minutes after that, we heard another shot. Then silence. But, still, every one was afraid to go across the river. Several hours later one man went across the river and found them both. Double Runner had killed his lover and then himself. They made one great big box for both of them and buried them together."

As with any society in the midst of a transition, violence was common and life uncertain. Acclimation was difficult, and, like many other children, Mary attempted to run away from authority. "I ran away with a girl named Josephine White Man," she recalled. "We traveled a whole day on foot, but were caught late in the night. We had a fire to keep warm and that's how the Catholic Fathers found us."

In her teens Mary was matched and wedded to an older man, a perfect stranger named John Ground. The date was August 12, 1899. Mary was told if she didn't marry John, she was never to set foot in her guardian's house again.

John was a good man she recalled. "He worked hard and never had to steal and we had some good times. Let me tell you a little story.

"You remember hearing about prohibition days? Anyone who wanted whiskey had to get it from Canada. Well this Indian family got a whole gallon of wine for two men and one women. When they got to customs, the husband told his wife, 'Now, when that officer comes you just act like you're in pain.' So, when the officer came out there and asked them where they were going, this man spoke up and said, 'My wife, she is sick; she's starting to labor; you've got to let us get to the doctor.' And that woman, she just acted like she was sick in the stomach. You see her stomach was 'swollen' out from the bottle hidden underneath her skirt. See how slick they got by."

Mary and John had 14 children and ranched together until he died in 1951. "Those were 52 happy years," she reflected. "Now I have about 300 grandchildren." And in 1983 a sixth-generation entered the family. Since that time, three other sixth-generation children have been born. In other words, Mary was a great, great, great, great grandmother.

Until just before her death in 1990, Mary remained active in traditional Native activities such as blessing the medicine pipe, a sacred Indian symbol, and Powwow dances. In the early 1980s, with the help of a granddaughter and an editor, she wrote a book titled "Grass Woman

Stories." In the book she related 14 different episodes she heard of or participated in while a young girl.

One of the stories in the book was about marriage. In this chapter, Mary said, "If the wives ran around and the husbands wouldn't punish them, their brothers would. They'd cut off their noses or ears. But sometimes, if a woman had been running around or they couldn't get along, a man would gather up the people. He'd get a stick and he'd say, 'This is my wife, whoever catches the stick, she's his.' And he'd throw the stick. The man who took it was her new husband."

Mary's stories are all rich in history and cover such diverse topics as trail-side birth, White Dog's death and Wolf Plume's lover. The publication is still available through the Museum of the Plains Indians located in Browning.

At the time I interviewed her, shortly before she died, Mary was 107 years old. Though she lived in a nursing home, her children made frequent visits, no small feat as they too were advancing in age. They enjoyed not only her presence, but someone to speak with in their native tongue.

"Ki-ta-ku-ta-ma-tsin," said Mary. "Come back. But better make it soon. The snow is getting deeper each winter and I fear I'll soon see again the tail of the last buffalo."

Bert Gildart has written more than 300 articles over the past 30 years, and has been published in such magazines as Field and Stream, National Wildlife, Travel Holiday, Travel and Leisure, and Smithsonian. He is the author of nine books, and has received awards from the Montana Press Association and the Outdoor Writers Association of America. Most of his work describes some aspect of the natural world. Bert often draws on his experience as a teacher and as a seasonal ranger in Glacier and Yellowstone National Parks. He usually illustrates his stories from his vast library of stock photos, to which both he and his wife contribute. The Gildarts live in Montana, not far from Glacier, their favorite of all parks. Bert was a participant at the 1999 Writers Workshop.

(Editor's Note: Members of the Blackfoot Nation living in Montana are called Blackfeet; in Alberta, they are named Blackfoot, as is the language spoken on both sides of the border.)

Sun Dance encampment, Blood Reserve 1997.   **Photo by Barb Grinder**

Spiritual Healing

by Heather Pringle

On an early spring day in 1975 an elderly rancher wrapped a woolen blanket around his waist and set off stiffly across a windblown parking lot, steeling himself to rescue the universe from a basement drawer in the Provincial Museum of Alberta.

A traditional leader of the Blood Indian Reserve in southern Alberta, Many-Grey-Horses had never set foot in a museum, much less roamed the shelf-lined aisles of a collection vault. On principle, he spoke no English. But a few months earlier, the elder had received an unexpected visit from a young white writer, Adolph Hungry Wolf, who had married into the tribe and taken up traditional Blood ways.

Folding his lanky frame into a kitchen chair Hungry Wolf had confided a troubling story. In a dream, he had seen the old man conduct a strange ceremony on the lawn of the Provincial Museum, spiriting away a shrine venerated by centuries of holy men, a sacred mystery known to the Blackfoot nation as the Longtime Medicine Pipe Bundle.

On the other side of the kitchen table the imposing old man listened intently. Several years earlier a tribe member had sold the sacred bundle to Provincial Museum officials in Edmonton for $3,000. Here researchers had untied its vermilion-streaked wrappings, laying out its tanned animal skins, its pouches of paints and its ancient holy pipe for display, relics of a long extinct plains religion.

But on the southern Alberta reserve, old-time religion was far from dead. Under a veil of secrecy, young Bloods had begun reviving the ancient rituals, calling for the return of one of their oldest shrines. To all entreaties, museum authorities turned a deaf ear. The mysterious bundle was too ancient, too fragile and now too valuable to be handed back to the tribe they explained; it belonged in a museum.

But as Hungry Wolf spoke, Many-Grey-Horses felt a kindling of hope. Among followers of the old faith it was said that the sun sent dreams foretelling the future. Sifting through Hungry Wolf's words, weighing their meaning, the old man made up his mind: in the spring he would wrestle the Longtime bundle from its intractable keepers.

Accompanied by Hungry Wolf and their wives, the old man crossed the museum foyer. Calling for officials, the Hungry Wolfs explained their party had come to take the bundle outdoors for prayers. Impressed by the elder's solemnity and unwilling to refuse such a simple request, the curators reluctantly agreed. Rounding up the holy pipe from a basement cabinet and its accessories from an upstairs display case, they handed them over and followed the small blanket-wrapped band a respectful distance as they filed past video cameras and security guards.

Outside, Many-Grey-Horses and his procession circled the museum, praying, and purifying the bundle. As they rounded the parking lot, however, the small troop swerved suddenly and made a beeline for a travel-stained truck, with the bundle firmly in hand. As he discerned their plan, Bruce McCorquadale, museum director at the time, charged after the raiders, exhorting them to surrender the treasure. Flushed with emotion, Many-Grey-Horses swung round to explain his claim. Since McCorquadale had never been initiated into the mysteries of the bundle, Many-Grey-Horses concluded, he had no rights to speak of it, much less dictate its fate. Nothing more remained to be said. Sliding into the truck, the old man ordered Hungry Wolf to drive off. Despite his months of worry, neither guards nor police appeared. Just as the dream had foretold, the small party screeched out of the parking lot unhindered - victors in one of the gentlest battles ever fought in the name of religion.

But the old man's stand was just the first step in a quiet revolution sweeping the reserves of southern Alberta and northern Montana. Among the Blood, North Blackfoot, North Peigan and South Piegan tribes - collectively known as the Blackfoot nation - young and old had begun embracing ancient beliefs with new fervor, forsaking the imported Christianity of their parents for the plains religion of their forefathers. Reviving the complex ceremonies of the past, they searched for new sources of personal strength and spiritual meaning.

Practised by all Blackfoot before the arrival of Europeans, the ancient religion sprang directly from the sun-bleached prairies. Like Christians, the prehistoric Blackfoot worshipped a supreme power, an ultimate mystery they called Napi, or the Creator. But as a culture of plains hunters living off the land, they chose to venerate not an anthropomorphic god, but the animating principle of life. Inspired by creation, the Blackfoot came to associate their supreme power with the sun itself.

Divine power was not limited to the Creator, however. In prayer, the Blackfoot called on a host of important spirits that effectively personified ecological processes: Windmaker, Coldmaker, Thunder. Moreover, as they watched the sun's power warm and light the world, they came to revere all that surrounded them - the antelope and grizzly that wandered the prairie, the sweet pine and spruce that shaded the western mountains, the siltstone and quartz that lined the rivers. All nature was enlivened by spirits and by living in harmony with them, the faithful practised what one expert has come to call "Indian environmental religion."

In return for their reverence, the faithful could reap special powers; through dreams and visions, animal Messengers called on the devout, bestowing important gifts from the sun — sacred lore for controlling fertility in the tribe, supernatural powers for mastering spring rains, spiritual strength for healing the sick. Over time, such powers came to be symbolized by specialized medicine bundles, collections of sacred objects passed from one tribal leader to another.

By opening the bundles in age-old ceremonies, keepers invoked their special powers for the benefit of all. "It was very rich and very complex," said Jay Vest, a Montana scholar in Native religious traditions and a devout believer.

But to early missionaries, the ancient faith seemed little more than superstition. From the lecterns of residential schools, they had rooted out traditional values and beliefs, planting Christianity in their place. Shocked by reports of Blackfoot sun worship, legislators prohibited the tribes' most important religious ceremony, the Sun Dance, and by the 1950s, only a handful of elderly Blackfoot kept its beliefs alive.

With the loss of ancient spiritual values, however, many young Blackfoot lost heart, sliding inescapably into an all-too-well-documented despond of alcoholism, violence and suicide. By the early 1970s it had become evident to many that Christianity offered little redemption, and a new generation of ceremonialists began gathering up the skeins of the lost past.

Today, along the rolling prairie of the Blackfeet Indian Reservation of northern Montana, elders conduct rituals of spiritual healing in tarp-covered sweat lodges, attracting supplicants from as far away as Arizona and California. On the Blood, North Peigan and South Piegan reserves, hundreds of faithful flock to tribal Sun Dances; dozens search for spiritual strength in the traditional piercing ceremony. And in living rooms and kitchens throughout southern Alberta and northern Montana, religious leaders are mapping out new battle plans for the protection of sacred rights and the return of sacred bundles and artifacts.

For years I had followed the revival of Blackfoot religion with more than casual interest. As a young museum researcher and display planner, I had watched Many-Grey-Horses and his band carry the Longtime bundle out the museum doors. In subsequent travels through southern Alberta as a journalist, I had come to know many Blackfoot. Beneath their appearance as ordinary Canadians, I glimpsed a fascinating, exotic culture; so when I received an invitation to attend the ceremonial opening of a medicine pipe bundle on the Peigan Reserve, I gladly accepted.

"This is like our New Year's," explained the then 39-year-old bundle keeper Reg Crowshoe. "You're welcoming the next four seasons — the rain, lots of berries, the animals, the birds, the universe - and you're helping to cure whoever is sick."

By tradition, ceremonialists unwrap their medicine pipe bundles as the first booming echoes of thunder are heard in the spring. But in recent years, keepers of the 12 remaining sacred bundles have begun staggering the ceremonies, permitting the faithful to attend as many as possible. Crowshoe's celebration had been scheduled for the last Saturday in June at his parents' home on the prairie near Brocket, Alberta. Here, a ragged row of pickup trucks and campers, bearing Montana and Alberta license plates, stretched over the prairie grasses, its passengers heading toward the house carrying cartons of tobacco, a traditional offering at Native ceremonies.

In the kitchen, Crowshoe's sisters presided, stirring vats of berry soup simmering on the stove. At the kitchen table, Joe Crowshoe, the family head, looked on approvingly. A highly respected spiritual leader, the furrowed elder had opened his own medicine pipe bundle a day earlier, and in honour of the weekend's double ceremony, his children and grandchildren had raised a small forest of tipis behind the house. Pitching the two largest tipis side by side, and pegging together their white canvas covers to form a connecting passageway, the family had constructed a large and eminently portable chapel. As I walked outside, I glimpsed a fire burning in its inner hearth.

An hour later, nearly 70 people had packed themselves inside the canvas church, and a hum of good-natured conversation filled the air. In the inner chamber, medicine bundle keepers, ceremonial assistants, Crowshoe family members, and a band of four drummers had squeezed elbow to elbow along blanket-covered mattresses; in the outer chamber, guests had crammed kitchen chairs into tight rows, leaving latecomers to spill out the doorway in two lines of lawn chairs. Near the entrance way, Reg Crowshoe surveyed the scene with his wife Rose.

A tall heavyset man, with long silver-streaked braids and a friendly, outgoing manner, Crowshoe descends from a long line of Blackfoot ceremonialists and spiritual leaders. But unlike those before him, this bundle keeper had come to his faith late in life. Attending residential school as a child, Crowshoe studied at the University of Calgary to become a teacher, before packing it in to return to the reserve. A series of dreams and visions had convinced him of his calling as a bundle keeper, but Crowshoe was far from ready. To care for such a sacred thing, he had to become immersed in traditional lore, apprenticing with elders. In 1975 he was deemed ready and after days of ceremony he returned to Alberta with the sacred Rider Medicine Pipe Bundle, transferred from an elderly Peigan woman in Montana.

Smoothing down the folds of a Hudson Bay blanket wrapped around his waist, Crowshoe asked his wife to bring the bundle from the house. With his father, and South Piegan spiritual leader George Kicking Woman, he watched as she carried the child-sized shrine into the tipi. Following in her wake, the three ceremonialists entered the inner chamber and took seats in front of a small altar — a square patch of cleared ground, half black with soil, half red with sacred paint. An assistant lifted a burning coal from the fire and Kicking Woman crumbled a handful of sweet-pine needles over it, filling the tipi with fragrance.

With slow rounds of sacred song, the three men took turns paying respect to nature, awakening the animals from their long winter's sleep. Calling on the birds in softly guttural Blackfoot, they asked them to come and peck at the strings that tie the bundle, thereby loosening it. Calling on the deer and the bear, they asked them to open the layers of skins and hides in which the sacred pipe is wrapped. As the afternoon shadows lengthened, the devout sat in rapt silence. At last, reaching into folds of flannel, Kicking Woman lifted up the stem of the holy pipe. With a gentle shake, he unfurled its streamers of eagle feathers and ermine skins, and a wave of emotion flooded through the tipi.

According to belief, all medicine pipe bundles descend directly from Thunder, the spirit that controls all rain, and hence all life on the arid prairie. In the long ago, say sacred stories, Thunder stole a Blackfoot woman from earth. Determined to win her back, her husband set off in pursuit and with cunning borrowed from Raven, he outwitted the fearsome spirit. To make peace, Thunder gave the man a sacred medicine pipe bundle. "When I first come in the spring," instructs the spirit in a version of the story published in 1892, "you shall fill and light this pipe, and you shall pray to me, you and the people. For I bring the rain which makes the berries large and ripe. I bring the rain which makes all things grow, and for this, you shall pray to me, you and all the people."

One by one, the ceremonialists arose to carry the pipe outside for prayers, greeting the spirit; as the last took a seat, the tension building all afternoon suddenly subsided. Several women ducked outside, returning with pots of steaming saskatoon berry soup. An hour later, as the last of the feast had been handed out — roast beef, bannock, Indian jam (a rich paste made from chokecherries), Rice Krispie squares, apples, oranges and juice — the ceremony resumed. In the inner chamber, Joe Crowshoe and Molly Kicking Woman took out pouches of paints. Rolling soft pellets of red ochre in their hands, the two elders painted lines along the celebrants faces and offered a blessing with the holy pipe or one of the bundle's animal fetishes.

Now those who wished to ask for some special dispensation — healing for a stricken child, perhaps, or sobriety for an abusive husband — entered the ceremonialists' chamber. Laying blankets on the ground, they donned shawls and took the holy pipe in hand. To the drummers thudding beat, they danced in small steps, turning to the four directions. Along the aisles, the celebrants prayed and made a sweeping motion with their hands, waving the powerful influence of the pipe towards their hearts. They were praying not just for themselves, not just for the Indian people, but for everyone and for the Earth and nature.

By seven o'clock, the last of the supplicants had come forward and Crowshoe brought the ceremony to a close. Taking out a thick rope of tobacco from the bundle wrapping, he asked his assistants to give a pinch to each of the faithful. Holding a few grains between their fingers, each offered a silent prayer, planting the brown flakes in the ground. A minute later, the assistants handed out packages of cigarettes and rolling tobacco. Crowshoe followed close behind, a broad smile playing at the corners of his mouth; the opening had gone well.

For some of the faithful, the gentle power of the medicine pipe ceremony will fall short of their prayers. Surrounded by tragedy and troubled lives, on unemployment ridden reserves, some will seek greater power through penance at the most prominent of all the Blackfoot ceremonies — the tribal Sun Dance or Medicine Lodge.

"If you're going through something and need some special help, if you've gone every place else and they couldn't help you, there's only one thing left," explained Gordon Belcourt, at the time the president of Browning's Blackfoot Community College. "That's the Medicine Lodge."

Belcourt had seen more than his share of hard times. On the highway outside his office, small white crosses huddled along the rolling prairie curves; on the town's shabby main street, ramshackle houses creaked in the wind and a drunk urinated against a paint-blistered fence. But despite the despair that hangs over Browning, Belcourt refused to give up hope. Born and raised on the Blackfeet Indian Reservation, he believed fervently in the restorative powers of the old faith. "There's nothing beyond it," he said. "The Medicine Lodge is the ultimate act."

It was no idle talk. In 1969, the young South Piegan and his wife vowed to raise the first Medicine Lodge on the reservation in 34 years. The outgrowth of many vision quests in the mountains, going without food and water for several days, Belcourt's pledge grew stronger. In the three decades since the last lodge had been raised, however, memories of the sacred rites had grown dim. To reconstruct the event, Belcourt canvassed the tribe's oldest leaders. "They kind of laughed and cried, because they thought it was dead," he said. "Then they said, 'Well, we've lost a lot of our people; a lot of our elders responsible for these ceremonies have died. Who's left?' "

Conducting a cultural and religious inventory, Belcourt and his helpers began tracking down those who still held crucial ceremonial rights. "And, lo and behold, we had all the people necessary to put on a Medicine Lodge," he said.

Even so, there was strong resistance to Belcourt's plans. Some called the proposed ritual devil worship, others warned Belcourt that he would be dead within a year. Nevertheless, the young academic went ahead. With the help of elders such as North Peigan holy woman Cecile Many Guns, Blood holy woman Annie Rides-at-the-Door, and South Piegan ritualist Mike Swims Under, the ceremony proceeded and more than 700 followers flocked to that first gathering. "We had no problems and that started a whole raft of things," said Belcourt. "We were having a Medicine Lodge once a year."

Fired by fervor, many began talking of resurrecting a related but highly controversial rite, also prohibited by authorities a century or so earlier. To obtain strength from the sun during times of personal crisis or danger, young Blackfoot men would undergo the piercing ceremony at the annual Medicine Lodge. In preparation, supplicants went without food and sleep, dancing to a drumbeat for four days, before entering a sacred lodge. There, a ritualist slit the flesh on their chests, threading the incisions with skewers attached to ropes strung from the lodge's center pole. Praying and pulling against the ropes, hallucinating in their exhausted state, supplicants danced until the ropes pulled free from their flesh.

But the last Blackfoot to perform the powerful rite had died years earlier. How could piercing be revived? After much discussion, a group of young Piegans journeyed to a Sioux reserve in North Dakota, where the practice had been preserved. Undergoing the rite with no ill effects, they proudly returned north and spread the secret.

The resurgence of the piercing ceremony grew slowly. In the fourth year 16 tribal members, including two women, took part. In addition, Sun Dancers left 50 to 100 flesh offerings, generally in the form of small strips of skin. "Our elders had taught us when you give part of your flesh and you suffer and you fast, that's the ultimate gift you can give the Creator," Belcourt explained.

Still, he admits the powerful ceremony offers no firm guarantees, no easy assurances of success. "Sometimes it works, and sometimes it doesn't. But what it does, we believe, is prepare a place for you on the other side. And your relatives will come and get you, and everything will be all right."

While rites such as the Medicine Lodge were reviving, the battle for religious freedom was far from over. Across southern Alberta and northen Montana, ceremonialists became locked in bitter debate with museum curators and private collectors over custody of some of their key articles of faith — birth control bundles, horse bundles, beaver bundles, water pipe bundles, and medicine pipe bundles. Scooped up at a time when traditional spirituality had fallen into decline, the holy icons now took pride of place in many museum collections, much to the frustration of Native traditionalists.

Without the bundles, you can't have the ceremonies, explained Hungry Wolf. It would be like a priest trying to perform communion without wine and wafers. In defense, some curators pointed to the great antiquity of the bundles and to the invaluable information they contained on the lives and material culture of prehistoric Blackfoot. Others saw themselves as stewards of the artifacts, to be held in trust for all Albertans, including Native people.

Belcourt's solution suggested that traditional Blackfeet could create new bundles. "The people who got them in the first place, 1000 or 10,000 years ago, got them through a vision quest, got them through fasting, got them through a process that we know a lot about. Individuals, young people, can still get that from the Creator."

But it will not be simple said Jay Vest. To obtain a vision, the faithful once journeyed to certain sacred retreats well known to the tribe, areas of spectacular and untrammelled wilderness. In recent years, however, many of the holiest areas, such as the Oldman River Valley, the Badger Two-Medicine Wildlands, and the Sweetgrass Hills have come under seige from mines, irrigation dams and oil and gas development. "The vision quest cannot be done in a place that's heavily used or disturbed," said Vest. To ward off such perils, traditionalists joined forces with local environmental groups and pressured for legislation to protect their religious rights. "The sacred land issue is critical," concluded Vest, "and I think it entails the sacred wildlife and plants too. If they disappear, so does part of the religion."

Even if such retreats can be preserved, however, some older believers question whether it will be enough to sustain the faith. As the prairie disappears irrevocably under a blanket of farmlands and fences, the experiences that gave rise to the plains religion, hundreds or thousands of years ago, may become harder and harder to obtain. In a religion that is based so firmly on the land, what will happen when the land itself has changed beyond recognition?

I thought about this question late on a Saturday afternoon as I walked along a windrow of hay and sagebrush behind the home of John Yellow Kidney, a spiritual leader among the South Piegan. A few days earlier the distinguished ceremonialist had invited me to attend his family's Saturday night sweat lodge, and as I cut down a prairie slope, I caught sight of one of his sons tending the fire for the sweat lodge rocks. Nearby, Yellow Kidney's daughter-in-law braided lengths of green sweetgrass, while her children played quietly by the tarp-covered lodge. In the distance the skeletons of three medicine lodges weathered in the sun.

It was a scene of peace and contentment, but such calm had not always settled over the Yellow Kidney family. As a younger man, the ceremonialist battled a serious alcohol problem, and his children fought similar battles with drugs. A decision to return to the traditional faith gave Yellow Kidney the strength to give up drinking and gave his children pause for thought. "They started looking at me and I was looking so good, and I was off alcohol, that they decided to start coming to these sweats," he explained over coffee one night.

By six o'clock more than a dozen adults and children sat quietly in the 120 centimetre high sweat lodge, the women dressed modestly in long sleeves and floor length skirts, the men stripped down to shorts. Along the western wall of the sweat lodge the ceremonialist and his wife Liz took their seats and after much good-natured banter and solemn prayer, the elder gave the sign to begin filling the lodge's central pit with the heated rocks. As the last of the gleaming red boulders had been carried in on a shovel, the tarp above the doorway was pulled down and the lodge went black.

In the darkness, water hissed on fiery rocks and waves of heat undulated through the lodge. In a deep sonorous voice, Yellow Kidney called on everyone to pray, and all around me a cacophony of loud, fervent prayer arose. Out of the blackness, Yellow Kidney began to sing a rising chant in Blackfoot, calling on the animal spirits to help those in the lodge. Other voices joined in, and, as the temperature rose, the pattern of prayer and song was repeated again and again. The stream of water flowing down my face became a torrent and my clothes clung to me, a sodden mass. Beside me, a child cried as the flap was lifted and the light of day briefly returned.

Three hours later, I felt as if all protective covering had been stripped from my body, leaving me bare. Leaning forward, Yellow Kidney asked each of the 20 or so people now packed together inside the lodge to explain why he or she had come. In hesitant, slow speech they told of marriage breakdowns, alcohol and drug problems, family illnesses, the desire to commit suicide. Some asked for prayers for the people on the streets lost to alcohol; one woman described the scene of a fatal car accident she happened upon that afternoon and asked for spiritual healing for the family of the dead, people she had never met nor seen. Surrounded by faces of nodding compassion, I was moved to tears.

In the darkness that followed, I was no longer listening to the prayers of others; I was speaking my own. Scorched by heat, I lost track of time and an eternity passed. As last, Yellow Kidney called for the flap to be lifted. A stream of moonlight flowed through the door, lighting the steam that hung in the air and silvering the faces of everyone sitting there. We were each of us reluctant to leave, to break the gentle magic of the circle.

In the end, we filed out, shaking hands warmly with people whose names we did not know, a community now of friends. I headed back up the bowl of prairie with only starlight and a half-moon to guide me, but I no longer had any fears for the future of Yellow Kidney and his faith. As long as nature holds a grain of mystery, as long as shattered lives remain to be healed, holy men like Yellow Kidney will sing and pray the world into balance, just as they have always done.

'Spiritual Healing' was originally published in Equinox magazine.

Heather Pringle *has been writing about nature, the environment and the ancient past for nearly 17 years. A National Magazine Award winner, she has travelled extensively in the pursuit of good stories, from the coasts of Newfoundland, where she listened to tales of the now extinct Beothuk, to the caves of the northern Yukon, where she pored over the relics of North America's earliest known inhabitants. She has published two books, Waterton Lakes National Park and In Search of Ancient North America, and many magazine and newspaper articles. Heather participated in the 1997 Writers Workshop.*

When the Waters Rose

by Barbara Grinder

Tuesday, June 6, 1995 started out like any other day for Milo and Ada Chytil. Their daughter Joanna went off to school in Pincher Creek and Milo and Ada did the chores. Two cows, expected to calve soon, were on the farmstead, as were the family's horses, another cow and her new calf. The other cattle were out in the fields. It was raining, as it had been off and on for several weeks, but the rain was coming down hard.

The Chytils, along with Ada's brother Jake Beemsterboer, run a small cattle, hay and grain farm, at Twin Butte, Alberta, about midway between Pincher Creek and Waterton Park, along Highway 6. The 13.5 acre farmstead lies in the valley of Drywood Creek and holds a small feedlot, a barn, a corral, assorted outbuildings and the Chytil's house.

At about four in the afternoon, water from the creek started entering the corrals. "I wasn't really worried," Ada recalls. "I grew up in Holland and I'd seen minor floods before. I didn't think there was any danger."

A short time later Ada got a phone call telling her to prepare to evacuate. Drywood Creek was rising fast and a small dam on the Shell Waterton Gas Plant property was going to break.

"At that point, I guess I wasn't thinking too clearly," Ada said. "I started throwing some clothes into suitcases, grabbed our saddles and bridles, gathered up the dogs, and put everything into the station wagon."

Joanna was home from school and helped her uncle move the animals to higher ground. Milo, a Shell employee, was working overtime with many of his colleagues to limit the damage near the plant.

Within a short time after the dam broke, water in the house's basement was nearly to the floor joists. The creek had breached its banks and the stream was creating new channels across the soft, bare ground of the farmstead, destroyed buildings and taking everything in its wake. "I remember walking around and feeling devastated," Ada said. "Milo didn't get home till 1:00 a.m. that night. He came back to a scene of utter chaos."

"We'd only had the property about a year," Milo explained. "We knew there had been floods here before, but we figured they couldn't have been bad, because the old log buildings were still here."

Built in the late 1870s, the log structures were part of the original Drywood Ranch. The flood destroyed these historic buildings, as well as the corral and other outbuildings close to the creek. It also left a metre-

On June 6, 1995 Drywood Creek left its channel, turning this corral into a lake; erosion washed away the hillside. **Photo by Barb Grinder**

deep layer of gravel, silt and debris on the lower portions of the family's land. In all, estimates of the damage came to over $125,000.

I first met the Chytils a week after these events, when I was interviewing area residents about the damage they'd suffered from the flood. I also talked to Ed Sinnott who farms 1200 acres along the banks of Pincher Creek, about five kilometres below the Oldman River dam. Sinnott had similar damage on his property, where the high waters took out large sections of streambank and washed away a small bridge.

In the mid-60s the creek which flows through his land had been diverted by the provincial government and the land where the Sinnott house now sits was considered safe. "That's why we built the house there," Sinnott said. "Now flood water has annihilated our basement and it looks like the creek wants to reclaim its old channel. We still can't use our household water supply."

Sinnott told me the rains had eroded his topsoil, delayed his seeding, carried the fertilizer and manure he'd spread into the stream basin, and ruined hay crops that were already growing. "There's so much debris in my alfalfa, I'll have a hard time cutting it. And the haying season's been ruined," he added. "I'll be lucky to salvage any for silage. I'm just watching my livelihood go down the drain."

At the Pincher Creek Hutterite Colony, west of the Sinnotts, 34 calves and 24 cows were swept downstream to a watery grave, just some of many hundreds of farm animals lost to the flooding rivers in the region. Mike Gross, one of the colony leaders, said they'd get nothing from a government compensation program hastily set up to cover property lost in the flood. "The government adjustor told us they wouldn't cover anything that could have been insured, but wasn't. But who insures their livestock against the possibility of a 100-year flood?"

In the town of Pincher Creek one of the main bridges across the stream was totally destroyed and several homes along the creek were lost. It would be more than a year before the bridge was rebuilt. In the rural municipality of Pincher Creek, another 16 culverts and small bridges were ruined, causing farmers who used them to detour many miles to get from one field to another.

It would be more than 24 hours before the river crested at Lethbridge, at a record 8.44 metres. The Highway 3 bridge was closed as water lapped over the top deck. Officials there were concerned about damage to the sewage and water treatment plants, but the wisdom of the city's decision 30 years earlier to remove all residential development from the river valley was now obvious. Liz Saunders, at the time the director of the Helen Schuler Nature Centre, said there was a lot of damage to the river valley system of parks and trails, but it was also an exciting opportunity.

"The flood deposited huge piles of debris that voles and mice love to nest in. And we'll probably see an increase in the numbers of shorebirds and water fowl who'll use the little islands and gravel bars created by the flood." There were other, more important benefits to the flood as well. Cottonwood seeds along the Oldman and other rivers would have a chance to germinate, brush piles that had accumulated for years in the valleys would be washed downstream, and new layers of silt would be laid down, allowing other plants to take hold.

Stewart Rood, a biologist at the University of Lethbridge, said he'd been worried for the last few years that the Oldman Dam was controlling the river's flow to the extent that cottonwoods couldn't regenerate. About three quarters of all the birds that live here rely on the cottonwoods for at least part of their life cycle," Rood said. The flood would also help deer, beaver and other small animals that lived in the river valleys and used the riparian habitat.

Waterton park wardens also viewed the flood as a mix of good and bad. The alluvial fan at Blakiston Creek was being renewed and expanded, providing improved habitat for the park's elk and deer. The same processes of regeneration that were happening in the Oldman basin, were happening along the Waterton River and its tributaries.

Nonetheless, the park closed down for four days, so wardens could deal with ruined bridges and roads, curtailed power and phone services, and the threat of contaminated water. Near the townsite campground, emergency crews scooped up sand and gravel washed into Upper Waterton Lake from Cameron Creek, then used it to fill in sections of road the flooded stream had washed the gravel from. Portions of highway as large as a kilometre long and a half metre deep had been washed away on the Red Rock Road and Akamina Parkway. At Goat Haunt ranger station, at the south end of the lake in Glacier National Park, floating debris piled up many feet high along the shore, pushed there by strong winds blowing from the north. Docking facilities were damaged, as were parts of the deck at the interpretive display. As the lake level rose, the Waterton marina was inundated, forcing the cruise boats to tie up to the trees lining the far side of Emerald Bay. Cottages along the lake were knee-deep in water.

We witnessed all this damage and left the park just an hour before they closed the entrance road. Already water was lapping the highway in places, coming onto the road at Emerald Bay, much too close for comfort as we crossed the bridge over Blakiston Creek.

My husband and I had driven to Waterton from our home in Hill Spring that morning to see how Cameron Falls looked with so much water coming down. It had been raining hard, steadily, for several days. Going to the park on Highway 800 we'd seen water streaming off many fields in huge muddy sheets, filling irrigation ditches, roadside borrow pits and in some places, pooling on the road itself. At the Belly River Crossing, Mami Creek was braiding new channels and eventually would totally demolish an old house that time and neglect were already razing.

The spring 1995 rains were extraordinary in a region that typically gets about 20 inches of precipitation a year. In a region better known for its droughts, we'd had a wet autumn, a snowy winter — the snow pack in the mountains was huge - and a wet spring. Rains were moderate but steady throughout May, filling drainage basins and water tables. More than 20 inches had fallen west of Pincher Creek at the home of Bob Lyons, district agricultural officer. In Cardston, Ted Nelson received 25 inches in the month before the flood. The downpours of early June had no place to go except across the floodplains.

Though property damage was in the hundreds of millions, there was no life lost in the '95 flood. That wasn't the case 31 years earlier, when what is generally considered the worst flood in the area's recorded history occurred in the foothills areas of southern Alberta and Montana. Eight people in Montana and one Albertan died as a direct result of the June 8 and 9, 1964 flood. On the east side of Glacier National Park and in Waterton, more than ten inches of rain fell in two days, accompanied by a spell of warm weather that melted the winter's high snow accumulation.

Torrents of water poured down Divide and Kennedy Creeks in Glacier, wiping out roads and bridges. In Waterton the lake crested nine feet above its normal level and the townsite was evacuated as flood waters rose past Waterton Avenue. The Akamina Parkway was closed for repairs for the summer and many cottages were destroyed.

Since then, Divide Creek and Cameron Creek have been bermed and re-channelled and both parks have emergency flood plans in place. Warden Brent Kozachenko says, "the park's position is that flood events will occur on a regular basis. We'll do what we must to assure the safety of park residents and visitors, but floods are a part of the natural cycle."

A shorter version of this story was published in The Western Producer, July 1995.

__Barbara Grinder__ is the co-founder and coordinator of the Waterton - Glacier International Writers Workshop. Trained as a geographer, she has been managing editor of the Banff Crag and Canyon, a college journalism instructor, and the founding publisher/editor of the Waterton - Glacier Views. Barb has written for many publications, including The Western Producer, and the national aboriginal newspaper, Windspeaker. She works as a freelance writer/editor from her home in Hill Spring, Alberta where she does technical editing and publication design. She recently won the Premier's Award of Excellence for her work on the Canada-Alberta Environmentally Sustainable Agriculture Committee's report, Agricultural Impacts on Water Quality in Alberta.

On the Trail

Hiking is probably synonymous with a visit to Waterton and Glacier national parks. It's the activity that starts most fishing, picnicking, or camping trips, and a way to enjoy the parks beyond their front fringes. Whether you hike for the sheer joy of travelling through beautiful terrain or to get to a particular lake, peak or camping spot, it takes some effort. But even if the trip's a struggle, reaching one's objective can make it all worthwhile and memorable.

Trail companions can also make a hike worthwhile. In "Waterton Memories" Robert Campbell takes his young son on one of their first hikes together, where they share the joy of being in the mountains. Valerie Haig-Brown tells of three different fall excursions with her partner and regular hiking companion in "On the Quiet Edge."

Dan Vichorek has a somewhat irregular hiking partner in Death-on-the-Trail Trudy — a friend who likes to make the same hike each time they go out together. But Dan has a somewhat irregular sense of humour too, so they make great companions.

Not that there's anything wrong with repeating a hike. You begin to understand the succession of flowers, plants, birds and animals that live on a particular valley or ridge top and get to know a place in all its seasons and moods. Trudy Harrold captures two of those moods - and the special ambience of misty, rainy, mountain days in her poetry.

Fishermen frequently repeat their hikes, to test out the best spots. Unless, like Wayne Norstrom, they're shrewd enough to get someone else to go in ahead and scout out the place, especially when it's a mile-high lake. Dave Butler has undoubtedly walked into British Columbia's Akamina-Kishinena area more than once, but in "Adding a Jewel to the Crown" he tells about a special hike to this provincial park to commemorate a special occasion.

David Finch's hike up Mt. Head in the Kananaskis started out as an ordinary outdoor excursion, but turned into a truly memorable occasion when he met one of those brief summer storms that sneak in over the Continental Divide and give rise to the notion of mountain weather - if you don't like it, wait five minutes. In "The Day the Mountain Roared" Dave comes to understand a little more about how nature works, to his discomfort and amazement, but winds up with a fine tale to tell.

Hiker at Wall Lake, Akamina Ridge, Akamina - Kishenina Provincial Park.
Photo by Dave Butler

Adding a Jewel to the Crown

by Dave Butler

We tramp up and down the crowns and cols of a ridge that seems endless. Beneath a sky of deep high-altitude blue, we know that ridge-walking just doesn't get any better than this. After five hours of repeated ascents and descents, my hiking partner and I finally sit with our backs against a human-sized cairn that some unimaginative surveyor has labeled Border Monument #9. From this vantage point — the 2418 metre summit of Forum Peak, about as far south and as far east as anyone can get in British Columbia — we're tempted to play a game of "Twister, the Wilderness Edition." Put one foot here and it's in British Columbia. Place the other foot over there, and it's in Alberta. Reach your hand down there, and it's in Montana.

Our efforts on this late summer morning have carried us into the core of Akamina Kishinena Provincial Park, one of British Columbia's newest and most exciting protected areas. The Akamina Kishinena, or "AK" as it's known locally, resembles a mouse lying along the U.S. – Canada border, its nose pointing west and its tail upright along the boundary between B.C. and Alberta. Nearly 110 square kilometres, the

AK sits on the northern edge of Montana's 4,000 sq. km Glacier National Park. To the east, it's connected to Waterton Lakes National Park through two mountain passes, South Kootenay and Akamina, both of which are ecological, historical and recreational links.

The AK "is a very distinct piece of British Columbia, quite different from parks in the northern Rockies, or places like Mount Assiniboine," says Wayne Stetski, Kootenay District Manager for BC Parks. Stetski was pleased when the new park was added to a list of protected areas in the Kootenays, a list that includes larger parks like Mount Assiniboine, the Bugaboos and the Purcell Wilderness Conservancy. "What matters to me is that as large an area as possible is protected in this part of the Rockies."

The park consists of nearly equal portions of open alpine terrain and spruce-fir forests, and sits wholly within one of the 110 eco-section units into which B.C. has been divided. This same unit includes forests of pine and spruce in the Flathead River valley at elevations as low as 1100 metres, through mid- to high-elevation stands of Engelmann spruce and sub-alpine fir, up to windswept alpine terrain above 2500 metres. The new park also protects a variety of geologic features, the Akamina and Kishinena Ridges and the massive rock walls, pyramidal peaks and lake-filled cirque basins associated with them, that are international in their significance. And the AK preserves habitats for plants and wildlife found nowhere else in B.C.

This land of roadless valleys, together with Glacier and Waterton Lakes National Parks, is home to one of the densest grizzly bear populations in North America. The estimated 2.3 bears per 100 sq. km is an impressive assemblage of omnivores that shows no respect for provincial, state or national boundaries.

The July 1995 designation of the AK as a provincial park culminated a series of attempts that go back as far as 1917. In that year, the federal Superintendent of Dominion Parks recommended that the AK be included in Waterton Lakes National Park. His suggestion fell on deaf Ottawa ears. A succession of park managers made the same suggestion in 1927, 1938 and again in 1962.

This narrow chunk of the Rocky Mountains is now the most recently protected gem in a piece of geographic jewelry known as the "Crown of the Continent." George Bird Grinnell, an American conservationist who founded both the National Audubon Society and *Field and Stream* magazine, coined the term after realizing that waters from these mountains flowed into three of the largest river systems in North America — the Saskatchewan, the Mississippi and the Columbia. With a pair of bigger and higher-profile national parks as its next-door neighbours, the AK seems in an enviable position. Its two flanks are now guarded, and in the minds of many, the AK will always be considered a de facto part of the larger park complex. Wayne Stetski thinks that the park's major role will be, in reality, to "play its part in an internationally significant protected land mass."

In fact, when the AK park was established, the surrounding parks already had an impressive reputation in the world of protected areas. The Waterton-Glacier pair became the world's first International Peace Park in 1932. In 1976, the United Nations named the area a Biosphere Reserve. Finally, UNESCO designated the Waterton-Glacier International Peace Park a World Heritage Site in 1995. It joined an illustrious list that includes national parks such as Banff and Yellowstone, and provincial parks such as Mount Assiniboine and the Tatshenshini-Alsek.

From our inspiring viewpoint on the summit of Forum Peak, we spy on unsuspecting canoeists as they explore Waterton's Cameron Lake, 800 metres directly below and to the east. We swivel our binoculars in an arc to take in the checker-board prairie fields far to the northeast. To the south, we gaze across the Canada – U.S. border at the most northerly and wildest section of Glacier National Park. Our eyes stop at a wide swath in the sub-alpine forest – the international boundary. Keeping this border defoliated, a requirement of the International Boundary Commission, seems an unnecessary and rather ironic dissection of an international park dedicated to peace. Finally, to the north, our eyes follow the divide between B.C. and Alberta as it meanders through Akamina Pass, over Mount Rowe and Festubert Mountain, and on to South Kootenay Pass and the headwaters of Kishinena Creek, all in the AK's northern end.

It is this unparalleled visual smorgasbord that has repeatedly drawn Janice Strong to the AK. An avid outdoor photographer and hiker, Strong is the author of a popular hiking guide to the East Kootenay. "Visually," she says, "the park appears vast. Everywhere you turn it's all different, and it's all big." Of the last time she sat atop Forum Peak, Strong says: "it was as if we were sharing the countries, without feeling as though we were crossing any borders."

Akamina Kishinena is a name most Westerners won't recognize even if used properly in a sentence. It acknowledges the park's native history. Akamina is a Cree word for benchland or mountain pass, while Kishinena is thought to be the native name for white or balsam fir. Cree, Blackfoot and Kootenay peoples, travelling across the Rockies to trade and hunt buffalo, used South Kootenay Pass as a regular route.

One of the first white men to travel the area was Lieutenant Thomas Blakiston, of the famed Palliser expedition. Helped by Kootenay native guides, Blakiston crossed South Kootenay Pass (which he called Boundary Pass) from west to east in September 1858. Despite the fact that he climbed through the pass in two feet of snow, wearing only thin moccasins, he had the presence of mind to stop and measure its elevation. Using the best equipment available at the time, his rough calculation was only a few hundred feet short of the 2100 metre figure that we use today. Since Blakiston's visit, loggers, miners, trappers, and hunters have explored the valleys, ridges, and lakes. Along the way they abandoned cabins, sawmills and oil wells. Some of the AK's colourful place names arose from the antics, explorations, and wrecks of these early white visitors. A pair of trappers who tried to eat the leathery tail of a beaver named Beavertail Lake, just east of Starvation and King Edward Peaks. Giving up in frustration, they supposedly left the tail spiked to a spruce tree as a warning to future culinary explorers. Pack-mule Lake received its name after a hapless pack animal tumbled down the steep north side of Bennett Pass, scattering itself and its load over a grassy slope above the lake.

Akamina and Kishinena are not just the largest creek drainages in the AK, they are also the names of the two most impressive ridges. It is along the undulations of Akamina Ridge that we have laboured this morning to reach Forum Peak. These two spines of weathered rock, running east-west along the southern part of the AK, are the dominant features in the Clark Range, the easternmost range of the B.C. Rockies. They are also the upper edge of the Lewis Thrust, a unique geologic feature that is at its most obvious and most awe-inspiring in this region. The Thrust began to move about 85 million years ago, when a wedge of rock – several kilometres thick and hundreds wide – was shoved up and over softer rock. Since then, erosion and glaciation have slowly stripped away the upper surfaces of the original wedge.

Along the crests of both ridges, and in their massive, forbidding northern faces, ancient sedimentary rocks lie exposed in their original bedding layers, some horizontal and others slightly down-warped. These consist of green and red argillites, sandstones, siltstones, and limestones, estimated at 800 million to 1.6 billion years old. Along the ridge, we find rocks the size of dinner tables. Their surfaces hint at the processes by which they were created. There are ripples from waves on ancient beaches, and mud cracks formed by the drying rays of the sun millions of years ago. These extraordinary ridges provide a hiking opportunity that's unmatched in all the Canadian Rockies. Janice Strong says, "That's because Akamina Ridge is so big and so safe, you're not feeling as though you're on a really narrow ridge, always wondering where your tripod legs are, or where to put your feet. You can see forever from up there."

As we retrace our steps westward along that ridge in late afternoon, we walk the line, literally, between North Kintla Creek on our left and the Akamina Creek valley on our right. From the ridge, we peer down at a family of four, unaware of our presence, as they picnic on the open shores of Forum Lake. Farther along the ridge, the green of our tent at the Wall Lake backcountry campsite seems tantalizingly close. Yet it's 700 meters below us, at the base of a wall so steep that it shows on topographic maps as a thick dark smudge. That's never a good sign for a tired hiker.

There's also a trio of mountain bikers on the edge of the Wall Lake lagoon. Like most visitors to the lake, they carve a few boot-ski turns on the perpetual snowfield at the lake's west end. For a few moments, they disappear into an ice cave, a popular but hazardous attraction that becomes accessible at the end of most summers. Like these cyclists, more people each year discover the AK through Waterton Lakes National Park.

Although Akamina Pass is only a 20-minute walk from a paved highway, the AK continues to retain its solitary wildness. "It's not that well known yet by those who come to use Waterton," says Wayne Stetski, "so you can still find many quiet places, and you can still get a sense of wilderness fairly quickly."

We pause for a sip of water before leaving the ridge via the trail down to Wall Lake, a route lush with wildflowers even in August, then spread our map and air photos on a patch of red argillite. It's a last chance to identify landmarks from one of the best viewpoints in the park. From here, there's no question that the AK is big and wild. To the west, we pick out the nunatak in the headwaters of Kintla Creek, its shadow pointing directly at us like a beckoning finger. Still within the AK, just north of the US border, the nunatak is a dramatic rock pillar, draped with a threadbare vegetative rug. Shaped like a loaf of bread, it rises above the surrounding terrain, almost completely untouched by the forces of glaciation.

On our last night at Wall Lake we carry steaming cups of sweet tea down to the pebbled shore. Only the rings of feeding trout break the lake surface. Just below the crest of Akamina Ridge, far above us, a solitary mountain goat crosses a precarious ledge. The setting sun drops behind Bennett Pass, creating a distinct line between dark and light that inches up the wall above the lake. Finally, for only a moment, the uppermost layer of Akamina Ridge – likely a band of the red argillite that we used as a map table earlier in the day – glows crimson with the last light of day before joining the rest of the park in deepening shade.

I pick up a piece of that same rock from the edge of the lake and turn it over and over in my fingers. One side is smooth, the other rough with the indentations of raindrops that fell from an ancient sky. Akamina-Kishinena Provincial Park, like this piece of red stone, is a wild and rugged jewel that preserves millions of years of Rocky Mountain history. The jewel has finally taken its rightful place in the Crown.

'Adding a Jewel to the Crown' was first published in the summer 1996 issue of Beautiful British Columbia.

Dave Butler *is a writer and photographer from Cranbrook, B.C. who works and plays in the Rocky Mountain Trench. His work has been published in Beautiful British Columbia, Explore, Nature Canada, BC Outdoors and Pacific Yachting, and he writes a regular column for Inside/Outdoors, the newsletter of the Outdoor Writers of Canada. His photographs have appeared on calendars and web-sites, and in publications from Grolier, Nelson, the B.C. government, and Tourism Rockies. He is also a professional forester and biologist. Dave was a participant in the 1995 and 1997 Writers Workshops.*

Waterton Memories

by Robert Campbell

I have visited Waterton Park several times each year since 1967, when I first moved to southern Alberta. The park has been a refuge for my family and me, a place to rest, to heal, to recreate, to just hang out. When friends or relatives come to visit us we almost always take them to Waterton. We often refer to it as *our* park. And there have been times when we've felt we were the only people in the park, especially in late fall or early spring. We have come to view the park as a place of retreat, solitude and renewal.

My memories of the park are rich and varied: the first family cook-out, opening our tent flaps on an early July morning to six inches of snow, spotting elk, incurring the wrath of a bull moose at Cameron Lake, or trying to get a small group of Cub Scouts to sleep on a star-filled night at Crandell Lake. The park has helped me shape my views towards nature and the environment. It has helped bring our family closer together.

My fondest memory is of a hike I took in late August of 1971 with my oldest son Rob. It was his eighth birthday and we had camped overnight at the campground that was then at Cameron Lake. We arose early, had breakfast and drove back to the townsite. We parked our car at the start of the trail and began our journey. I was somewhat apprehensive since I didn't know how well Rob would respond to this adventure.

Autumn was in the air. The sky was a brilliant blue that somehow seemed bluer when viewed as a backdrop to the mountains. By the same token, the aspen leaves seemed more golden when set against azure skies. The air was pine scented, crisp and clean, and it hinted at a warm day ahead. I walked slowly up the trail, not wanting to out-pace my small son. What struck me as I walked was the quietness. Aside from an occasional swirl from the treetops caused by a light breeze, the only sounds were our muted footsteps.

As we looked south along Upper Waterton Lake, glistening white gulls glided lazily overhead. The lake was still and deep, dark blue. Occasional yellow butterflies paused to drink dew drops from blades of grass. The sun warmed our backs. It was a day when Waterton was on its best behaviour.

Walking calms the turmoil of the mind and this walk was no exception. A calmness came over me and I became more aware of the natural beauty around us. I felt that this was where I should be, at this time, with my son, in this place.

Rob, being curious beyond measure, wandered along picking up tiny stones and throwing them, running helter-skelter around me, stopping to poke a tiny stick into a small hole in a rock. "Will we see any bears?" he asked. "Probably not," I replied. We walked further, hand-in-hand in an immense and pervasive silence, stepping carefully to avoid roots and stones that might trip us. We both turned as a light breeze skimmed through the treetops and started the golden aspen leaves delicately trembling on their branches. A chipmunk darted across our path and disappeared into the underbrush.

As we walked, the stillness gave way to a barely discernable muffled background noise. At first, I thought it was the wind picking up. Then for the first time on the hike, Rob began to run ahead of me as if he sensed some unknown treasure ahead. For a minute I lost sight of him. Then from the sound, I knew we were nearing the falls. As they came into view, I saw Rob standing on the footbridge, his arms raised outwards toward the water as if giving a benediction. "This is beautiful. I like it here," he said, taking my hand. We both stood in awe, on this sacred spot – water cascading over rock, rushing downward to its ultimate destination, Hudson Bay.

I felt buoyed as the mist from the falls delicately caressed our warm faces. We stood in a state of curiosity, reverence and wonder. The quiet we had experienced along the trail had been replaced by a symphonic crescendo of water over rock. My mind came to silence – thought ceased. We were no longer observers of the scene; we were part of it, experiencing an epiphany of nature - of water, sky, mountain and forest. I was renewed and filled with gratitude and awe. Rob stood in wide-eyed wonderment.

I've had many experiences in our park over the years since, but my first encounter with Bertha Falls is still the benchmark for measuring the quality of these experiences.

Walking the trails and paths of Waterton has given me an appreciation of the complexity, interdependence and fragility of ecosystems. But beyond that, each time I enter the park — spring, summer, fall or winter — I sense an overpowering presence that extends beyond the natural wonders of the place. What to call it, I'm not sure. Nature, God, Creation — it's a transforming presence that I can only experience and appreciate in wildness. Bertha Falls was the beginning of that appreciation.

Robert Campbell is a storyteller, workshop leader and meditation teacher, and has worked as a health care administrator and management consultant in various parts of Canada, including the Northwest Territories and Alberta. He is currently works a health promotion specialist for the Chinook Regional Health Authority in Lethbridge, Alberta. He is on the board of directors of the Alberta Wilderness Association and the Southern Alberta Environment Group. Bob has degrees in English and Education from the University of Lethbridge and a Masters in Adult Education from Saint Francis Xavier University in Antigonish, Nova Scotia. He was a participant in the 1999 Writers Workshop.

Canoeist on Cameron Lake, Waterton.   **Photo by Bruce Masterman**

On the Quiet Edge

by Valerie Haig-Brown

The warm sunny days of Indian summer make it seem impossible there will ever be winter, but experience tells us differently here on the edge of the Rockies and there is an urgency to be outside. All summer there were chores to be done, or too many guests, or the garden (alas, now almost over) needed weeding instead. Now, a day or two around the house and garden and what isn't done seems much less insistent. It becomes absolutely necessary to go hiking.

First, the annual fall climb up the 400-foot cliff into Lineham Basin. At this time of year, the only other obvious inhabitants of the basin are some bighorn rams, grazing their way across the scree, looking fat and ready for winter. The larches are as golden as you could possibly ask. There is not a breath of wind, so they and the dark evergreens are reflected to perfection in the five small lakes. In the shallows, fish skitter away as we walk along the shore, but farther out there is rise after rise all afternoon. We both fish for a while, stop to eat lunch, and then I realize that dream I always have on the way up in the morning on any hike.

Somewhere ahead is a patch of dry moss or grass or warm rock where I can stretch out with my pack for a pillow, feel the sun and the wind in the right combination, and snooze for a few minutes after watching the clouds sail by. Today I find a mossy hummock and indulge myself in one of the great small pleasures of life.

Then, back to fishing. John goes one way, I the other to explore the big lake. I don't have much hope for my sloppy casts on the glassy surface and after a few minutes I prove myself right. John returns and on his first gentle cast catches a fish that has been cruising back and forth in front of me. Oh, well. John catches a couple more nice ones while I supervise from high on the scree slope, watching the clouds slide in over the Continental Divide and send shadows across the green and gold of the trees and the red and grey of the rocks. Finally, it is time to gather ourselves for the descent of the cliff and the trek out to the car before dark. And that's one perfect day.

This is the year we have a friend's canoe. The weather goes on being perfect – one sky-blue day after another. A few more chores done so the conscience is easy, and we set off for a second outing, to try our hands at the paddles. We have both done a little canoeing – John in the North and I as a child on Vancouver Island – and we have talked a lot about getting ourselves one, but the moment has never been quite right.

We look first at Upper Waterton Lake, but there is a chop and a few whitecaps. We would have liked to explore a new shoreline, but it seems wiser today to follow the middle lake, whose shore we skated along several times, a few winters ago. And here, high cliffs shelter what would otherwise be the windiest part of the route.

I am surprised almost immediately by how shallow the channel is between the Upper and Middle Lakes. I have walked the shoreline. Why did I assume it would be deep? Perhaps because I know the big lake is very deep – the deepest in the Canadian Rockies. We paddle past the cliffs to the beach at Wishbone, on the east shore, and climb around on ridges that are part of a wall that once held the glaciers back until they carved the big lake basin. We eat our lunch and watch half-a-dozen windsurfers scoot back and forth below us like exotic butterflies. Then back to the canoe to paddle on down the lake.

I always think of the people in the wagons travelling across the prairie day after day when I fly or drive so easily across that great plain. Here on the lake, I think of voyageurs paddling endlessly to gather furs. It's easy for us. We are well fed, well rested and we have picked our day. There is no urgency and we will not have to portage. And we are two in a small canoe with no load beyond our lunch, a couple of jackets, the binoculars and the camera. But there must have been days when those hard-working men also had the wind at their backs, the sun over their shoulders, and a good long stretch of calm water that gave them a chance to enjoy the rhythm of their stroke, the sound of the canoe's ripple, and the sight of blue skies and distant mountains.

A slop gets up on the way back, but the wind is warm and we paddle steadily on with no difficulty. One great bald eagle circles up and away from us as we approach, followed by three immatures. We cross the lake and meet the immatures close up again. They sit, wings spread, on the wind just above their perches and then glide off back down the lake. A white-tailed doe and her fawn come down the beach to drink and watch us a few minutes before heading back into the bush. The fawn flashes its tail as though it's being careless to amble away without a warning signal. Or is it practicing for real dangers? The wind is behind us on the last leg and we slide onto the beach. Another perfect day.

The perfect days don't last forever, of course, but we manage another good hike and possibly an even better day of canoeing. This time we put in on the Lower Lake and paddle upstream where we can see fish swirling about beneath us. I snooze on some smooth round rocks on a bar while John catches a fish.

When we pull the canoe out of the water, we feel fulfilled and resolve yet again to get our own. But there's no rush. It will soon be winter.

Valerie Haig-Brown is a writer/editor who has lived on the northern edge of Waterton for the last 20 years. She is the author of Deep Currents, a biography of her parents Roderick and Ann Haig-Brown, and a co-author of Waterton and Northern Glacier Trails. She has collected and published four books of her father's writings since his death in the late seventies. Valerie has worked in educational television and as a staff editor for several well-known Toronto-based magazines. An avid walker, she has traveled most of the mountains and valleys in the Waterton area and has participated in all three Writers Workshops.

Fly fishing on the Elk River, British Columbia.   **Photo by Wayne Norstrom**

Wayne Norstrom *has been writing about having fun in the great outdoors since 1980. His irreverent brand of humor and helpful tips on hunting and fishing have appeared in Buckmaster, the Alberta Hunting and Fishing Magazine, Outdoor Canada and many other publications. When he's not out in the woods, he can be found at his day job, as a wildlife technician with Alberta Fish and Wildlife, or reading from his extensive library on wild places.*

The Mile High Club

by Wayne Norstrom

It wasn't a pretty sight. The scree slope Colleen and I were crossing was super heated by the noon sun and I was soaked in sweat from the climb and the height. Rocks, kicked out by my stumbling feet, slid, rolled and then bounced into nothing, and I knew it wouldn't take much for this tired old angler to do the same. Hell, even the sheep trails were below us — way below us. What was I doing here anyway?

I had been lured into this miserable situation by promises of spectacular cutthroat fishing, and pushed there by Colleen, who actually enjoys exercise and high places. At just under 8,000 feet elevation the oxygen-depleted air and summer sun were having their way with me. My pack had gained in weight with every foot of elevation and my little four weight Loomis rod felt like a telephone pole. I soldiered on, but I wasn't having fun.

It goes without saying that once we'd climbed to the top of the ridge, we had to go down to reach the lake. Dropping over the compulsory cliffs and sliding down last winter's snow banks we finally reached our destination. I flopped on the blanket of wild flowers and sucked up a couple of litres of water from a small seep along the lake's edge.

Lying there on the water's edge things looked better. Mountains surrounded us in all directions, the alpine meadows were blanketed in flowers, and on a nearby scree face a ewe and lamb were moving into higher country, not wanting to share the basin with a couple of anglers.

On the lake a fish surfaced. "A riser, Colleen" I said. "There's a riser." Maybe the effort was going to be worthwhile after all.

It was. I spent the afternoon tossing a barbless Stimulator to cruising cutthroats. It was classic fly fishing with the trout coming from the depths to the surface, first as shadows, then as real fish. They sucked down the fly with a small *plop*. These weren't big fish, they seldom are in these high, cold, tough environments. But man, are they pretty! The fish ranged in color from silver to irridescent green, with sides that were often brilliant orange or gold. I released them all.

The tranquillity of the day was suddenly broken by the arrival of a pack train. They gave me that condescending look horse people reserve for those who are relegated to boot leather for transportation, but suddenly that changed. "Hey, he's caught one," someone yelled. I played the fish with a little extra show just for them, then flipped out my fly and did it again. In minutes I had company. It turned out one of the dudes was an avid angler. I lent him my rod and almost had a fight getting it back.

"I've never seen anything like it," he exclaimed as he released another fish. "I didn't know there were fish up here." He had hit the subject of high country lake fishing right on the head — mile high fishing is a hit and miss business, with a lot of the lakes being total misses.

The afternoon got even better when we were able to pass that pack train on the way out. Colleen and I hopped and slid, straight down the scree slopes, while the horses had to be led along a series of switchbacks, taking the long way home. It just doesn't get much better.

One of the things I've learned about high country fishing is never to walk in first. I'm old and weak, but smart enough to let somebody else go ahead of me to scout out the territory. I had heard of a high lake in Waterton that was a winner every year, producing a lot of fish. Colleen and I were determined to try it and on a hot day in July we were all set to go. At the trail head we met a couple of hikers coming out.

"Been up to Goat Lake?" I asked.

"Yeah, lots of snow up there. It's still froze over," they replied. "It was cold camping, but we saw a nice grizzly. And there's no one there."

Well. I'm here to say there were two less that day. We eventually made it up to the lake a couple of weeks later, but had limited success with the fish. There were lots of cutthroats swimming around, but they were having little to do with me. So much for slow-witted, uneducated high mountain trout.

Trips into the high country can be beautiful but brutal. In late September Colleen and I walked into a high country lake in southeastern B.C. The poplars were turning yellow and the high tamaracks were shades of gold. Snow blanketed the ground and made things wet, but stories of big trout had me pumped. The lake was only a couple of hours from the road and the cool temperature made for an enjoyable trip. The fish were there in good numbers but without the size I had expected. Still it was a good day. Until Colleen fell on tough times.

She was balanced on a big rock, fishing a cliff face and had actually hooked into one of the big ones the lake is famous for. I readied the camera while Colleen worked on the fish. As she lifted a large, brilliantly colored cutthroat from the water it came off the hook. "Grab that fish, Colleen" I yelled, "it will make a great photo." Colleen grabbed, the trout flopped, and both of them were in the lake.

The fish submerged, but Colleen managed to keep her head above the water. I pulled her out by the parka hood. (Luckily she had dropped the rod on the rock.) Although Colleen claimed the water wasn't cold, the fact she immediately ran a hot bath when we got home said otherwise. If we'd had to cross a lot of open, windswept slopes she could have been in trouble. As it was, she gained some good experience.

Mile high lakes aren't for everyone. It helps if you enjoy flower-painted mountain meadows, the whistle of a marmot, or the sight of a grizzly. But an angler also has to be in good shape, have fit partners, and have certain mental deficiencies - like wanting to bathe in ice cold water.

'The Mile High Club' was originally published in the June 1999 issue of Western Sportsman magazine.

KEW

Between the months of April and October, when the Peace Park grizzly bears are not in hibernation, it's wise to keep beer and other alcoholic beverages under lock and key. (Most writers opt to drink their booze, to keep it from the bears.) Grizzlies have a natural affinity for liquor and a keen nose to sniff out caches of booze. Many a visitor and resident has been awakened from his slumber to find a herd of grizzlies in the beer fridge. Once the bears start on the booze, it's best to let them finish as they can be bloody mean drunks.

Off to Avalanche Lake with Death-on-the-Trail Trudy

by Dan Vichorek

Suddenly, I snap awake from a snooze in front of my television and I'm thinking about Avalanche Lake in Glacier Park. I can almost smell the pines and feel the chill breeze sweeping down from Bearhat Mountain.

What this probably means is that I'm about to get a telephone call. It will be my friend Trudy and she will say from some unpredictable but faraway location, "I'm going to be there tomorrow, can we go to Glacier?" For Trudy, going to Glacier means going to Avalanche Lake.

This is not a romantic friendship: Trudy is a generation behind me and only occasionally pretends to take me seriously. I have been a friend to her and her family since she was 11. She doesn't live around here, has no roots at any particular place, disappears off my radar screen for a year or two at a time, never writes or calls. Sometimes a college student, sometimes a productive citizen, sometimes a freeloader on her father, she ricochets around the western hemisphere on no identifiable itinerary. Occasionally she shows up at my place without advance notice and immediately says, "Can we go to Glacier?" And so we do. And if we can possibly manage it, this means we have to walk in to Avalanche.

Trudy's first visit to Avalanche was not a happy one. It came about when she was going through some sort of childhood fits and her mother decided the kid needed fresh air. Learning that a friend was headed for Glacier Park for the weekend, Trudy's mom sent Trudy along.

Turned out, the guy was going to hike to Avalanche. Trudy was not exactly outfitted for hiking. As she recalls, she had on a little dress with long cotton stockings, a thin jacket of a type that was popular in the third grade that year, and some sort of fashionable shoes. She'd still rather freeze and be fashionable than be comfortable and out of style if there's anyone around whose opinion might count. Mine doesn't. She tells people I wear the same clothes all year.

The man in charge of Trudy on that first trip to Avalanche got along with kids mainly by ignoring them and their problems. He wasn't worried about Trudy's city shoes and thin garments. Nope. He set off briskly for Avalanche and told Trudy not to lag or a bear would get her. She recalls that she was not a happy hiker. She tried sulking, howling, and refusing to move, none of which got her anywhere. When she fell behind, her companion kept going and was soon out of sight. She was then inspired to catch up, only to start howling again.

Soon enough, she had more to howl about. It was early summer and halfway into Avalanche they ran into deep, wet snowbanks. Her companion plunged on, heedless. Trudy was soon soaked, and her fashionable shoes were threatening to disintegrate.

Somehow, she avoided hypothermia that day and made it safely to Avalanche. Oddly enough, contrary to all common sense probabilities, she remembered the lake as a place of serene, mystical beauty, mist rising off the water, clouds shredding in the crags overhead.

Years later, when she was relying on me to provide her outdoor experiences, she couldn't remember the name of the place, but wanted me to guide her back there. She remembered the hike in as being about 10 or 12 miles, which didn't help me figure out where it was. Several times we hiked in to other lakes looking for her lost paradise. We drove past the Avalanche trailhead many times, hurrying by to avoid the crush of tourists queued up to walk the popular Trail of the Cedars.

Then, one year as we were driving along Lake McDonald, Trudy demanded access to an outhouse. We stopped at the Avalanche Trailhead, and when she saw the Trail of the Cedars, she remembered the spot. Paraphrasing Brigham Young, she said, "This is it."

So now when the strange rebounds of her life bring her into this vicinity, we hike to Avalanche. She has never again seen it looking just the way it did the first time she saw it, but as she says, it is never without a mood; never a mere slack puddle in the woods at the foot of a mountain. Though she is totally a city person these days, devoted to the things of the city, Avalanche Lake is a place she can go, and get her groove back.

On one hike to Avalanche not long ago, I was making fun of the terrible temper she had demonstrated on her first unwilling hike to Avalanche. (I do this carefully, since she still has that same temper). Reflecting on the difficulties of that day and her disintegration from fashion plate into a sort of water-soaked mutt, I said, "I think we could have called you, 'Death-on-the-Trail Trudy.'"

"And we could call you 'horse's ass' Vichorek."

"Well, we could," I said quickly, "but if you'll just listen for a moment I'll tell you why you should be flattered." Then I told her about "Death-on-the-Trail Reynolds. Trudy is readily distracted by a good story. My long years of telling her stories that were completely true, partly true, or total fabrications led her at one bounce in her life to become a journalist. A newspaper journalist, which I told her was the only kind to be.

On one of her newspaper assignments, she was detailed to a large airport to get a story about some eminence who was arriving. Waiting on the tarmac for the eminence, she was swallowed up by a rowdy crowd of television reporters who shoved her out of the way to get their cameras in the best spot. Being shoved out of the way was all it took for the alter ego, Death-on-Trail Trudy, to emerge. If they wanted shoving, shoving they would have. That night, Trudy's father casually mentioned that he had seen her on TV. "You looked like a real bitch," he said.

"Ah, you made me proud," I said.

"You were very helpful with my career," she said.

"You mean, when I told you to always get at least two sources for every story, and always follow your instincts?

"No, I mean the way you showed me to brace my feet, one behind the other in the direction I was going to shove, and to grab my elbows and lock my arms in front of me when I attack. Those television guys with big cameras on their shoulders go over like bowling pins."

"As I recall, that advice was intended for use in playing basketball."

"And who was it that told me that life is a game?"

* * *

The lake was moody and dimpled on the day we finally made it to Avalanche, with gentle soaking rain from low, motionless clouds. Waterfalls unseen in the fog were roaring off the cliffs, delivering icy runoff to the lake. At the lake we lingered, examining pebbles on the lake bottom, looking for loons, not talking, until we were miserably wet.

On the way back to the trailhead, I stepped to the side of the trail to avoid a large puddle just as a ranger came into view. She reprimanded me for stepping off the trail, and delivered the usual lecture about trail damage, the duties of responsible hikers, and so on. I had given Trudy this same lecture many times (though I never insisted she walk through the middle of foot-deep water in her color-coordinated hiking boots). After the ranger left Trudy said "You ought to be ashamed."

Later, as I sat shivering under a tent flap guzzling schnapps-laced hot chocolate, Trudy asked me, "So was there really such a person as Death-on-the-Trail Reynolds?

"Yes there was," I said authoritatively, and then shut up and sat silent for some time.

"So you gonna tell me or not," she finally said.

* * *

Albert Reynolds was one of those hard-as-nails guys that populated the west a hundred years ago. He was a logger by profession, and came to Montana in 1871 to look for trees to cut down. He and his wife Sarah had a house at 319 Blake Street in Helena.

"I went and looked at that house," I told Trudy.

"Figures. You're the only guy I know who would ride a bus three days to look at a place where Hemingway once fished."

"It wasn't just any place. It was the big Two-Hearted River."

Anyway, Reynolds was working in the timber in the Flathead when the national forest reserves were created and he decided to retire into government work as a forest ranger. He met the qualifications, which, according to the founder of the Forest Service, were that he "must be able to take care of himself and his horses under very trying conditions; build trails and cabins, ride all day and night; pack, shoot, and fight fire without losing his head... All this requires a very vigorous constitution. It means the hardest kind of physical work from beginning to end."

After years of 16-hour days in the woods, Al Reynolds thought this government work would be like a vacation. He spent his first years as a forest ranger in the Flathead forest reserve, transferring to Glacier Park when it was set aside from forest lands in 1910.

Despite his advancing age (61), Reynolds at this time was still a prodigious hiker. He saw no inconvenience in having to walk 17 miles each way to get his mail, winter and summer. It was probably somebody who tried to keep up with him who first called him "Death-on-the-Trail."

"I'd like to see him walk to Avalanche Lake in the snow while he was wearing a schoolgirl dress and strappy little shoes."

"He probably never really appreciated how hard it would be to walk in deep snow in a dress."

"So what finally happened to this guy?"

"He froze himself up on a walk back home from Waterton where he had gone to see his friend, Kootenai Brown, who was superintendent of Waterton Park. He tried to snowshoe 17 miles home when it was 42 below. Froze his feet, then got pneumonia and that was the end of him."

"When did this happen?"

"In January, 1913."

"So who exactly was Kootenai Brown?"

"He was a tough old bird who met all the criteria as a protector of the wilderness on the Canadian side. For example, he once shot a man in Fort Benton."

"And that was good?"

"Oh yeah. You know how you used to complain about not being taken seriously? In Kootenai Brown's days, a dead man on your resume would help people to take you seriously."

"Why'd they call him 'Kootenai?'"

"His real name was John George Brown, and that's no kind of name for a colorful western character."

"So why 'Kootenai?'"

"I guess he spent a lot of time over in the Kootenai drainage and got named after the country. By the way, did you know 'Kootenai" gets spelled three different ways? Canadians spell it 'Kootenay,' The Kutenai Indians spell it 'Kutenai," and we spell it 'Kootenai.'"

"And why is it that I am so interested in this?"

"I'm not sure. Maybe it's because in some parts of the world they fight wars over stuff like that."

"Oh yeah, like, we're going to fight a war with Canada."

"Not many countries live cheek-by-jowl and never get into a scrap. It's kind of a miracle."

"I guess we just don't care as much as we should about spelling."

"It's not only spelling. Most countries argue about their boundaries. We never have, to speak of. Did you know that Americans and Canadians jointly surveyed the boundary across the plains? From Lake of the Woods to Waterton, they surveyed it together. They built hundreds of rock piles to mark the location of the boundary. In later years, we checked those rock piles and discovered that out of all the hundreds of them, only one was actually on the legal boundary."

"Is that true?"

"I believe it is."

"So neither Canadians nor Americans knew how to survey?"

"They were pretty close. The point is, nobody got their throat cut over it."

"I'm dying to hear more interesting facts about our relationship with Canada"

"Your sarcasm is noted, but as a journalist you should know the importance of whiskey in international relations. In the early days, western Canada was lacking in whiskey, so American entrepreneurs brought it up from the Missouri River port at Fort Benton and sold it to the locals. Business was good, because, of course, it was illegal."

"They were selling it to Native Americans?"

"They weren't carrying ID cards. They may have been Native Canadians."

"Eventually, Dudley Do Right ran off most of the entrepreneurs and locked up the rest. Then, in the 1920s, Americans went temporarily crazy and made whiskey illegal. Fortunately, the Canadians retained their sanity and put on additional shifts at their distilleries. American entrepreneurs brought the Canadian product across the line, not fretting about the possibly imprecise alignment of that border, and business was good. Also colorful. Big Packards loaded with booze were dodging the Revenue men in the frozen grainfields up by Havre, in the service of a thirsty nation."

"That was a nice hike today," Trudy said, tiring of ancient lore. "I don't know why you never bring extra clothes. You always get wet and then sit around drinking and shivering. Don't you ever learn?"

"You know," I said, pouring some more schnapps, "it's kind of a shame that we set aside all this land as a park when the only place you're interested in is one lake."

* * *

And now the phone rings, and I find myself as in a dream returning from a great distance. The waking dream is hard to shake off, and the last part of it to leave is the anxious illusion that I am wet and have mud on my feet. And then the voice on the phone: "I'll be in town tomorrow, can we go to Glacier?"

Dan Vichorek says he was born a long time ago in Livingston Montana, in a hospital that was won in a poker game. He was graduated from the University of Montana with a degree in journalism, and says he inexplicably worked as a reporter in Billings, Montana, and in Chicago. He currently works as a technical writer for the state government in Helena, Montana and produces a humor column for several small publications. He has written for Montana Magazine and is the author of five books on Montana history, including Montana's Homestead Era and Montana's Cowboys. Occasionally he finds time to write letters to newspaper editors to alert them to conspiracies and to deplore progress. Dan was a participant in the 1999 Writers Workshop.

Misty morning in Waterton.   **Photo by Kirk Harrold**

Trudy Harrold *retired from a career in educational consulting to develop a small in-home writing and publishing venture, Aspengrove Communications, focusing on history, ecology and learning. She writes poetry and has written a book for the Lamont Health Care Centre.*

Kirk Harrold *has professionally explored many areas of photography, specializing in theatre archival work. He has a background in the sciences and enjoys the challenges of photographing nature's changing moods.*

The couple farm near Lamont, Alberta. The Harrolds were both participants at the 1997 Writers Workshop.

Mountain Suite

Excerpts from a song cycle

by Trudy Harrold

MOUNTAIN RAIN

Everything changes when it rains here.

Curtains of grey transform clear sky,

Rock turns to mist-ephemeral outlines of sleeping giants.

Trees sharpen their looks with dark wet trunks

Against brilliant green cloaks,

Dripping a thousand jewels.

MORNING MIST

Rising from the river,

Hanging from the sky,

Ghostly apparitions of mist frame treeline profiles,

Outline rock, and hide faces of mountains

In an ever-changing game of hide and seek.

Mountain goats above Baring Falls, Glacier National Park.

Photo by Bert Gildart

The Day the Mountain Roared

by David Finch

It started out simply enough: jump on a mountain bike and ride up Flat Creek trail to scout out the north side of Mount Head, the highest peak in the Highwood Range of the Canadian Rockies.

Cowboy friends said they had walked up the north side, carrying rifles no less. In their cowboy boots. If they can do it, so can I. Besides, I had climbed Holy Cross Mountain just a week before and it was only a few metres shorter than Mount Head.

From noon until 3 p.m. I worked my way up the ridge, looking in vain for an easy route up the north side of this pile of rotten rock. Finally, I reached a cliff I couldn't climb and spent some time taking in the view, as a few grey clouds scudded across the top of the mountain. Then I set off back down the ridge.

Suddenly. . . Ouch! I needed protection for my hands and head. Gloves would ease the pain. Boxing gloves. Welder's gloves. Winter mitts. Even my biking gloves, put on the wrong hands upside down would have helped. So would my bike helmet. But they were at my bicycle a half kilometre away and more than a hundred metres below, across a creek that was swelling with each passing second as a violent, noisy, lightning-filled hailstorm vented itself on the tiny valley of Head Creek. Staggering down the slope, I winced as the hail beat my head and pounded my shoulders. Finally, I ducked under a tree long enough to cut a conifer branch and stuff it into the hood of my anorak to protect my skull from the hailstones.

Sounds of madly rushing water greeted me as I reached the creek that I had stepped across easily just a few hours earlier. It had swollen dozens of times and was changing as I watched into a torrent of chocolate brown tumult, floating with hail. Carefully, I waded the raging flood and found my bicycle under a tree. I pulled the branch from my hood, donned my helmet, stuffed smaller branches into my coat sleeves to protect my hands and set off.

Up the steep bank I carried my two-wheeled steed, wondering how a horse would react to such a storm. More than 20 centimetres of hail lay on the ground, like slushy ball bearings through which I pushed my bike down the trail to the first of five creek crossings. Though badly swollen, the first ford was wide and less than knee deep so I plunged through, intent on getting to my last river crossing at the Flat Creek and Head Creek confluence as soon as possible, knowing the Flat could be even more flooded than its minor tributary.

Lightning crashed. Thunder boomed. Hail staccatoed the ground, the water, the rocks, my back and my arms. The bicycle bell played its own wild tune as hail pummeled it too.

Just short of the second creek crossing I felt a sudden wind. Stronger than the hailstorm, it swept over me from the side. Then came an unearthly howl, like a ghost from a scary thriller. I looked to the left and watched as a small dry gulch a few metres away from the main trail began rushing with clean water. Then it changed.

From high up the steep canyon wall, a torrent of mud and rock cascaded down the tiny watercourse. Prudently, I moved off the trail, away from the growing debris flow, marveling at its power and sound: it howled like a wounded animal and growled as it pushed gravel and large boulders across Head Creek, damming it in just a few seconds. Three times I moved across the valley to get away from the landslide, watching in amazement. When it stopped, the rubble pile was big enough to fill a large house, its basement, and a three car garage.

Unsure what to do, I set up a small tarp to wait out the storm. As the deluge continued, I saw clear sky to the east and west. But above me, and to the north and south, black clouds, lightning and more hail sat stalled over this small valley.

At 5:25 p.m., I made a decision. The storm had been bombarding Head Creek since about 4:00 p.m. and I was still more than 20 kilometres from my vehicle, under a storm that was not about to move. Unless I did move, I would be stuck.

I packed my tarp, hefted my bike and waded several braided watercourses that were draining the dam across Head Creek. Then I crossed the landslide itself and rejoined the trail. Unable to ride through the deep hail, I pushed my bike. But I was not alone.

Ahead on the trail were footprints. Large footprints. ROUND footprints. A bear was running from the storm too, desperate to escape the hail. Blowing my whistle and with bear spray close at hand, I pushed on to the next crossing. The bear tracks disappeared.

After a kilometre I began riding. As the storm continued pounding the valley behind me, I anxiously approached Flat Creek. Finally I came around a bend to an amazing sight. Where Head Creek entered from the southwest, a roaring tide of brown muck overspilled its banks, tearing at everything it its path. Flat Creek, however, was unimpressed, flowing clear and calm. There was no hail in the valley of the Flat.

After a snack and a drink, I sped down the gravel track to my vehicle, doing the morning's two hour ride in less than 50 minutes. As Mount Head receded behind me, I looked back at the storm, illuminated by lightning, the canyon white with hail.

"Isn't nature vicious?" commented a friend as she served me a wonderful hot meal an hour later in Longview.

"No, I don't think so," I replied as we watched the storm continue toward the mountains. Hot prairie air had collided with a moist, Pacific weather system that brought cooler mountain air over the front ranges. The result was a stalled lightning and hail storm in a small valley where the Canadian Rockies meet the Great Plains. With or without me and the bear as witnesses, the extraordinary storm and landslide would have taken place. There was nothing malicious in the natural events that occurred on that afternoon of July 30, 1998. I was just a lucky hiker, given a front row seat at a geological event.

David Finch is a consulting historian and the author of several books on the history of the Canadian west, including Glacier House Rediscovered. He co-authored Fields of Fire and The Great Oil Age, on Canada's petroleum industry, and Legendary Horsemen, Images of the Canadian West. David lives in Calgary with his wife and daughter. He participated in the 1999 Writers Workshop.

Mountain Reflections

With pavement behind and the peaks ahead, each visitor to the Peace Park region enters into a more quiet, timeless place. Here, no glass holds back the wind and no walls keep out the cold. We move at the same pace as other creatures and are immersed, completely, in the natural world which gave birth to humankind and in which we can yet find our truest selves.

Reflecting on who we are, how we relate to one another and to the communities and ecosystems that enclose us, is an intrinsic part of a journey home to the living wild. Stephan Legault explores a montane landscape north of the Peace Park — the Whaleback — and visits with a walker from a previous century. Together they consider the timeless value of wildness and walking, and celebrate the dimension of humanness that enables us, from time to time, to rise above ambitions and greed; to set aside and protect special wild places such as the Whaleback or the Peace Park.

Debby Gregorash visits an even older and more timeless friend each time she returns to the Peace Park. Her essay contemplates the nature of the Divine as it is reflected in wild nature, and the nature of human goodness as reflected in our choices with regard to Creation. In "Of Predators, Prey and Other Matters," Margaret Chandler reflects on our relationship with wild creatures and the places they rely upon for survival, in a too-short visit to the North Fork of the Flathead River.

Most of us travel to the mountains as visitors, taking time out from lives that really have little day-to-day connection with wild nature. Our estrangement from nature can lead to artificial understandings of it, based more on bias than experience. But Elaine Sedlack's relationship to the Peace Park has lasted decades, and her reflections upon this place reflect an intimacy and personal concern that can only come out of the melding of a human's history with that of a landscape.

Like many others who love and value this place, what these writers see reflected back when they gaze into the rich, wild beauty of the Peace Park region is, ultimately, part of their own souls.

Winter aspens, southern Alberta.   **Photo by John Russell**

A Wilderness New Year

by Elaine Sedlack

I roll over on the metal bunk and peer drowsily out the small window of the cabin. In the thin, early morning light I can see soft snow flakes floating to the ground in the seemingly unceasing pattern that began in early December and has by now obliterated our ski tracks from yesterday. The early morning chill creeps into the corners of the cabin and I sink deeper into my warm sleeping bag. I was never very good at being the first person up in the morning so I'll just lie here in the warmth until Art gets up and lights the fire in the wood stove. He is sleeping in the other lower bunk and up above, in the top bunk, almost buried in his sleeping bag, is our son John. During the night the trees outside cracked like rifle reports, warning us of the cold.

We have chosen to ring in the new year this way since moving to Walton Ranger Station three years ago. We cannot drink and party all night and still get up and ski the next day. We left the ranger station yesterday about three in the afternoon to ski in here before dark, carrying steaks and a bottle of wine for dinner, along with sausage and eggs and fruit bread for breakfast, and a trail lunch. This cabin has become a haven for us, away from the ever-ringing telephone and knocks on the door at all hours of the night that often accompany this kind of weather.

I snuggle down in my sleeping bag, contented and at peace, and soon have drifted into that delicious second sleep that is all too rare in my busy world. When I awake again, it is to the familiar sounds of the wood fire crackling and snapping, and of Art preparing breakfast.

I lie in my bunk and think about the old time rangers who stayed in this cabin, one of a string of buildings which provided shelter for them on their foot or horse patrols before the highway was completed along the southern edge of the park in the 1930s.

This particular cabin is different from the others, more refined, with some modern touches. The story says it was built clandestinely by the field rangers who felt they needed a cabin at this site, though the administration disagreed. Over a period of time, whenever other building or remodeling projects were taking place, the rangers simply ordered a few more pieces of lumber, or roofing, or an extra door or hinge. When they had stockpiled sufficient materials, they gathered at this site and put up the Fielding cabin. I often wonder how long the cabin was standing before the administration discovered it. I bet it was quite a shock to the first administrator who rode up the trail and found a cabin standing where none should have been. I wouldn't say relations between the field rangers and the administration have improved much through the years.

Fielding cabin is board-sided, with two glass, shuttered windows, a shingle roof, and a real door. It is approximately 12 feet square. Inside are two sets of metal bunk beds, a table, four chairs, a cabinet for dishes, a wood stove for heat, and a separate wood stove for cooking. What seems most out-of-place is a large, white-enameled sink which, unfortunately, doesn't drain into anything but a bucket on the floor. In the center of the floor is a trap door that leads down to a small cellar where canned food is stored to keep it from freezing and from wildlife.

I like the efficiency of the cabin - just enough dishes and pans for one meal. Two buckets — one for drinking water and one for washing water which is dipped out of the nearby creek — and always candles and kerosene lanterns. It is a humble reminder that people can live simply.

Art has been busy working while I lie here daydreaming. I can feel the heat from the wood stove and see the steam rising from the water kettle. There is now warm water to wash up with, so I gingerly crawl out of my sleeping bag, put on my clothes, and dash out the door to visit the outhouse. A blast of cold air smacks me in the face as I run down the path. Ten degrees below zero!

I hurry back to the warm cabin, wash up, and sit down to eat. By the time breakfast is over, dishes washed, and the cabin cleaned up, the thermometer outside reads zero. It's a good temperature for skiing - not unbearable but cold enough to keep the snow feathery soft and forgiving. We put on gaiters, jackets, hats, and mittens, grab our packs, wax and don our skis, then head up the trail to the slopes of Elk Mountain.

The trail travels through the forested fairyland. Each branch of every pine tree is laden with snow giving the spruce trees a perfectly conical shape, the envy of any suburban landscaper. Even the bare branches of the aspen trees by the cabin are frosted with three inches of snow, balanced precariously, waiting for the first whisper of wind to send flakes floating to the ground. I glance at my sleeve and am delighted to see that each snowflake that lands there is a perfect stellar crystal, each one a different work of art. They cascade lightly off as I move my arm, and remind me of the paper snowflakes we made as children to decorate the windows at home and school on the drab Chicago streets.

When I was growing up I always wanted to live in a place where the snow stayed on the ground all winter without turning to grubby-looking grey slush. I tried Ann Arbor, Michigan, but after four years at the university, I was convinced I had not gone far enough north. I moved to Minneapolis, Minnesota and though the snow did stay all winter, it still became drab between snowfalls. Here in Montana, finally, I found real snow, six or seven feet of it, always fresh and bright and inviting. Here not only does the snow stay all winter, it starts the end of October and lasts until the first of May. And even in June and July there is still snow on the ground at Logan Pass. In fact, it often snows in July and August. I remember one July 4th morning at West Glacier, when we woke to find six inches of snow covering the ground!

With Art leading the way and breaking trail through the new snow we soon reach the gentle open slopes of Elk Mountain. Down below to our left is Fielding Creek buried under a blanket of snow. Ahead, the trail switchbacks down to Ole Creek about three miles from the cabin. On our right, the gentle lower slopes of Elk Mountain beckon. Clumps of trees dot the open slopes. Above, the slopes steepen and rise to the summit of Elk Mountain. These gentler slopes are a good place to practice telemark turns. We drop our packs, climb the slope, and ski down, then climb again and repeat the cycle until we are tired. The total silence of the snow-covered hills is broken only by the squeaking of Art's ski binding and the gentle swish of skis sliding through powder snow. Then we pick up our packs and ski back to the cabin for some hot chocolate and lunch.

Too soon it is time to leave the cabin and ski down the trail and back across the railroad to reality, which in this case is snowmobiles roaring up and down the snowbound road to the highway.

The Ole Creek Grizzly and A Wilderness New Year, both by Elaine Sedlack, are excerpts from a work-in-progress about her experiences in Glacier.

__Elaine Sedlack__ is a public health nurse in Flathead County, Montana and has had a close association with Glacier National Park for more than 30 years. Her husband Art was a park ranger and Elaine served for many years as an official volunteer, working to upgrade the park's emergency medical services. She has also served on the board of directors and as Flathead Chapter president of the Montana Wilderness Association, and has written many articles on conservation issues for MWA. Elaine is also the author of The Nordic Skiers' Guide to Montana. She was a participant at the 1995, 1997 and 1999 Writers Workshops.

Rendezvous With a Friend

by Debby Gregorash

When I wake up here on the prairie, east of Lethbridge, Alberta, I look to the east, toward the rising sun. After greeting the big orange ball and thanking it for another day full of potential, I look to the southwest, towards Waterton Lakes National Park. Some days I cannot see the mountains, but today the Rockies stand tall above the horizon.

At sunrise, the higher mountain peaks, 100 miles away, were clothed in snow that reflected a rosy pink. I attached our scope to the tripod and took it out to the deck off the upstairs bedroom. Waterton's peaks stood tall and clear and beckoning. From Chief Mountain, in Montana's Glacier National Park, I gazed north and could see Sofa Mountain and Mount Vimy. The mountains made my longing heart squeeze.

Though 70% of the area's wildlife has disappeared due to cultivation, the prairie is still a place of biodiversity. The land is full of native mixed-grass prairie, pronghorn antelope, grouse, and myriad small predators. A few bison live in a fenced pasture four miles to the north. On the odd moonlit night we can hear a small pack of coyotes. In winter, flocks of procrastinating geese forage in the stubble field next door and a pair of Swainson's hawks resides here in summer. Nonetheless, when the mountains call, I must go.

Frank gave me a quiet grin when I told him I absolutely had to be in the mountains. "I have to write a little essay about Waterton and I really need to be there, to take notes," I informed him,

"You'll be home before dark?" he asked. I nodded.

"Have fun, and don't forget your camera."

What a guy! He does not share my unabashed obsession with nature, but he at least understands it.

As I packed my daypack with camera, binoculars, paper, pens and snowshoes, I felt like I was embarking on a rendezvous with a secret lover. But I was meeting an old friend or mentor, someone who nourishes my body, mind and spirit and gives me hope. This someone is the universe's Creator, but is my own self as well. Perhaps this is what is meant by, 'being at one with God.' Like a holograph, each part of the picture is also the whole. I am an insignificant part of the whole natural world, yet I am the same as the whole earth.

I am made of the stuff of rocks, trees, grass and shrubs. The elements I contain flowed through heroes of history as well. I feel free to imagine myself as a Kootenay trader, a Blackfoot woman tending her fire, a hunter, artist, writer, supreme lover, and modern pilgrim on a vision quest. I rendezvous with my creative spirit and my ancient soul.

For me, Waterton Lakes National Park is a refuge for life, which I figure is the manifestation of God. I do not have to seek sacredness in Waterton. The Creator, the Artist, is everywhere in the wildflowers, grasses, trees, rivers, brooks and animals. The native religions say that even the rocks contain spirits.

When at last I reached the park gates, Waterton's typical blasting wind was keeping the elk herd in the trees where I couldn't see them. But I didn't have to see them to feel their presence. Knowing they were there was satisfaction enough. I would not see a bear or wolf that day either, but they were around. Perhaps the wolves were inspecting the elk I couldn't see; the bear curled up beneath an exposed mass of roots, dreaming bear dreams, as the fierce wind curled snow over its hiding place.

Up Akamina Parkway, I stopped at one of the trail-heads and put on my snowshoes, then trudged into the woods to a little hideaway where I dusted off a log, sat, closed my eyes, and listened. The wind moaned a chant in the treetops and lodgepole pines creaked as they rubbed together.

A distant chickadee called its flock and they shyly approached, tree by tree, to see what the human was doing in their natural cathedral. I thought I heard a raven caw, far away. The raven is my totem according to native friends. Sitting on that log in the peaceful woods, I imagined the dark-eyed, dark-cloaked bird coming to settle on a nearby branch, lecturing me, telling me in a crusty voice what I must do to save its sacred home.

Then the real raven spread its wings, lifted off its perch, and disappeared into the forest. I returned to the trail and plodded along to another hidden spot for contemplation. Here the snow-covered stream gurgled and giggled, like children gossiping under a downy comforter. I parked myself on a boulder and looked around.

A few chewed stalks of the summer's bear grass poked up through the snow; shrubs were bent out of shape by white pillows balancing on their branches. Further away, the wind was whipping snow off the mountain peak. The sight surpassed anything my imagination could give birth to, but the view, the solace, the silence, and the sweetness of the air made me feel suddenly melancholy.

Why do we humans pester, poke and tear into Mother Earth the way we do? How can we staunch the wounds of man's progress?

In the marvelous buffer zone called the Castle Wilderness area, north of Waterton Park, a valley lies vulnerable and under increasing attack by recreational expansion schemes. Part of the Castle was once scheduled for protection, but the looters have won out so far. In other regions of the Castle Wilderness, more madness is evident where four-wheel drive and all-terrain vehicles infiltrate old access trails.

How can we trigger a change of heart? How can we stir a soul or baptize a new belief system? How can we get other people to weep over nature's wounds and fight for its survival? The death of God's wilderness will be the death of us all — if not our bodies, then at least our souls. What an empty world this would be without nature!

The hours flew by. The sun was about to make its exit behind the tall, dark steeples of rock and it was time to head home to the prairie. As always when I leave Waterton Lakes National Park, I peeked in the side view mirrors, and said tender good-byes to the darkening and shrinking hills behind. And I promised that I would rendezvous again, soon, with those great granite anchors of my soul.

Debby Gregorash has written about agriculture and the environment for many years and is especially interested in people's spiritual connections with the land. She has had a column in the Sunny South News, a Taber, Alberta weekly, for 11 years, and has had articles published in Harrowsmith, Encompass magazine and the Western Producer. She recently wrote a book on the history of the Lethbridge Northern Irrigation District. Debby has a Diploma of Agriculture from McGill University. She has participated in all three Writers Workshops.

Of Predators, Prey and Other Matters

by Margaret Chandler

It wasn't an easy decision to make. As intrigued as I was by the offer to attend a field camp on predators and prey, it involved some convoluted travel planning that went something like this. Saturday afternoon: depart the writers' workshop in Waterton to attend a wedding that evening in Calgary. Sunday morning: drive south again, to Glacier Park, Montana, wedding hangover in tow, via Waterton Park to pick up two other camp participants in need of a lift. But the invitation to "let the prey, the predators, the scavengers, and the land teach us about life in this remote wilderness" was an unusual one, so by Sunday evening we were pulling into the field camp headquarters of the Glacier Institute at the western edge of Glacier National Park. Traversing the Livingston Range with a full moon on the rise was enough to convince me I'd made the right decision.

We knew little about what awaited us, always the best arrangement. Upon arrival, we acquainted ourselves with rest of the group — a motley and delightful assortment of both aspiring and seasoned journalists and photographers. Within the hour we were absorbed in a slide show complete with a bantering commentary. Mountain lion tastes like lean pork and lynx isn't bad either. Wolf kills have a musty pee smell. Pink marrow is a good sign; red marrow is a sign of malnourishment. Bears will den to die, but most other predators will live until they starve. How refreshing to learn about another kind of predator far removed from the ones I'm familiar with in the urban tangle.

Our host Jamie Jonkel was a man who invites respect. I marveled at how different our lives are. I track words and examine budgets and puzzle over intricacies of magazine production. He tracks footprints and examines scats and puzzles over how the predators communicate with each other. I can command my screen to connect me instantly anywhere in the world; Jamie can pause by a cottonwood and contemplate all the creatures that have passed by that morning. My world is immense and remote, his minute and immediate.

Equally fascinating was Jamie's cohort Rasim. As far as any preconceived notions of a bear biologist can be made by the uninitiated, Jamie fit the bill. But I wasn't prepared to be instructed in the ways of the wild by an exotic-looking intellectual New Yorker of Albanian descent. Obviously, we were in for a treat.

The next morning we set off on a great adventure. After stopping for supplies in the rustic hamlet of Polebridge, we headed up the North Fork Road until Jamie and Rasim decided it was time to abandon the vehicles and get into some serious bushwhacking. All the while Jamie charmed us with anecdotes that made the stunningly beautiful landscape seem less unfamiliar. The animals aren't that different from us after all. They've got their own idiosyncrasies and their own social dynamics. "Wolves are just like a bunch of bankers. There's always somebody trying to bump them out of the community," Jamie chuckled.

Rasim teased him for spending so much time in the wild that he's become more like a bear than a man. With Jamie's somewhat gruff yet gentle manner, there's some truth to it. In the manner of any self-respecting animal, time was never an issue and I took my cue from him. I knew we only had a couple of days to spend in this river valley paradise so I let myself fall into the eternity of the present. By the end of the first day, I'd learned more about identifying prints and sniffing out kill sites and matching the creature to the hair than in all my days prior. What the heck had I really learned in school? All the education I've had, I've never once figured out just how smart the bear is. And I'd certainly never learned that dried moose scat makes a fine incense.

The next day was more of the same and none of us could get enough. After an exhilarating tramp through meadows of golden grass, followed by a hard slog through more dense brush, we ended our day at the North Fork of the Flathead River. I dared myself to go in for a swim. What bliss to swim the third week into September. After all that bushwhacking my arms looked like I'd had a close encounter with an energetic mountain lion kitten. I reveled in the cool waters.

That evening we were all tired but elated. Nothing would have suited us better than to spend a few days more in the company of Jamie and Rasim. There was so much to learn. Instead we slipped into the local liquor vendor and bought them a decent bottle of whiskey. As we drove reluctantly home, we imagined them tending the fire, savouring the whiskey and scheming their next foray up the North Fork.

I'm still no bush savant. On a hike recently I stepped squarely in what looked, in retrospect, like some interesting scat. Cougar? Lynx? Bobcat? I didn't know. But the natural world is now alive in new and mysterious ways. As Jewish poet and philosopher Solomon ibn Gabirol puts it, "Of what avail is an open eye, if the heart is blind?" My time in the North Fork valley was time well spent. I'm not as myopic as I was, and my heart is open wider to the wonders of this world.

Margaret Chandler is a freelance writer and the editor of Encompass, Alberta's Magazine on the Environment. She can also be heard regularly on CBC Radio's Midday Express as their environmental columnist. She has a B.A. in History and a Masters in Adult and Community Education and combines her passion for language and writing with a commitment to environmental education and communication. Margaret has participated in both the 1997 and 1999 Writers Workshops.

Hoary Marmot, Highline Trail, Glacier National Park.

Photo by Bert Gildart

"I wish to speak a word for Nature,
for absolute freedom and wildness."
Henry David Thoreau

Walking the Whaleback
with Henry David Thoreau

by Stephen Legault

The words Whaleback, walking and wilderness should, in the language of every Albertan, be synonymous. Each of us might at least once step over the crown of a windswept ridge above Camp Creek or Bob Creek and face into the gale that blows steadily from the west. We could stand there, leaning — as Sid Marty might suggest — into the wind and feel it buoy us. We might choose to hike upwards on that ridge until the foothills burn the respect reserved for mountains into our thighs and calves, and then, at its apogee, we could sit as still as possible in that wind and merely watch. We could sit and look out over distance, a distance in all directions not possible anywhere else in the province.

If each of us did that, at a time spaced well apart from other Albertans so that we might also taste solitude, then there would never again be a question of the Whaleback's worth. Never again would the Alberta government — whose only interest seems to be short-term economic gain — consider letting oil and gas companies and loggers pillage the Whaleback. There would be no debate, because the people of Alberta would have tasted a place wild and free.

But the people of Alberta will not come. And, I'll admit as I hoist a pack from the tailgate of the truck onto my too thin back, that suits me just fine. I'll enjoy it for them. Somebody's got to do it.

I tighten the waist belt with several sharp tugs and feel the weight of the pack transfer from my back to my hips, also too thin, and only marginally stronger than my shoulders. I tug also on the shoulder straps, snugging the pack into my body where it will not throw me off balance on the walk ahead. Although it is July, this is the first time this summer that I've put on anything more than a day pack. I haven't even taken a step and I feel as though I might fall over.

My companions are likewise shouldering packs, adjusting caps and sunglasses and otherwise making ready for a four day "saunter" in the Whaleback. There are five of us together here on the flats beside a bend in Camp Creek. Four of us standing — Jim Wood, Margaret Scaia, Jack Loustaunau and I — and one of us tucked into the outside pocket of my backpack, wrapped protectively in a zip-lock bag. Though dead for some 100 years, the fifth member of our hiking troupe is very much alive in the spirit of this landscape. In the pocket of my pack is an abridged version of Henry David Thoreau's essay *Walking*, bound neatly in a volume no larger than a pocket calculator.

And so the five of us set off, stepping gingerly across Camp Creek where it takes a tight bend below a steep ridge. The water is clear and cool, in places a foot deep. We step from rock to rock, but not before submerging, in a quiet backwater eddy, four bottles of beer.

This is one pleasure I could not forsake — the joy of finishing a hike and returning to creek-cooled beer. The brown bottles are submerged in the water, noses upstream like fat, brown trout, and large flat stones are placed on top to prevent them floating down stream.

Only four? Well, Henry David will have to forgo this pleasure. History has it he was never much of a drinker anyway.

The creek curls around the bottles, carrying on towards the Oldman River beyond. We cross the creek and start up the steep hill beyond it. Henry David pipes up:

*He who sits still in a house all the time may be the greatest
vagrant of all; but the saunterer, in the good sense, is not more
vagrant than the meandering river, which is all the while
sedulously seeking the shortest course to the sea.*

This righteous indignation is easily ignored as the four living,
breathing, panting members of our expedition plod like draft horses up
the steep grade of the ridge. We follow a seldom used track abandoned to
the weeds and the wilderness. Hardly a saunter by Thoreau's standards.
Henry David hastens to add:

*For every walk is a sort of crusade. . . It is true, we are but
fainthearted crusaders, even the walkers, nowadays, who
undertake no preserving, never-ending tours, and come round
again at evening to the old hearthstone from which we set out.
We should go forth on the shortest walk, perchance, in the
spirit of undying adventure, never to return, prepared to send
back our embalmed hearts only as relics to our desolate
kingdoms. If you are ready to leave father and mother, brother
and sister, and wife and child and friends, and never see them
again — if you have paid your debts, and made your will, and
settled all your affairs, and are a free man — then you are
ready for a walk.*

In justification for coming round again at evening, I can only say
that the creek-cooled beer is reason enough. As for Henry David's
demands for earthly abdications prior to setting forth on "the shortest
walk in the spirit of undying adventure" I must insist that the very act of
walking itself creates the freedom so dear to Thoreau. With each step we
take, we pace out the distance between our daily affairs and the freedom
so beloved by the man immortalized in the zip-lock in my pack.

Panting we reach the top of the rise and, thrashing our way through
a dense stand of tangled shrubs, gain our first view of the earth beyond.
And here we come face to face with the crusade to which Thoreau was
alluding. Here we see the earth spread out, vast, wide and open. We
huddle a moment among a few giant Douglas fir, looking west over the
valley of the Oldman River where it splits the spine of the Livingstone
Range and snakes across the nearly level plain between foothill ridgelines.

The crusade is the thirst to know this place; the desire to understand, by walking over this land of all up or all down, the secrets and treasures of this landscape.

From the grove of Douglas fir we angle up a long, undulating and nearly bald extension of Livingstone Ridge, which creates a clean break between the Front Ranges of the Rocky Mountains and the foothills and prairie to the east. While the going is certainly not difficult in the technical sense, the ridge is steep in places, and my pack, overloaded as is my custom with camera, lens, tripod and film, feels as if I were carrying a cow. But this is no excuse, and the truth of the matter is, I'm falling out of shape. I have allowed myself to become chained to desk and computer, and have seldom taken a walk this summer, except for my daily stroll around the woods behind my home, just for the pleasure of the motion. Henry David would not approve.

> *I think that I cannot preserve my health and spirits, unless I spend four hours a day at least — and commonly more than that — sauntering through the woods and over the hills and fields, absolutely free from all worldy engagements...*
>
> *I, who cannot stay in my chamber for a single day without acquiring some rust, and when sometimes I have stolen forth for a walk at the eleventh hour, or four o'clock in the afternoon, too late to redeem the day, when the shades of night were already beginning to be mingled with the daylight, have felt as if I had committed some sin to be atoned for. . .*

Thoreau knew well the powers of healing that come with a walk in the woods, and he took to them every day for their medicinal powers. I too have looked up from the heaps of papers, files, articles, reports and press releases on my desk from time to time and — seeking relief from this stew of bureaucracy and insanity — taken refuge in the woods.

Late in the afternoon we reach the crest of the ridge. The sun, obscured by cloud for most of the day, sinks low in the west, casting long, soft rays of light across the rolling hills. On a previous walk along this ridge the sun shone bright, and at this apex I looked out across a world bathed in light thick as honey. That light curled around the hills, and pooled in the meadows as Camp Creek curled around river stones, worn smooth with time and the creek's endless patience.

Now, as then, we can look far out to the east and see the humpbacked spine of the Whaleback itself, an area that extends from the Whaleback Ridge west across three or four rows of foothill ridgelines, and their corresponding meadows and creeks, and ends at Livingstone Ridge. It reaches from the Oldman River in the south to Chaffen Ridge in the north. It is a region that hunters, guide-outfitters and other conservationists have worked for 30 years to protect .

The Whaleback Ridge derives its name from its form. Thirty kilometres long, it is a series of humps that look like the vertebrae of a whale's spine. Each rise is shadowed to the east with open stands of Douglas fir. In the dales between each undulating rise are thick groves of aspen. The windward slopes are bare, having been pounded by Chinook winds for time eternal.

Beyond the Whaleback to the east are the Porcupine Hills. These rounded domes are flowered with a combination of mountain and prairie species, and are not foothills at all, but the gentle swell of prairie sediments that have bulged as the great tectonic forces that crumpled the Rocky Mountains pushed from the west. The Porcupine Hills, cut into two halves by Willow Creek, have both unique and painfully common characteristics in Alberta. What makes them unique is that ecologically they represent a union between the prairies and the mountains. Looking south from my vantage point high in the foothills, the Porcupine Hills trail off into the distance. The furthest humps appear as a pod of whales.

What makes them common is that, like the Whaleback region — and almost ever single square inch of provincial land in Alberta — they are under threat from the oil and gas industry, logging interests, and from over-grazing.

It was in and around these hills that 14 wolves from the Livingstone Gap pack were slaughtered in 1994 -1995. Accused of killing cattle, the wolves were legally trapped, shot and poisoned with strychnine. Alberta Fish and Wildlife assisted with the killing. While one or two wolves might have been guilty of this crime, the Livingstone Gap pack and several others were nearly eradicated.

We rest while a cold wind trips across Livingstone Ridge, a kilometre to the west, spills down its eastern slope and over our perch. On the summit of that ridge is a fire lookout, closed as an inspection by binoculars shows. What a view the lookout must have had, the rugged Continental Divide, with Tornado Mountain, to the west, and this hopelessly beautiful sea of folded stone and sky to the east.

In the evening we make camp in the south fork of Miles Coulee. In a grove of Douglas fir and spruce, we pitch tents against the possibility of rain. I sleep open to the night under a Douglas fir until about two o'clock in the morning, when thick drops of rain chase me into the tent. It takes Jim so long to untangle himself from a makeshift mosquito net that I am soaked by the time I crawl into my sleeping bag.

Morning comes and with it sunshine. We take a leisurely breakfast, and after filtering water for our bottles from tiny Miles Creek, we walk down the valley.

We have no definite plan for our hike. Our maps are opened regularly, and our plans changed nearly every hour. Our only intent is to see as much country as we can in the four days we have. Henry David explains his position on our apparent lack of direction:

> *My vicinity affords many good walks; and though for so many years I have walked almost every day, and sometimes for several days together, I have not yet exhausted them. An absolutely new prospect is a great happiness, and I can still get this every afternoon. Two or three hours walking will carry me into as strange a country as I expect ever to see.*

The world of Concord, Massachusetts, of Walden Pond where Thoreau took residence for two years and two months, and of New England in general in Henry David's time, was a much different world than that we walk through today. From the late 1840s through the early 1860s, when Thoreau wrote, New England still contained a good deal of wildness. Though not the rugged mountain wilderness of Alberta and British Columbia, it offered a man of Thoreau's inclination an opportunity to examine untouched country each day of his life. For Thoreau that could mean walking the same trail through the woods many days, and seeing it differently each time. It was a familiarity with country that is not common at the close of the twentieth century.

The necessity of open country, and the gift of the opportunity to explore it, as Thoreau did in the woods west of Walden, and as we are in the Whaleback, is the true measure of wealth. Richness is not a provincial budget surplus bolstered by the sale of oil and gas leases, it is open country with all its endemic species still intact. Wealth is the exaltation that accompanies exploration — on foot, and for no other purpose than the discovery of the land's own beauty and majesty.

From Miles Coulee we angle north again, up another ridge that ends near tree line in a saddle between two buttes, each severed through by slanting limestone, crumbling in upon itself. The day is bright and sunny, but the wind is strong, forcing us to lean into its cold bite. We find a place between the two buttes, sheltered from the gusts that threaten to topple us, and eat lunch.

Thoreau said that wilderness and wildness were tonics, better than any medicine we could take to prevent, and cure, the ills of society. What Henry David so gently warned long ago, we are coming face to face with today, the loss of wilderness. Did we listen to the bard of Walden Pond? It would appear, across much of the North America, that we did not.

In Alberta less than one percent of lands held by the province have received protection. The national parks — Banff, Jasper, Waterton, Wood Buffalo, and Elk Island — inflate the percentage of land protected to around nine percent. But many of these lands are not protected at all. The ills of Banff and Jasper National Park are well known. Those ills are knocking at the door of Waterton Lakes National Park, and Parks Canada, the federal agency responsible for national parks, seems more than willing to open that door. Elk Island National Park, east of Edmonton, is too small to offer anything but zoo-like protection to the elk and bison that make their homes there. And Wood Buffalo, massive and certainly significant, has fallen prey to logging inside the park boundary and the harmful effects of upstream dams on the Peace River.

In Alberta, the province has set aside natural areas as one classification of protection, but development inside those protected areas is occurring three times faster than on lands adjacent to them. No piece of

Alberta earth is safe from the tentacles of the oil and gas industry. No sooner is a protected area established — such as the recent case of Fort Assiniboine in central Alberta — than the provincial government issues or renews permits to build oil and gas pipelines, drill for petrochemicals, or harvest timber. Protection, Alberta style. Thoreau agrees:

> *Nowadays almost all man's improvements so called, as the building of houses and the cutting down of trees, simply deform the landscape, and make it more and more tame and cheap. . . At present in this vicinity, the best part of the land is not private property; the landscape is not owned, and the walker enjoys comparative freedom. But possibly the day will come when it will be partitioned off . . .*

The earth that I look out on from our lunch stop is mostly public land, and thanks to the ranchers and private land owners that surround it, access to this domain is still relatively simple. But in other places in Alberta, ranchers who own grazing leases have been known to bar access to "trespassers" on public land, sparking a debate as to who has the legal right to use lands owned by all Albertans, but leased by a few.

After lunch we drop from the ridge, out of the wind, and into the woods at the headwaters of Jackknife Coulee. Here we walk along a valley floor that opens into a broad meadow of grasses with cow parsnip six feet tall along the creek. We thread our way along the creek for several kilometres, watching for sign of moose or black bear. We find a good deal of scat and tracks, and remember that the Whaleback region offers the last large expanse of intact Montane grasslands and forests in Canada.

This is an ecosystem that attracts vast numbers of wildlife. Warm winds blow throughout the year — though the chill in this July air seems to suggest otherwise — brushing the winter pasture of elk, moose and deer, and the wolves that hunt them, clear of snow. It is a melting pot of vegetation, a transition zone between mountains and prairies. As a result, it attracts song birds in droves. It is truly a national treasure, one that all Canadians should be proud to call part of our national heritage. One that every Canadian should defend.

We make our second camp in a grove of aspens and lodgepole pine, bordered by a fine meadow of tall grasses, beside an arm of Jackknife

Creek. Late in the afternoon we light the stoves and brew hot tea, and in the liquid light of summer I sit with my back to an aspen and converse with Henry David about this troubled west. A west, it would seem, that Henry David dreamed of often, but never saw. A west that Thoreau, for all his vision, could not have foreseen. Speaking of the direction he prefers to walk in — west — he says,

> *The future lies this way to me, and the earth seems more unexhausted and richer on that side... Eastward I go only by force; but westward I go free.*

Here Henry David adds a crucial word or two about his notion of the west, and comes as near as any writer has to encapsulating the notion of the necessity of nature to the human soul.

> *The west of which I speak is but another name for the Wild; and what I have been preparing to say is, that in Wildness is the preservation of the World*

Late in the afternoon, the light already slipping down the shoulders of foothills and ridgelines, Jack and I walk up the creek, then take a steep climb over rocks and through meadows to the summit of a ridge. From our vantage, we look far out over the prairies, and back at the mountains, and watch clouds whose bellies are flat and dark drift lazily over the earth. The sun tickles the tall grass in which we lounge, and the wind blows steadily. We cast our eye over what is left of the west, and recall what Henry David has said of the state of the human link between our soul and all that is wild.

> *Life consists with wildness. The most alive is the wildest.*
>
> *How near to good is what is wild!*
>
> *Give me for my friends and neighbors wild men, not tame.*
>
> *Here is this vast, savage, howling mother of ours, Nature, lying all around, with such beauty and affection for her children.*

Jack and I return to camp, light a small fire out of the wind and prepare our dinner. In the dusk that drifts in, my thoughts return to the high ridge above, and the sweeping view of earth and sky. Here I am reminded abruptly of the connection between our regard for a wild place like the Whaleback, the health of humanity, and the gentle affection a New England bard had for the fine art of walking. If we cast these things away and leave in their wake only a civilized world, then what makes us most human will be lost. And with it, our humanity. And so I fall asleep, with my face to the stars, the wind filling my dreams with hope.

On the third day of our walk I return to the present. Each walk I take I resolve, again and again, not to become consumed by the conflicts of protecting wilderness. And each walk I take reminds me of the need to work tirelessly to preserve what I love.

Above all, we cannot afford not to live in the present. He is blessed over all mortals who loses no moment of the passing life in remembering the past.

Very true, Henry, but what about the lessons that the past has taught us? My first trip into the Whaleback was only four years ago. I had learned of the threat by Amoco — a huge U.S. oil and gas company — to drill 20 gas wells in the Whaleback. I learned also of the band of local ranchers, craftsmen, hunters and anglers who had stopped them. I came to the Whaleback for a few days of walking to see what it was people like Judy Huntley and James Tweedie were fighting for so valiantly. When I left I vowed that if the bulldozers ever returned, so would I. It is this remembered past, the insults and defilements, that we must recall in order to prevent the re-occurrence of such threats.

The day is cold and windy as we cross the divide between two forks of Jackknife Coulee. After dropping our packs in a meadow where we will camp the night, we wander north to the banks of White Creek, and look into the Chaffen Ridge region. More windblown foothills, more deep forests of fir and pine and aspen. More wildness. More threats.

Evening again, dinner and a fire. The air temperature is around five degrees Celsius this July night. The sun dips below the ridge, casting long shadows from the grove of aspen in which we camp. We sit up, talking and laughing, telling stories and filling our bellies with hot food and drink. Henry David retells this tale:

We had a remarkable sunset one day last November. I was walking in a meadow, the source of a small brook, when the sun at last, just before setting, after a cold, gray day, reached a clear stratum in the horizon, and the softest, brightest morning sunlight fell on the dry grass and on the stems of the trees in the opposite horizon and on the leaves of the shrub oaks on the hillside, while our shadows stretched long over the meadow eastward. . . a light as we could not have imagined a moment before, and the air also was so warm and serene that nothing was wanting to make a paradise of that meadow. When we reflected that this was not a solitary phenomenon, never to happen again, but that it would happen forever and ever, an infinite number of evenings, to cheer and reassure the latest child walking there, it was more glorious still.

Unable to decide whether or not it would rain, I sleep half in and half out of the tent, my face pressed against the roof of the world, my body snug inside layers of down.

Morning comes, bright and clear and windy still. The wind never stops a moment, and I wonder how it is the sky could blow relentlessly without stopping even for a breath? Today is the last day of our walk — we four and Henry David can feel civilization lurking beyond the hills.

We follow Miles Coulee downstream, crossing the creek in places where the banks have been severely eroded, or where some fool with a four-wheel drive has driven along the stream, tearing up the riparian edge so valued by plants, animals and fish. The closer we come to civilization, the greater the degree of stupidity we see.

When we reach the wide rolling valley of Camp Creek the trees gently pull back, and hills open up and are bare. We see a lone horseman in the distance. We see two red-tailed hawks high overhead, circling, calling, hunting. We see fences and barbed wire and gates. We see small herds of cattle, persistently munching the grassy meadows.

The walk from here to the trucks is along a flat valley bottom, but Jack and I choose to climb a bald ridge for one last view. After a 1000 foot gain we sit in the wind, looking over the country that for the past four days we've traveled. We can see in the distance Thunder Mountain, always on the horizon, dark now in the shadow of clouds. Below us is the serpentine course of Camp Creek, twisting through meadows and groves of aspen which shudder in the wind. That creek will lead us back to the trucks, which will carry us back to the work week, to responsibility, and to the fight to protect this sacred and holy place. Camp Creek holds as corollary for this, four cold bottles of beer, and the promise that, thanks to the ongoing efforts of a few dedicated locals, the Whaleback will be here when we need to return to it. At least for one more year.

If I could, I would stay here. Every time I walk this landscape of foothills I think I should never leave. So far, I always do. Coming into this country is like coming home. And though home means many things to me, this place is certainly one of them. Sometimes we have to walk a long way to find our true home. Sometimes it's right under our noses. Maybe someday I'll stay.

'Walking the Whaleback with Henry David Thoreau' was first published in the 1999 edition of the Canadian Alpine Journal. The article was a finalist for that year's Andy Russell Nature Writing Award, held in conjunction with the Waterton - Glacier International Writers Workshop and is part of a collection of essays Stephen is currently compiling.

Stephen Legault *is a writer, photographer and conservationist, and the Executive Director of the Canadian Grass Roots Environmental Effectiveness Network (GREEN), based in Canmore, Alberta. His writing has appeared in more than 20 different magazines and journals, including Outdoor Canada and Canadian Wildlife. He is currently working on a book of essays titled Earth and Sky: A Foothills Journey, about the foothills of Alberta.*

Living in Nature

National parks used to be thought of as living museums: places that would be protected against change so future generations could see 'living vignettes of primitive America." But in the real world, parks sometimes prove to offer only the illusion of protection.

Park boundary lines can't hold back change any more than they can hold in elk, bears or tourists. If we're going to protect our parks, we need to look at how we live in the surrounding landscapes too.

When we organized the first writers workshop, ecosystem management was already evolving from concept to practical reality. The many interconnections between protected parks and the things that go on around them were attracting more and more attention from park managers because it was plain that protecting biological diversity – and meeting the needs of people to learn about, enjoy and coexist with natural things – can't be seen as something that happens only in national parks.

Kevin Van Tighem's "Ghost Forests" shows how human decisions distant both in time and space can have devastating impacts on even the most carefully protected forests inside park boundaries. Don Meredith further explores the illusory nature of boundaries, and the importance of borders in nature. Both offer hopeful suggestions for reconciling our flawed past with our future.

"Hope on the Range" takes this discussion across the park border to look at one of the biggest threats to nature emerging in the landscapes that surround the Waterton-Glacier International Peace Park: the loss of open spaces to real estate development. David Stiller's cautionary tale "Fragmentation" offers some good reasons not to contribute to the conversion of scenic ranchland into tiny acreages. Even so, the process is already underway. Both David Stalling and Donna Fleury describe some of the things concerned citizens are doing to keep mindless change from threatening the wild places and wild things visitors to the Peace Park region currently take for granted.

Taking things for granted is a subtext in Andrew Nikiforuk's hard-hitting essay "Our Home and Native Land" in which he argues that we cannot build a sustainable relationship with our home places as long as we continue to discount the environmental costs of the big changes we impose on the landscape. Living in nature will never be easy in our crowded world; perhaps national parks and their neighbours can help teach us how, while also inspiring us to try harder.

Clark's nutcracker.

Photo by Kevin Van Tighem

Ghost Forests

by Kevin Van Tighem

It's usually late spring before you can hike in to Forum Lake. Tucked up against the base of cliffs that form part of the Continental Divide, ice often blankets the lake well into late June. Its cirque faces northeast, sheltered from the high elevation sun. Most years, snowdrifts linger in the shady timberline forests well into July.

Morning mist tangles the tree tops and drifts in shredded tatters along the walls of ancient rock that loom above the lake. Wraithlike and jagged, the whitened spars of dead trees rise high above the darker canopy of fir trees. Varied thrushes whistle eerily. A raven croaks. Later, the sun will break through and burn a brave brightness into the mountain morning, but for now the timberline basin feels like a place of ghosts.

It *is* a place of ghosts. Bleached arms bent, dead whitebark pines stand mute and still, lifeless reminders of a time not long past when this basin echoed to the rasping cries of Clark's nutcrackers and the chatter of red squirrels. Most of the timberline giants have died over the past half century, starving the subalpine forest of its annual bounty of oil-rich pine seeds. A century ago, grizzly bears followed their noses from one squirrel midden to another in this part of the Canadian Rockies, raiding the treasure troves of whitebark seeds. Today's squirrel middens contain a more trivial bounty of fir, spruce and lodgepole cones; today's grizzlies have to make do with other foods. In Yellowstone and Jasper National Parks where whitebark pine stands have yet to suffer the fate of Forum Lake's whitebarks, other grizzlies still rob squirrels.

Hike to timberline anywhere in the Rocky Mountains along the 49th parallel and the same picturesque ghost forests of whitebark pine snags will greet you. To those who don't know the story behind the dead trees, they seem to speak of little more than the difficulty of life up high near timberline. To those who know why the spectacular high mountain pine trees are dying out, however, the dead snags are mute testimony to the dark side of twentieth century conservation.

"Whitebark and limber pine forests are functionally extinct in the Waterton-Glacier International Peace Park," says American ecologist Kate Kendall. With biologists from Parks Canada, the U.S. Forest Service and other agencies responsible for managing the pines' high country habitats, Kate Kendall has studied the on-going die-off of one of the most spectacular – and ecologically important – of Rocky Mountain trees. Now, in what seems to some like a desperate race against time, she is working with those same colleagues to help the trees save themselves.

Unlike the better-known lodgepole, jack and Ponderosa pines, the whitebark (*Pinus albicaulis*) and its lower-elevation relative the limber pine (*P. flexilis*) are members of the stone pine group. They bear their needles in bunches of five and produce large cones with nutlike seeds the size of a cherry pit. Stone pines are circumboreal, with several species in Europe and Asia. Most grow in semi-arid environments, often on rocky ridges and outcrops, where their deep roots and drought-resistant needles enable them to cope with limited water supplies. Although few other trees can compete with these specialized pines in their rugged habitats, the frequent fires that are a natural feature of dry landscapes help reduce competition further by burning up seedlings of upstart fir or spruce trees. Stone pines have fire-resistant bark and, by using up the available water near them, minimize the grasses and other fine fuels next to their trunks.

Perhaps the most remarkable aspect of stone pine ecology is the interdependent relationship between the trees and the nutcrackers – curve-billed members of the crow family. Whitebarks and limber pines are synonymous with the Clark's nutcracker, a raucous and sociable black-and-grey bird somewhat smaller than a crow. Nutcrackers rely on the energy-rich pine seeds to feed their offspring. Since cone crops vary in productivity from one year to the next, however, the birds need to hedge their bets by gathering pine seeds when they are abundant and hiding them for later retrieval when they may be scarce.

Nutcrackers use their stout beaks to pry seeds out of pine cones. Tilting its head up, a nutcracker will stash each seed in its gular pouch – a hollowed-out space beneath its tongue. Once it has five to ten seeds, it flies to an open slope up to several hundred metres away, lands on the ground, pokes a beak-length hole in the ground and empties its gular pouch into the hole. A couple of quick pokes and the hole is covered. Calling sociably as they flock back and forth between treetops and caching sites, flocks of nutcrackers work compulsively for hours on end.

Dianne Keane, an ecology professor at the University of Colorado, studied nutcracker food-caching behaviour as part of her Ph.D. studies. She estimated that an individual nutcracker may gather and store up to 90,000 seeds in a single summer. Experimenting with captive birds, she found that their spatial memory is nothing short of astounding. Using sticks, rocks and other markers as reference points, her study nutcrackers were unfailingly able to retrieve every seed they had cached. Only if researchers moved one of the markers did the birds fail to find their hidden food supplies.

Nutcrackers, however, are over-achievers. Their food-caching behaviour far exceeds the needs of the average nutcracker family. Of the 40,000 to 90,000 seeds each nutcracker hides it may retrieve only a third. Pine seeds are critical food for nutcracker nestlings. The birds retrieve enough seeds to ensure the survival of the next nutcracker generation. The seeds that remain behind ensure the next generation of pines. Each stash of seeds is at the ideal depth for germination. Because nutcrackers choose sunny, open slopes — they particularly favour recently-burned sites — the sprouting seedlings enjoy abundant sun and little competition from other plants. The relationship between nutcracker and pine, in other words, works to the advantage of both parties: a classic symbiotic relationship.

It's a relationship that's in trouble however, partly due to the misguided enthusiasm of North America's early forest conservationists.

During the early years of the twentieth century, Americans became concerned about the rate at which timber barons were devastating that nation's forests. President Theodore Roosevelt established national forest reserves to protect what remained and hired Gifford Pinchot as the first head of the U.S. Forest Service. Pinchot, a staunch believer in conservation – the philosophy of wise use of natural resources – set about to change the way American forestry was done.

In Canada, Prime Minister Wilfred Laurier organized several Forestry Congresses to promote a similar change in management philosophy for our forest estate. Gifford Pinchot was an honoured guest at the first Canadian Forestry Congress in 1906.

Among the changes to forest management that arose on both sides of the border with the establishment of public forests and forest management agencies, was a move to improve the quality of North American trees. Pinchot and others felt that North American forests were little better than raw materials, sorely in need of improvement through management. Selective breeding and progressive techniques of forest culture were among the ways foresters determined to improve native forests. Since some of the best available silviculture expertise of the day was in Germany, scientists in Pinchot's agency shipped seeds and seedlings of North American trees overseas to be improved by selective breeding in German plantations. Among the species that went to Europe were eastern and western white pines – five-needle pines that, unlike the related limber and whitebark pines, produce high-quality lumber.

When the "improved" trees came back to North America they brought a hitchhiker – white pine blister rust. Blister rust is endemic to Europe, where pine trees long ago developed resistance to its ravages. North America's five-needle pines, however, had never been exposed to the fungal disease. With no built-in resistance, our native trees were – and are – extremely vulnerable to infection. Ironically, scientific forestry in the service of wise use proved more devastating to North America's five needle pine forests than the ravages of the nineteenth century's unbridled commercial exploitation. Eastern white pine forests have yet to recover from the combined devastation of over-cutting and blister rust.

Only an aggressive breeding program to select for rust-resistance has saved western white pine forests from vanishing.

The commercial value of the white pines at least motivated foresters to try and undo the harm they had unleashed upon this continent. Lacking any economic value, however, wind-gnarled limber and whitebark pine forests were left to die. Death by blister rust is a slow, insidious process that begins with rust spores infecting a single branch, then gradually killing that branch as the fungus spreads down the tree's vascular system to the trunk. Blister-like swellings girdle the trunk at the base of the infected branch, gradually killing the top of the tree. After several years, the tree finally dies completely. Since slow-growing whitebark pines may be a hundred years old before they produce their first cone, the disease often kills trees before they get a chance to reproduce.

Gnarled and scenic, the growing number of dead snags up near timberline went unnoticed for many years because the attention of foresters was focused on economically productive forests farther downslope. A third of all the whitebark and limber pines in the Waterton-Glacier International Peace Park were already dead before Kate Kendall and her research associates began to investigate the problem in the late 1990s. More disturbing yet, from half to almost 95% of trees in the surviving stands were infected with blister rust and, consequently, doomed to early death.

Blister rust has been in western forests for almost a century. Its spread has been uneven. While the worst damage is concentrated along the 49th parallel in a fan-shaped area extending from near Vancouver to the Waterton-Glacier International Peace Park, whitebark pine forests farther north and south have yet to show much sign of damage. In Jasper National Park, flocks of nutcrackers greet tourists at the base of Mount Edith Cavell; on the slopes above, the rounded tops of healthy whitebark pines dominate a forest that shows no sign of infection. Yellowstone National Park is similarly healthy, although early signs of blister rust infestation have ecologists there worried. The endangered grizzly bears of the Yellowstone ecosystem rely on whitebark pine nuts that they excavate from squirrel middens for critical summer food. If blister rust devastates Yellowstone's high-elevation forests, ecologists fear the ecosystem's capacity to support grizzly bears will be drastically reduced.

Nobody knows whether whitebark pines were once as important a bear food in the more badly infected regions along the 49th parallel. Two mid-century biologists reported sign of grizzlies feeding on pine nuts, and during her 1997 field investigations in Waterton, Kate Kendall found bear scats full of limber pine seeds. For the most part, however, whitebark pine stands were already suffering heavy mortality before anyone started asking questions about the role their cone crops might play in Rocky Mountain ecology.

The late twentieth century, however belatedly, brought an awakening interest in non-commercial forest values among government agencies and conservation groups. A heavily-attended 1997 conference in Missoula, Montana drew forest experts from numerous agencies and universities together to plan strategies for saving the threatened whitebark ecosystem.

What's needed, all agreed, is for whitebark pine populations to be given the chance to develop rust resistance. Some agencies like the U.S. Forest Service and B.C. Ministry of Forests have selective breeding facilities which they have used, in the past, to develop disease-resistant strains in other western trees. At least in the U.S., whitebark pine breeding programs are already underway. The problem with growing rust-resistant seedlings in nurseries, however, is that most die once transplanted into natural habitats. Given the sheer geographical scale of the problem, selective breeding is unlikely to make a big impact.

Canadian and U.S. national parks, unlike neighbouring multiple-use agencies, are mandated to work with natural ecological processes. Park vegetation specialists in both countries are now looking to prescribed fire as a way to kick-start natural selection of rust resistance. They point out that, if it weren't for aggressive fire control programs, lightning strikes would have maintained a mosaic of various-aged forests at timberline through the twentieth century, rather than the aging stands that dominate today. Without frequent fires, subalpine fir and other shade-tolerant trees eventually crowd out the sun-loving whitebarks and, ironically, expose them to the risk of death from much more intense fires fuelled by the dense foliage of the ingrown forests.

The least rust-resistant whitebark pines in most stands are already dead. Although nutcrackers stash seeds from those that have survived the twentieth century, mortality among pine seedlings is high in the timberline environment. Only on recently burned slopes where conditions are ideal for regeneration do high numbers of pine seedlings successfully sprout and grow. For vegetation ecologists like Kate Kendall and Kootenay National Park's Rob Walker, small burned patches offer the best hope of filling the mountain landscape with young whitebark pines. All of those, inevitably, will be exposed to blister rust spores. Most ultimately will die. Those whose genetic make-up keeps them immune to rust attack, however, will grow and, in a few decades, begin to produce new generations of pines with increasingly high rates of rust resistance.

The key is to get lots of young whitebarks growing while the dwindling supply of old whitebarks are still producing enough seed. And the challenge is getting the okay to set fires in scenic, high-elevation forests. Land use managers are understandably timid about letting their staff start forest fires that might upset a public brainwashed by Smoky the Bear. Even more worrisome is the thought that some fires could escape and burn neighbouring commercial forests, farmlands or other property.

Rob Walker feels there is little cause for nervousness with well-planned prescribed burns. He conducted Canada's only whitebark pine restoration burn to date. The 12-hectare prescribed fire near the Crowfoot Glacier in Banff National Park went off flawlessly in October 1998. "We know it was an intense fire," says Walker. "We got 100% crown scorch and more than 70% organic soil loss. Monitoring so far shows excellent herbaceous regeneration. We won't know how well we met our pine objectives until we get a good cone crop year and that hasn't happened yet."

Farther south, forest managers in the Bitterroot National Forest near Missoula, Montana have already found prolific whitebark pine restoration in experimental units they burned in the early 1990s. Rob Walker is planning a larger fire in Yoho National Park's isolated Sodalite Creek valley and his colleagues in other Rocky Mountain parks have similar plans on the books.

"One thing that works in our favour that I hadn't originally anticipated," says Walker, "is how dry the sites actually are. You think of them as cool and damp because they're at timberline but they're usually quite well-drained. The other thing is that we have our choice of many topographically isolated sites where talus and rock can be used to keep the fires from spreading."

In British Columbia, some forestry companies have recently taken an interest in working with the B.C. Ministry of Forests to restore whitebark pine stands there. Most whitebarks grow above the operability line – the elevation contour where it is uneconomic to log. Even so, logging companies often use fire to get rid of logging slash in cutblocks just downslope from whitebark stands. Late fall slash burns, deliberately designed to burn upslope into whitebark pine stands, could play a future role in creating patchwork openings full of young, regenerating pine trees. Given the role that commercial forestry considerations played in unleashing the blister rust problem, there is a kind of symmetry to the idea that commercial forest companies might have a role to play in undoing some of the harm.

The silent snags reflected in Forum Lake's icy waters stand as a silent reproof to the hasty arrogance of early forest conservationists, and a continuing challenge to the current generation. Twentieth-century forest management resulted in the slow, insidious devastation of an entire forest ecosystem. If twenty-first century forest management fails to reverse that decline, the price of failure will be measured in Clark's nutcrackers, squirrels, grizzly bears, and the spreading silence of those high-mountain ghost forests. It is a haunting challenge.

Kevin Van Tighem is a four-time winner of the Outdoor Writers of Canada Environment Writing Award, and the author of eight books and hundreds of articles on conservation, wildlife and outdoor themes. His 1997 anthology of personal essays, Coming West: A Natural History of Home, has been widely acclaimed and has won several awards. His guidebook titles include Bears, Wild Animals, and Predators. Kevin is the conservation biologist for Waterton Lakes National Park and a skilled hiker, hunter and wildlife observer. He has served on the executive committee of the Alberta Wilderness Association and the Federation of Alberta Naturalists. Kevin lives in Waterton and is a co-founder and coordinator of the Waterton-Glacier Writers Workshop.

border: an outer part or edge.
boundary: a bounding or separating line

On Borders and Boundaries

by Don H. Meredith

The scent wafted up from the valley on the eddy of a warm upslope breeze. It tantalized the nose of the bear grazing on the new, succulent, green grass in the meadow, reminding him how a full belly felt and tasted! Yes! The taste of rich sweet meat watering his mouth. He remembered the last time he had tasted such meat. It was with his mother somewhere down this slope. The hunting had been easy, the meat not as fast as it was up here. Without further consideration, the grizzly bolted from the meadow and bounded downslope toward the source of the scent.

On his way through spruce and pine forest, he crossed a narrow swath of cut bushland that marked the park boundary and entered a region where the risk to his health had suddenly increased. The boundary of Waterton Lakes National Park didn't matter much to the bear. Sure, he had learned from his mother that somewhere down this valley he had to be more careful. Feeding on calves or dining on a pile of grain had consequences that were different from those up in the mountains. In the valleys, such activities could land the bear in a dark tunnel out of which he might have to make a many-day trip to get back to his home in the park. Or worse, it could mean sudden death at the hands of a conservation officer or angry rancher. But like all bears, grizzlies are opportunists, and the opportunity to gorge himself after a long winter sleep was too important to miss.

But what was that on the air now coming over a low ridge? Another scent? Yes, but this one was richer than the one he had been following. It too was sweet and equally mouthwatering, but it had an overwhelming pungency that told the bear it came from meat that was already down, did not have to be hunted and would easily fill his belly at little cost.

He made a left turn and skirted the slope, following the tantalizing odor up an adjacent valley. Once again he crossed the swath cut through the woods, and once again he ignored it. The scent's increasing strength overpowered all thought. That is, until he reached a familiar opening in the woods where he had dug for roots in the past. He suddenly remembered that this is where a much larger boar had run him off last year. It had been a close call, and he didn't want to repeat the incident.

Coming to a stop at the edge of the woods, he carefully sniffed the air, trying to distill other scents from the potent odor of overripe flesh. He did discern a different scent, but not that of another grizzly. Bolting into the meadow, he finally saw what he was after at the far end — the carcass of a cow elk. Something was shaking the front end. As he approached, the bear huffed a warning. The bloodstained face of a coyote rose from behind the carcass and stared in shock at the approaching bear. In less than a heartbeat, the coyote spun around and rocketed out of the meadow. The bear made a quick inspection of the carcass, making sure no other grizzly had yet laid claim to it. All he smelled was the rotting flesh, the coyote and some slight acrid scents on the hide that were more familiar to him downslope, where the slow meat lived.

Later that summer and higher in the mountains above the elevation where it is too cold and dry for trees to grow, a small least chipmunk also smelled a tantalizing scent on an upslope wind. It was the scent of overripe Saskatoon berries down in the trees. However, another more pungent odor told the little rodent that she dare not make the trip to harvest those berries. The latter scent was that of her larger downslope neighbour, the yellow-pine chipmunk. That species holds the territory from tree-line down, while the least chipmunk holds the territory from tree-line up into the alpine meadows and rocks. Individuals of both species know the boundary that separates them as if it had been drawn on the rocks with a paint brush. To cross that line and trespass would invite a fight the least chipmunk knew she could not win. She ignored the Saskatoons and continued foraging for the scarcer blueberries just ripening in the sprawling alpine meadows. There, if she caught her yellow-pine neighbour foraging, she knew she could drive the intruder back into the trees despite her smaller size. Why? Because those meadows were dominated by the least chipmunk's scent and there were no familiar trees for the yellow-pine chipmunk to hide in.

Borders and boundaries play roles in all our lives, whether grizzly bear, chipmunk or person. We humans, however, often design borders and boundaries that don't make a lot of sense to a grizzly bear or chipmunk. Take the international border between the United States and Canada, that also separates Glacier National Park in Montana from Waterton Lakes National Park in Alberta. On a map it follows an arbitrary straight line that on the ground crosses alpine meadow, forest and grassland. Its position is well understood by the people who populate each country. It marks cultural and historical differences that are highlighted each time a person crosses from one country into the other. But to a grizzly bear, chipmunk or migrating Canada goose, the international border is not a consideration.

We humans like our borders and boundaries to be neat straight lines with sharp square corners that look orderly on paper. View agricultural or urban land from the air and the pattern is apparent. Roads, fences, streets and alleys crisscross the landscape as evenly as possible, going to great lengths to ignore the topography. When the topography can't be ignored, such as at streams or cliffs, it is done so reluctantly — borders and boundaries quickly returning to the pattern as soon as the terrain allows.

Even the curvature of the earth is reluctantly acknowledged by our land survey systems. So-called "correction lines" jar the regular pattern of squared plots of land, reluctantly acknowledging the planet is not flat — as if we have to be continually reminded that Christopher Columbus wasn't a liar.

The natural borders and boundaries in our wild lands are not such slaves to mathematical regularity. Streams, cliffs or mountains change and indeed create these demarcations in many ways. The varying amounts of moisture, light, temperature and soil quality, all control what lives where.

Change one factor and a boundary might move. Fish require water to live in streams. But if the clearing of shoreline vegetation raises the temperature of the water in a stretch of stream, certain fish, such as the bull trout, might find it difficult to get enough oxygen to live there. Thus, a boundary is created in the water, across which the trout will not go.

What's a boundary for one species might just be a convenient border for another. In the mountains, a south-facing slope might be too dry for trees to grow because of the exposure of the slope to the sun. However, such conditions might be ideal for the growth of grasses and other plants that feed bighorn sheep, elk and ground squirrels. Near the boundary of this grassland, where conditions begin to permit the growth of shrubs and trees, there is a variety of food for certain birds, mice and chipmunks. These animals can find berries, seeds and grasses all in close proximity to adequate cover to protect them from predators and the weather. Deer also find this edge between the two plant communities to be ideal for browsing on woody vegetation and grazing on the softer grasses.

Some human-made boundaries are recognized and used by wild animals. For example, the Waterton elk herd knows the east boundary of the park very well. In the summer, it will range in and out of the park in search of plentiful green grasses. But in the fall, when the grass has turned brown and hunting season opens outside the park, it grazes within the park boundary where no hunters wait in ambush.

While this boundary benefits the elk at a certain time of the year, they readily ignore it and other boundaries when it suits them. In the winter, after hunting pressure subsides and grass in quantity may be difficult to find, elk will leave the park and jump fences to get at stacked hay in ranch yards. This can be a severe problem for ranchers, who lobby government for extended hunting seasons to keep the elk at bay.

Waterton and Glacier parks protect unique mountain ecosystems. But the concept of ecosystem itself is an attempt by people to put a boundary around things. Ecosystems are abstract concepts of our scientific imaginations that attempt to describe the processes and relationships among living things and their environments. Unlike the pieces of land we surround with fences, nowhere can you actually point to an ecosystem. You can only point to what lives in it or the landscape that supports it. But the actual system runs in the background, only revealing pieces of itself, (for example, photosynthesis, transpiration, disease, or a grizzly bear feeding on an elk carcass,) when we are lucky enough or persistent enough to see them.

Thus, saying that a national park protects ecosystems may or may not be true. It depends on how we define the ecosystems. If we define them as distinct pieces of territory, then yes, those whose boundaries are within the park are protected. But the reality is that most ecosystems are not limited by man-made boundaries. Indeed, ecosystems adjacent to one another, such as a south facing grassland and a pine forest, are so interconnected with threads of relationships that it would be difficult to tease one from the other.

The ecosystem in which the least chipmunk resides can be defined as the distinct treeless alpine zone that runs along the backbone of the Rocky Mountains. It is not bound by park or other arbitrary boundary. It is, however, defined and bounded by the forest ecosystem below it. Similarly, the forest that is home to the yellow-pine chipmunk is not restricted by arbitrary boundaries. Of course, outside the park, we attempt to cut this system into easily defined blocks to satisfy our hunger for wood fibre and lumber. But the system is resilient and over long periods of time it will replace the trees.

The ecosystem that supports the grizzly bear is much larger and broader than those that support chipmunks or elk. Indeed, the grizzly bear uses many ecosystems and illustrates the arbitrary nature of defining this abstraction of the mind. For the grizzly bear will graze and hunt elk calves in grasslands, hunt marmots and ground squirrels in the alpine, feed on berries and carrion in the forest, and dine on grain and hunt beef calves on ranches. So, is that one ecosystem or several?

Similarly, the ecosystem that supports our species is a conglomerate of many. We get our water from alpine and forest; our food for the table from grasslands, forests and water bodies around the world; and our air, recreation and food for the soul from everywhere. In turn we have a significant effect on most ecosystems, even in parks that purport to protect them. Just our sheer numbers on trails and in townsites affect the movement of animals, the distribution of plant life and the quality of the air and water in and outside the park.

If the borders and boundaries around these ecosystems are so arbitrary, should we bother protecting them in our parks and other protected areas? Of course. The fact that we've placed boundaries around certain areas demonstrates that we've recognized their importance to our well being. But in terms of managing an ecosystem so it will survive and maintain the widest variety of plant and animal species, we need to consider the arbitrary line we've drawn on paper to be more of a border than a boundary. That is, we must recognize the interconnected nature of ecosystems and manage them accordingly.

Waterton Lakes National Park, "where the mountains meet the prairie," illustrates this very well. The prairie that supports the ranch lands enters the park from the east. Deer, elk and grizzly bears freely range the ranch lands. People benefit from them all. To maintain these benefits, ranchers, park and wildlife managers are working together to solve problems, in organizations such as the Waterton Biosphere Reserve. Steps are taken to protect hay stacks. Hunting seasons are augmented to reduce elk depredation. Grizzly bears are discouraged from hunting calves in the spring by the placement of road-killed deer and elk in the mountains.

Yes, borders and boundaries play roles in all our lives. But those roles vary from place to place, animal to animal, plant to plant, ecosystem to ecosystem. If we understand what constitutes a border and what constitutes a boundary, we stand a greater chance of keeping the variety of life we have in this world — a variety that keeps us whole by reminding us there's more than one way to earn a living on this planet.

Don Meredith *works for Alberta Environment as the Coordinator of Information and Education for the Fisheries and Wildlife Management Division. He received a PhD in Zoology in 1975 and has worked on projects in the High Arctic, northern Alberta and the Rockies. He writes two monthly outdoor columns: "On the Scree: notes on an outdoor ethic" for the Alberta Outdoorsmen and "The Great Outdoors" for the Edmonton Sports Scene. His work has been published in Canadian Geographic, Western Sportsman, Alberta Fishing Guide, and the Edmonton Journal. His young-adult novel, Dog Runner, won the 1990 Writers Guild of Alberta Award of Excellence for Children's Literature. Don was a participant in the 1997 and 1999 Writers Workshops.*

Our Home
and Native Land

Andrew Nikiforuk

I own land in southern Alberta and not long ago I made a presentation to the MD of Pincher Creek about air pollution from an industrial hog factory. The operation in question raises 600 sows and produces sewage equivalent to a town of 1200 people. It legally stores this waste in an open lagoon in one of the world's windiest geographies. As a result, many ranchers I know can smell pig waste downwind of this operation as far away as seven and a half miles.

I have nothing against pigs, but when produced on industrial scale, pig dung is a highly volatile substance. It also contains 250 compounds neither my neighbours nor Ralph Klein would ever choose to breathe on a daily basis, including ammonia, hydrogen sulfide and carbon dioxide. Alberta Agriculture pretends that this problem is merely a nuisance, but my neighbours and I know this enterprise has unwittingly and thoughtlessly depreciated something we all hold dear: clear air.

In purely economic terms, this new operation has damaged natural capital. It has fouled a free good, created a local air quality deficit and made many of my neighbours nauseous and ill. It has also diminished land property values and, by implication, property taxes for the municipal district. These kinds of negative costs are now occurring throughout the province and irrevocably changing the landscape of Alberta. My pig quandary also symbolizes an increasing tension between Alberta's booming industrial economy and Alberta limited heritage economy – the initial natural dowry bequeathed to us by Creation.

Neither government nor the media talk openly about this heritage economy or accurately report its depletion. Economic boosters tend to dwell on the province's low tax rate, diminishing debt load and healthy growth rate. These are formidable accomplishments. As a long time fiscal conservative, I supported many of these measures long before it was popular to do so. But the happy economic statistics we hear every day are one-sided and make up only one column in the ledger. There would be no boom or debt reduction if Albertans weren't digging into what Ralph Klein calls "our treasure trove of natural resources." Man-made capital depends on natural capital and it has always been so. A refinery cannot prosper without access to petroleum deposits and a pulp mill cannot thrive without a dedicated forest reserve.

As such, Alberta's heritage economy is the foundation of our house, the source of much of our income and the provider of services essential for pleasurable living. But the man-made economy that has so energized Calgary and Edmonton these days is drawing heavily upon our heritage bank account. The Alberta government, the trustee of most of our natural capital, has not only allocated 90 percent of our resources to one or more industrial enterprises but stubbornly refuses to reinvest in natural capital for future generations. This kind of planning is both short-sighted and uneconomic.

The drama of our maligned heritage economy is most pronounced in the boreal forest. This is where our $28 billion oil and gas industry is now duking it out with the province's $5 billion forest industry. It is largely a silent wrestling match and one whose details would appal most Albertans if accurately reported.

As every school child knows, Alberta's northern forest carpets half the province and accounts for nearly a tenth of Canada's northern taiga - a fabled and riches-laden land that provides nearly $70 billion worth of free services every year in terms of oxygen-making, carbon- holding, fish-breeding, moose-rearing, water-cleaning and yes, some of the world's finest fibre-making. What's unique about the boreal is that it performs the same ecological services as the Amazon rainforest, with only a fraction of the species. It is a model of efficiency and one many industries and governments could well emulate. Unfortunately, Stockwell Day doesn't keep track of the wide array of natural services that the boreal, or the foothills, for that matter, provide to Albertans.

The current conflict dates back to the hurried and careless allocations of timber made in the 1980s. Just about every stick of wood outside a provincial or national park is now scheduled to be clear-cut within the next 70 years. The Alberta Forest Producers Association (AFPA) warned the government as early as 1991 that the province's timber supply numbers weren't reliable and that there had been serious over-allocations. As the AFPA recently noted, "over-allocating the resource creates problems not only for government but for industry 15 to 20 years into the future." It's also lousy stewardship. The government has compounded its poor timber math by failing to calculate just how much forest massive fires, global warming, international conservation commitments and aboriginal land claims would also subtract from the supply. (To be fair many of these demands were not entirely predictable a decade ago.) And it forgot about the petrochemical industry, now one of the biggest wood hewers around.

Two recent reports on the mayhem in the boreal clearly document that Alberta now treats its forest the way teenagers use an instant teller machine on a Saturday night: all withdrawals and no deposits. In fact, a 300-page opus by Alberta Environmental Protection (*The Final Frontier: Protecting Landscape and Biological Diversity with Alberta's Boreal Forest Natural Region*) concluded that less than nine percent of Alberta's frontier forest could be called wilderness any more. What's left lies mostly in Wood Buffalo National Park.

Based on 10 year-old data, the study reported that more than 75 percent of Alberta's 4005 boreal townships (a township is roughly 93 square kilometres) now sport oil wells, while more than 71 percent have been fragmented by roads. Government data also shows that at least 72 percent of the forest has been leased for drilling, logging, mining and sometimes all three at once. Road densities in the boreal are now eight times higher than that recommended by the U.S. Forest Service to conserve big game animals such as grizzlies. In addition, agriculture has cut another two million cubic metres of trees, an ongoing development that gives Peace River country the distinction of having a deforestation rate on par with that of the Amazon.

Such fragmentation has shattered the forest like glass. In fact, only five percent of Alberta's forests now stand in blocks greater than nine square kilometres. A nine square kilometre block fits nicely into downtown Calgary and takes up no more that one-tenth the size of the city. Like Brazil, Alberta has eaten its wilderness capital with gusto.

A wilderness interrupted by roads and other industrial signposts can no longer be considered wild. In fact, laissez-faire is good policy for wilderness and markets alike. A fettered wilderness works no better than a fettered market. Nature works best when managed least.

But neither industry nor government is prepared to let the boreal be these days. In some parts of the forest, such as Alpac's forest management area, oil and gas activity now removes more trees than Alpac. This explains why Alberta's Environmental Protection Contravention website is crowded with the names of Calgary-based oil and gas companies. The petroleum industry pays three times as many fines for unauthorized use of public land as do logging firms.

Unlike forest companies, the oil patch and frontier farmers don't have to replant what they cut. In fact no one can predict how much of this felled forest will ever grow back. In simple terms, Alberta's forest industry depends on trees that the oil and gas industry and "other stakeholders" are gobbling up at an unsustainable rate.

The messy situation in the boreal has a companion in Special Places, a made-in-Alberta conservation project that started with the noblest of intentions. When Ralph Klein kicked off the project in 1992, the idea was to create a network of protected places that would serve "as the province's lifeline to an ecologically sustainable future." Special Places was supposed to be a sacrosanct wilderness savings account and a reinvestment in natural capital. In 1994, a blue ribbon public advisory panel of conservative Albertans, (with nary a wild-haired environmentalist in the bunch,) recommended the protection of five percent of Alberta's landscape by the year 2000. They noted that these protected areas should come in big chunks and be connected with wilderness corridors. The public advisory panel understood that wilderness, like currency, needs to flow if it is to retain any value. At the same time, both government and industry realized that the completion of this network would fulfill a number of national and international conservation commitments and bring some environmental peace to the province.

To date the government has achieved none of its conservation targets and has won no peace on the environmental front. Instead of protecting five percent of the land mass as Albertans requested, the government reduced the target to 2.8 percent. An independent audit by the World Wildlife Fund based on government data found that Alberta Environment has saved less than a third of this diminished goal and achieved only seven percent of the specific targets for core protected areas. Any industry with a similar performance record would now be out of business.

Special Places has been a clear failure for two reasons. For starters, a strong made-in-Alberta ideology stymied the program from day one. Unlike most industry leaders I know, many provincial politicians regard conservation as a form of "sterilization." Men such as Ty Lund, Steve West and Ken Kowalski believe that protecting the landscape from industrial development is just wrong. These individuals practice a 19th century land creed that is purely utilitarian: abuse it or lose it. Wild economies, natural capital and the beauty of Creation apparently offend these men. Yet any reading of opinion surveys indicate that their sentiments are rare if not fanatical viewpoints in a province that boasts Canada's largest population of park users. For a government that prides itself on innovation and flexible thinking, their ideology remains a public embarrassment.

In addition to active government opposition, Special Places faced another hurdle: the reality that more than 90 percent of Alberta's landscape has already been committed or promised to industry. Rather than come up with innovative solutions that permitted lease exchanges, conservation incentives or royalty credits, the government has simply denied the existence of a problem. This approach has irritated Albertans and the Canadian Association of Petroleum Producers (CAPP) alike. In fact government has steadfastly ignored a consensus document by CAPP and conservation groups that agreed industrial activity within Special Places sites was incompatible with preservation goals.

The enduring woes of the Special Place program are perhaps best illustrated by the plight of the Chinchaga. It contains a unique patch of old growth forest in the foothills just west of Manning, where grizzlies still fish and caribou forage. The government has identified the Chinchaga as one of the last possible sites for establishing a large protected area in Alberta's foothills.

An industry-dominated advisory committee for Special Places recommended that the Chinchaga, already fragmented by industry, be spared any more drilling or cutting. Conservationists have pressed for protecting Chinchaga's old growth forest, the richest and rarest part of the hills. And Daishowa-Marubeni International Ltd. wrote that it does not "...wish to harvest in this area if it is being considered for protection," but their request for an alternate license has not been acted on. The government's response is a proposal to save a local peat bog.

Another example of the province's assault on our heritage economy concerns the government's plans to expand intensive livestock operations. Although exporting meat makes far better sense than shipping grain, the government proposal has generated more grief than joy in rural Alberta for four reasons: its scale is unrealistic; it came without an adequate regulatory framework; it totally discounted costs such as noise, flies and air pollution; and it didn't properly account for existing demands on natural capital.

Let's start with the scale of the plan. Four years ago, the province proposed doubling cattle production to 10 million and tripling hog production to eight million within the next 10 years. Thanks to subsidized water from irrigation projects, Alberta is already one of the world's top beef exporters and North America's fifth largest feeding centre for beef.

Unfortunately, success in this industry means big manure piles. Alberta's feedlots and hog barns now produce manure equivalent to the untreated sewage of 48 million people. "Feedlot alley" - home to 1.3 million animals in the area north of Lethbridge - produces more waste than the cities of Calgary and Edmonton combined. However, I have yet to see a plan on how we will economically deal with double that amount of dung without damaging soil, air and water quality.

Current production levels have already created some formidable problems. A recent $4 million study on the impact of farming on Alberta's waterways found that more than half of 27 streams in key agricultural production areas typically exceed guidelines for phosphorus, nitrogen and disease-carrying bacteria. These compounds feed algae growth, kill fish and force local towns and cities to develop costly water treatment systems. The findings confirmed what a great many rural Albertans already suspected: feedlots, cow-calf operations, seasonal feeding areas and improper manure disposal already pollute rivers and streams at levels higher than anticipated.

The intensive livestock industry has also taken a toll on rural Albertans' health. A recent survey in Picture Butte and Brooks looked at concerns about air quality among 234 adults. Both towns support intensive livestock operations. The results were sobering: more than 75 percent of the respondents in both towns said that they were bothered by "unpleasant odours." And more than 40 percent of the respondents in both communities felt that air quality was affecting their own health. A recent Iowa study identified the reason for these concerns. It found that people living two miles from hog factories suffered from a higher incidence of respiratory diseases, as did the people who work in the barns. None of these public health costs have been factored into the expansion plans.

When government announced its big push for increasing livestock population, it did so in a regulatory vacuum. Intensive livestock developments have been built in the last four years without any clear framework other than a voluntary manure code which isn't enforced. Half of the province's rural municipalities have endured chronic complaints about bad manure practices, water contamination, increased traffic, dead animals, and foul odours. At one point in 1998, almost every newly proposed hog operation was contested in court by angry farmers who didn't want to shoulder the environmental costs of poorly planned developments.

Although the government belatedly introduced legislation to deal with many of these issues, the proposed law is weak. The promoter of expansions, Alberta Agriculture, is also responsible for enforcing the rules of expansion. Citizens don't trust governments that govern without checks and balances. Both Regional Health Authorities and Alberta Environment should have the power to deny approval to animal factories. Local governments should also have the right to impose and enforce higher standards than those now proposed by the province. Last but not least, the government needs to recognize that odour is really air pollution.

Albertans, by and large, are not comfortable with our collective assault on the heritage economy. I haven't met a rural or urban citizen in the last year who didn't express some unease over the scale of developments now transforming our rivers, forests and foothills. And I haven't even mentioned recreational developments, the density of oil and gas developments or the flaring issue. As economist and Christian philosopher Herman Daly recently observed, it isn't good form to hand back to God the gift of Creation in a degraded state, capable of supporting less life, less abundantly, for a shorter period of time. This is not a legacy Albertans want to leave to their children.

'Our Home and Native Land' is an amalgam of two articles, originally published in Alberta Ventures magazine and Outdoor Canada.

Andrew Nikiforuk *is an award-winning investigative journalist and the author of many hard-hitting books and articles on contemporary Canadian society and the environment. He writes for Canadian Business, Canadian Geographic, Equinox, Outdoor Canada, the Calgary Herald and other publications. His books include The Fourth Horseman: A Short History of Epidemics, Plagues and Famines, and Running on Empty: Alberta After the Boom. Andrew participated in the 1997 and 1999 Writers Workshops.*

Fragmentation

by David Stiller

Southwestern Alberta's share of the Rocky Mountains is one of the most hurried topographical transitions in North America. It's where the mountains meet the prairie. In several short kilometres the landscape leaps hundreds of meters skyward, from grass-covered prairies to wind- and ice-carved peaks.

The eastern side of the Rockies, known as the Front, extends from the Yukon to New Mexico, but in southwestern Alberta and adjacent Montana, it also constitutes the eastern margin of what wildlife biologists refer to as the Crown of the Continent ecosystem. These 40,000 square kilometres of mountains, forests, and crystalline waters are home to grizzly and black bears, timber wolves, elk, moose, deer, and dozens of other species, winged and four-legged, fauna and flora, large and small, rare and common. The Crown's name derives from its location at the continent's hydrologic apex: from here rivers run south to the Gulf of Mexico, west to the Pacific, east to Hudson Bay.

In addition to hosting an array of wildlife, the Crown is one of the continent's most scenic environs. Its ragged mountains, jeweled lakes, thick spruce and pine forests, and fertile parks provide a visual kaleidoscope for the human eye. Canada's Waterton Lakes National Park and Montana's adjacent Glacier National Park are the Crown's crown jewels. Every summer hordes of tourists descend upon these parks in camera-toting waves, elated by the brisk air and arching sapphire skies. By mid-July, hotels, motels, RV parks, and campgrounds resonate with a continuous buzz. Restaurants and curio shops, closed and boarded during the winter, ply meals and trinkets.

But holiday cabins and second homes have begun to invade this landscape. Over the past two decades their numbers have increased to where they have concentrated like pockets of ground-hugging fog.

Perhaps, from the center of a lush, rolling park that is knee-deep in grass and dotted with aspen, you may see a spot that you covet. As a visitor, you may have enjoyed such relaxation and sensory delirium that you find yourself planning to move to southwestern Alberta or northern Montana, and telecommute to Toronto or San Francisco. Or you might be contemplating the purchase of a vacation home to use several weeks a year. Land is available, carved out of former ranches into parcels for holiday retreats and second homes. From the edge of the foothills' verdant forests, east-facing cabins and near-mansions overlook the prairies and the sunrise, or, looking back, provide spectacular views of sunsets and the Front itself; certainly tempting to those wanting a piece of Eden.

Before you plop down your deposit, however, think again. The Crown is in reality a harsh land. Its charms lessen with summer's end. Come autumn, conditions change. September winds gather strength somewhere far beyond the western horizon, then roar with sound and fury down from the peaks to the prairie, flailing the forests and flattening the grasslands. Gusts fling fist-sized rocks to the valley floors from the ridges. Look around and note the ready evidence. The trees appear harried and ragged. If you proceed with your idyllic plans, the roof of your proud new cabin could wind up in a Regina back yard, or in a wheat field near Minot. For that matter, the wind blows most of the time along the Front, diminishing only slightly during the summer.

If the wind is no deterrent, consider winter's bone-shattering cold. By October or November, Arctic air begins to creep mercilessly southward from Hudson Bay and the Territories and bunches up against the Front, often dropping the mercury to minus forty. Trees can freeze solid, then split with a crack like a gunshot. And when the cold has become nearly unbearable, a *chinook* swoops down from the mountains and tips the thermometer upside down. Overnight, a balmy breeze begins to caress the region and the air becomes spring-like. But it is only nature's tease. The cold always returns, whether in hours or days, for it is only November and months of deep-freeze remain. Chinooks are welcome respites from cold and snow, but their fickle nature can become annoying, even maddening.

Or ponder the mosquitoes. During late spring and summer they drive livestock mad. Cattle and horses shrug, twitch, run, and roll in the dust and mud in crazed efforts to avoid these indigenous winged carnivores. Without industrial-strength repellent, humans venture out at their peril. Strong breezes blunt their assaults, but only for a while.

In addition to wind, cold, mosquitoes, and a scarcity of espresso bars, an even greater reason why humans should not populate the Crown is because we constitute a unique menace to its wildlife. Our presence splits apart what have been calving grounds and winter range for millennia, and ranching country for decades. This process of fragmentation of the land threatens wildlife far more than droughts, blizzards, hunting, and park budget cutbacks. Characterized by increasing numbers of roads and human habitations, fragmentation dissects and subdivides wildlife habitat and makes it that much harder for species like grizzly bears to sustain the populations that make the region attractive in the first place.

And grizzly bears can be ill-tempered neighbors. They possess little regard for international borders or property boundaries of any kind, and a single specimen can require several hundred square kilometres to support its life style. They wander out of the mountains for spring green and summer berries and bump into unsuspecting humans. Such encounters frequently result in death, usually for the bear. But if you doubt their foul humor and are truly stupid, if you try to photograph one as if in a zoo, or feed one from your picnic basket, you may be batted across the landscape like a shuttlecock and the grizzly will consume your picnic without any demonstrable expression of gratitude. If your karma is truly bad, the grizzly may consume you. Cooperation may exist among provinces and states, or between the two sovereign governments, but not between prey and predator. In the Crown, humans can be prey.

Deer and elk and mountain sheep cannot readily survive mountain winters deep behind the Front. The snow is too deep, the cold too extreme. Without adequate browse to sustain them, winterkill — slow death from exposure — pulls down the weak. And if cold, snow, and starvation do not kill wildlife directly, their weakened condition makes them easy prey for predators. To outlast winter, most descend to lower elevations for their winter range and pursue forage outside park boundaries and protective forests. Ranching may be the best friend most wildlife have along the Front.

Although frequently it is the ranchers themselves who yield the land to the cancer of vacation home development, they do so because the land is worth more as recreational real estate than as pasture. In contrast to the myth, modern ranching makes few millionaires. Family ranches are commonly typified by sizeable amounts of land (some owned, much leased), perishable livestock, and a constant quest for ready cash. Cattle prices have been in the tank of late. Heavy debt loads are familiar to many. Ranchers wanting to stick to their calling find it difficult to accommodate non-agrarian neighbors into their ranching operations, each with his or her own fences and ofttimes conflicting lifestyles.

When ranching becomes too difficult, when the headaches become intolerable, some find an attractive alternative in selling out. Who can blame them for wanting the silver lining to a dark cloud of uncertainty?

Fragmentation is a circular phenomenon that spirals steadily downward to force, at least theoretically, potential extermination of threatened species. It encourages ranchers to sell and subdivide, which exacerbates the process, leading to even less wildlife habitat. If there is a simple solution to the problem, no one has identified it.

So visit the Crown if you must. If you value it, however, do not build or buy a house here. Instead, walk softly and educate yourself to the area's complex rhythms. Wear bug dope like cheap cologne and give wandering grizzlies a wide berth. In the end, when your holiday is over and your money spent, when swarms of mosquitoes begin spilling your blood, or when September's gales brush tree tops against the earth, return to your own distant pasture. Long before winter grips the Front and deep snows bury its remote valleys, weeks before starving deer and elk begin competing with cattle for the stem-cured prairie grass rising valiantly above the wind-crusted snow, you should be tucked snug before your fire, far, far away. If you do this, the Crown as you see it may survive; it stands a chance of being here when you or your descendants return. But if you succumb to the Crown's seduction and stay, if you build a house here on a small plot of land, it will die slowly, horribly, before your eyes.

David Stiller has written broadly on environmental issues in the American and Canadian West. His first book, Wounding the West: Montana, Mining and the Environment, was published in spring 2000, after three years of research. Educated in both the United States and Canada, he is a consulting hydrologist, and has worked privately and for the government on projects involving hard rock and strip coal mining, hazardous waste, municipal and private water supplies, and agricultural land use impacts on water quality. A longtime resident of western Montana, he now lives and writes near Niwot, Colorado, where he has watched Colorado's Rocky Mountain Front fill with vacation homes and condominiums, its wilderness lost to human encroachment. Dave was a participant at the 1997 Writers Workshop.

Bull Elk

Keeping Elk in the Crowsnest

by David Stalling

Nearly 4,000 elk roam the rugged mountains between Alberta's Waterton Lakes National Park and the headwaters of the Oldman River. In the heart of this vast elk country, in a narrow valley called Crowsnest Pass, lives Ted Michalsky, a man with a passion for elk and elk hunting. He killed his first elk when he was 15, back in 1947. This past fall was the first time in 55 years that he didn't purchase an elk tag. "My knees are in rough shape," he says. "I just don't do it any more."

He's killed some large, fine bulls over the years, a few that would score high in trophy record books. But his wife and hunting partner, Connie, killed the largest.

"We didn't bother to measure anything in those days, but it was big," he says. "We hung it on our gate, on the road coming into our place. One day a truck came in with a high load, hit the gate, busted everything."

But the loss of those old antlers doesn't bother him as much as the loss of elk habitat. That's why, back in 1984, he became the 32nd person to join the Rocky Mountain Elk Foundation, a Montana-based wildlife habitat conservation organization that now boasts more than 120,000 members.

"I've hunted a lot of years, and I figure I ought to put something back into it," he says. It's also why he's helping with local efforts and selling his own land to protect wildlife habitat around his home.

When winter snows pile high, a fairly regular occurrence in the mountains of Alberta, elk head down into the Crowsnest Pass for the sheltered, grassy slopes of its lower elevations. There's a river to ford, a highway to cross and some railroad tracks where, on occasion, elk meet an ugly fate with trains. For the most part, though, elk find plenty of room to winter. But that's beginning to change.

"We've got a lot of prime winter range," Michalsky says. "But if we lose that to subdivisions, the elk will be stuck on the highway and railroad tracks, and you might as well forget it."

It's a common concern all across elk country. In the Crowsnest Pass, people are doing something about it.

I met Ted Michalsky last fall during a half-day tour of habitat protection efforts in the Crowsnest Pass, a trip designed to provide story ideas as part of the Waterton-Glacier International Writers' Workshop. I saw first-hand the bunchgrass and sedge-covered slopes, Douglas fir forests and brilliant stands of aspen that make up the rich elk range in this beautiful valley. I also saw newly-built homes, foundations for homes to come, and "Land for Sale" signs tightening like a noose around the open hillsides that have, for so long, provided habitat for wildlife. And I saw, up close, a telling example of the wildness that yet remains in this valley.

If not fear, there is certainly apprehension when looking into the eyes of a wild grizzly from just a few feet away — even if the bear is sedated and confined to a 6-foot, cylindrical metal cage. The grizzly came as an unexpected bonus. We were riding back towards Waterton in a provincial government truck when one of our tour guides, Wildlife Technician Jim Clark of Alberta's Natural Resources Service, received a call on his radio. Two of his agency's wardens had just captured a grizzly, a large boar that had been raiding a rancher's grain, and they were bringing the bear to a nearby weigh station before releasing it back to the wilds.

"Want to go see it?" Jim asked.

Of course.

Grizzlies evoke strong emotions; fear and awe to name just two. Smelling the musky stench of this burly boar, seeing this mass of bone, muscle, claw and thick, brown hair, this beast that under the right circumstances might tear off your limbs and consume you, I also felt sorrow to see such an animal humbled in a cage with a radio-collar around his neck. But this bear, and others like him, have contributed to the protection of the habitat we had walked and talked about that very day.

By collaring and monitoring the movements of grizzlies, wildlife biologists like Jim Clark learn more about where the big bruins roam, identifying and mapping crucial pathways, providing information that can help guide the protection of what Crowsnest area residents have deemed worth saving: wildlife and wild country. If you can protect the pivotal habitat needed to sustain large, far-roaming predators like grizzlies, so the reasoning goes, you'll also save what's needed for elk, bighorn sheep, mule deer and most other wildlife.

Like many folks, I have enviously regarded Canada as a huge, sparsely-populated chunk of wildness; a place one might still live a wild, adventurous life as depicted in the tales of Robert Service and Jack London. After all, Canada encompasses nearly 3.9 million square miles coast to coast with a population of 30 million people. By comparison, 270 million people live in the 3.5 million square miles that make up the United States.

But back at the writer's workshop, I sat through a myth-shattering slide show by Larry Simpson, director of The Nature Conservancy of Canada's Alberta, Saskatchewan and Northern Regions. Simpson flashed a persuasive array of maps and statistics and gave us an uncomfortable dose of reality. Much of Canada is the proverbial land of rock and ice. There's still room for caribou, stone sheep, mountain goats and barren ground grizzlies. And certainly there are plenty of isolated communities surrounded by rugged wilderness. But the amount of Canada's arable, fertile lands — the grasslands that became croplands — fits into an area about the size of Montana and Wyoming combined. About 80% of that relatively small slice of fertile Canada has been altered by towns, homes, highways, ranches and farms. The 20% that remains sustains 70% of Canada's wildlife species considered imperiled or at risk.

In the Western provinces, Simpson divides the Canadian prairie into five "ecoregions," woefully listing what little remains of what once existed: tallgrass prairie, less than 1% left; mixed prairie, 24%; foothill fescue, 27%; northern fescue, 5%, and aspen parklands, about 8%. And most of these remnants — the lands most valuable to wildlife — are privately owned. Simpson identifies three major impediments to protecting these lands: a false perception among Canadians that they live in a big, wild place, a tax system that doesn't offer incentives for landowners to protect habitat, and a lack of wealth directed toward protecting wildlife habitat. Add it all up, he says, and trying to conserve wildlands "is like fighting Mike Tyson with one hand tied behind your back."

"There's not much still intact," Simpson says, "and of that which is, not much is protected. There's intense pressure occurring on our landscape. If we don't get more pro-active, most land with high wildlife and aesthetic values will be lost or compromised in the next 20 years."

In the Waterton vicinity, and that of Crowsnest Pass, Simpson says wildlife habitat is threatened most by subdivision and development of homes, what he calls a halo effect resonating out from Calgary.

Ron Montgomery, Crowsnest region habitat coordinator for the Conservancy, says that in the Pass, there's still time to save what's left. He compares the position the valley is in now to the town of Canmore a few decades ago. That mountain valley town, near Banff, has grown from a nearly defunct mining community of a few thousand people, to a city of 10,000, with a predicted growth to 30,000 in the next 12 years.

"We don't want to become another Canmore," is a statement I heard often on the Crowsnest Pass tour, a rallying cry of sorts from people who cherish wild country and wish to keep it that way.

Montgomery and Jim Clark are heading up an all-inclusive effort supported by the Rocky Mountain Elk Foundation in Canada, The Nature Conservancy of Canada, Alberta Environment's Natural Resources Service, Alberta Conservation Association, Alberta Fish and Game Association, the Public Lands Branch of Alberta Government, Foundation for North American Wild Sheep, community leaders, ranchers, coal companies, timber companies, real estate agents and others to control growth in their valley. The effort ties in nicely with the Elk Foundation's Crowsnest Pass Habitat Conservation Initiative, which seeks to conserve 600 acres of the most significant elk winter range in the valley through private land purchase and the use of conservation easements.

"This is not a land grab," Montgomery says. "People in our community simply want to protect open space, agricultural lands, wildlife habitat and associated lifestyles with a balanced approach. We're not going to oppose or box development every time it comes up; we're trying to plan and direct development so we protect wildlife values."

Montgomery believes there are only three to five years left to protect these crucial wildlife corridors along the Crowsnest River.

The Crowsnest River begins its descent from Crowsnest Lake near the Continental Divide, just south of Crowsnest Mountain, a jagged 9,138-foot limestone pinnacle along the Alberta-British Columbia border. From there, the river flows east, dropping through a steep, narrow valley past several small communities, once thriving coal-mining towns, some now barely hanging on, and a few catering to a new economy of tourism and recreation. The river runs first past Coleman, then flows through Blairmore (with 1,800 people, the largest town in the valley), and on past Frank, Hillcrest, Bellevue and Burmis, before leaving the valley and joining with the Oldman River. All in all, 7,200 people inhabit this slim valley, defined and confined on both sides by steep timbered hills of aspen and fir, and jagged peaks that reach elevations of over 9,000 feet.

Just past the turn of the last century, and within a few years of each other, Gordon Kerr's grandfathers, Albert May and John Kerr, arrived in the Crowsnest Pass. A hunter, conservationist and former director of Alberta Natural Resources, Kerr writes of his ancestors in a 1997 report he penned about the elk of Crowsnest Pass. He tells how his grandfathers befriended Jack Morden, a mountain man who later become one of the valley's first forest rangers. When Kerr's grandfathers arrived, the elk were gone — victims of unregulated market hunting. Morden told them the valley had once known an abundance of elk, recalling how one spring in the late 1800s, while traveling between Calgary and Crowsnest Pass, he "couldn't get away from the smell of rotting dead elk," laid low by a hard winter.

In the late 1930s, elk from Yellowstone National Park were released in the Waterton-Castle River Area. By 1953, the herd had grown enough to be a nuisance, raiding haystacks and crops. So the first modern hunt was held — a month-long winter season for depredating cows unaccustomed to being shot at.

"I turned 14 the year the Castle River Game Preserve was opened, and shot my first elk there on opening day," Kerr writes. "I will not elaborate here on the chaos of opening day or the month long harvest of elk. Suffice it to say a person could determine the location of the herds by following the sound of gun fire."

Through the next two decades, the herd reclaimed most of the nooks and crannies of the Crowsnest. About 40 are now year-round residents, and upwards of 250 elk winter there.

"General wintering range now is limited to approximately 11 square miles," Kerr concludes in his report. "Key or critical wintering range and escape cover is confined to about three square miles, but loss of that has been as great as 40 percent through human related activity."

Federal crown lands and provincial lands dominate the rugged landscape that frames the valley, but in between lies a two-to-three-mile-wide zone of mostly private lands, running east to west. To move north or south, elk and other wildlife must thread their way across this strip. For now, the spaces between settlements still allow wildlife free passage. But if their routes of travel are plugged with developments, crucial wildlife habitat — particularly migratory paths and winter range for elk, deer and sheep — will be greatly diminished or lost.

The government has mapped three *red flag* corridors — crucial swaths of wildlife habitat linking crown and provincial lands north of the river to public lands on the south. One zone sits between Crowsnest Lake and Coleman, another between Coleman and Blairmore, and another between Bellevue and Burmis. The goal is to keep development out of these crucial corridors, while allowing it elsewhere, giving the Crowsnest Pass room to grow while protecting wildlife, wildlands and a way of life.

Ted Michalsky has lived in the Crowsnest area for all of his 69 years, outfitting, logging, mining, trucking and whatever else he could do to get by. Ask him a question and along with your answer you'll likely learn a bit of local folklore and history, and possibly get a slightly tall tale or two in the bargain. When our conversation wound around to grizzlies, he told of a coyote that chased a grizzly up a power pole. Zapped by the power lines, the bear came out of the sky like a runaway grand piano. Both were found dead, he says, the charred bruin on top of the flattened coyote. Not surprisingly, Michalsky doesn't wrap grizzlies in a shroud of mystique. Here, the bears aren't endangered and can still be hunted.

"We have a good population here, and they don't seem to bother anyone, although we do have an occasional incident," he says. "In 1940, 1941, I saw grizzlies all around me when I was trapping with my Dad. I've been around them ever since. You either get used to them or your hair stands up all your life."

Michalsky purchased 124 acres of land in 1949, planning to mine limestone from a craggy peak just north of Crowsnest Lake. He never did. More recently, he considered opening a campground along the lakeshore. "Then I thought, 'What the heck do you want to do that for?'"

There's a cave on the property with clear spring water gushing out into the lake; the main source of the Crowsnest River. A few years back a large bottling company offered him a tantalizing sum for the site, hoping to bottle and sell the spring water. The offer got him thinking more about the value and future of his land. There are other caves on his property, some filled with petroglyphs and Indian artifacts. His land also helps sustain a migratory herd of bighorn sheep, supports quite a few mule deer, and provides fall habitat for elk and grizzlies.

"I didn't want to see it developed or cut up," Michalsky says. So he sold it — for much less than it would have fetched as a source of bottled spring water — to the Rocky Mountain Elk Foundation.

Recently, the Elk Foundation and The Nature Conservancy teamed up to acquire the 345-acre Kerr property two miles west of Coleman. Both the government and the Crowsnest Pass Elk Management Advisory Committee (made up of ranchers, biologists, community leaders and others to help focus and direct elk habitat protection efforts,) has identified the Kerr land as the core winter range in the Crowsnest Pass. The land's gentle, grassy slopes, and Douglas fir - aspen forests feed and shelter 250 elk during Alberta's harsh months. Developers had their eye on the property for 20-acre housing lots, and were willing to pay far above appraised values, but the Kerrs wanted the land to remain intact. The Nature Conservancy will retain title of the land, and donate a conservation easement to the Elk Foundation. The easement further protects the land's wildlife values by ensuring that the property is never developed, regardless of future ownership. The Foundation for North American Wild Sheep, Shell Oil and North Star Energy also helped with the purchase.

Just across the river from the Kerr property, the Elk Foundation acquired 76 acres of willow bottom, providing habitat for elk, moose and whitetail deer. The Municipality of Crowsnest Pass, which owned the land as three distinct sections, agreed to donate the largest of the three parcels, if the Elk Foundation purchased the other two. The deal was completed in 1998, again with the help of the Foundation for North American Wild Sheep.

The sheep foundation also helped the elk foundation acquire 75 acres of riparian habitat and elk migratory corridor west of Blairmore, purchased from Wilma Frayne, Ted Michalsky's sister. And the Nature Conservancy bought 160 acres of grassland and forests east of Bellevue, a habitat for elk, sheep, bears, wolves, coyotes, grouse and more.

Taken one by one, these projects seem modest. But as a whole, they are a significant way to keep the corridors open for elk and other wildlife. Time is short, a sense of urgency strong, but the job is getting done, thanks to the vision and cooperation of so many in the community.

"Meetings continue with landowners, stakeholders and the general public regarding our concerted effort to secure multi-species habitat within the three identified corridors," says Montgomery. "Our big challenge, as always, is to continue fostering a sense of ownership and stewardship among all parties, particularly the general public, to ensure that our habitat protection success continues."

This article originally appeared in the May/June 2000 issue of Bugle magazine, the bimonthly journal of the Rocky Mountain Elk Foundation.

David Stalling is the conservation editor for Bugle magazine, where he writes, solicits and edits stories about natural history, wildlife management and conservation issues. Born and raised in Connecticut, Dave earned a degree in forestry from Paul Smith's College in New York and served five years in a U.S. Marine Corps Force Reconnaissance unit. He later received a degree in journalism at the University of Montana, then worked for the U.S. Forest Service, first as a forest technician, later as a writer and public affairs specialist. David participated in the 1999 Writers Workshop.

Hope on the Range

by Kevin Van Tighem

Another April chinook is spilling down across the Alberta foothills. Prairie crocuses dance in the wind as they've done here every spring for centuries.

The wind sweeping out of Waterton Lakes National Park chases rippling waves through brown fescue. Trumpeter swans and Canada geese dot the quiet wetland below the crocus-covered ridge. A grizzly bear roots about beneath the nearby aspens, unearthing sweet glacier lily bulbs and pocket gophers. Two sandhill cranes strut and croak. The thin sweetness of a horned lark's song tinkles in the wind.

The grizzly emerges from the aspens and pauses to rub his heavy muzzle in the tangled bunchgrass. Unaware of him until now, several cows on the nearby ridge begin to bawl for their recently born calves. The bear watches with lazy interest as mothers gather calves and the herd crashes away into silver willow shrubbery along the base of the far hillside. Then he shakes himself and moseys down to the water's edge, investigating the odours to be found there.

Undisturbed by scent or sight of humans, he has spent all week here, in some of the most productive habitat occupied by grizzlies anywhere in Canada — a mosaic of rich wetlands, aspen forest and bunchgrass prairie. He cleaned up the remains of two stillborn calves earlier this month but it's mostly the greenery that interests him today.

The same combination of productive natural habitat and lack of human activity that makes this foothills a haven for bears, benefits the cranes and swans. Both will produce broods of offspring here later this spring. Amid the cow tracks down by the slough are the tracks of elk and deer. They, too, thrive in the solitude of the aspen parkland that stretches along the foot of the Rocky Mountains here beneath the chinook arch.

For those who visit nearby Waterton Lakes National Park, this diversity of wildlife and habitat might seem unremarkable. The spectacular, compact park — designated an International Biosphere Reserve in 1977 and a World Heritage Site in 1995 — is famous for its abundant wildlife.

These grizzly, cranes and trumpeter swans, however, are on privately-owned ranchland several kilometres east of the park. Much of Waterton's wildlife wealth is, in fact, less a product of park protection than of habitat ranchers outside the park have protected for more than a century. Almost all the region's sandhill cranes and trumpeter swans nest on private ranchland. Some rare plants — like blue camas and blue flag iris — are virtually unknown inside the park, but abundant on neighboring cattle pastures. Even grizzly bears — although their opportunistic feeding habits sometimes bring them into conflict with ranchers — are often more abundant on foothills ranches outside the park boundaries than inside Waterton.

Waterton is a paradox that confounds those who look for simple solutions to conservation challenges. Its wildlife abundance is at least as much the result of cattle ranching as it is of park protection. To many naturalists, the whole idea seems counter-intuitive: aren't cows bad? Don't ranchers kill predators? How can a park not only coexist with, but depend upon, cattle ranching?

"Make no mistake about it," says the Nature Conservancy of Canada's western field director Larry Simpson. "If the ranches vanish from the Waterton Front, there is no future for Waterton Lakes National Park."

172

Dave Glaister agrees, as might be expected of a man who's raised cattle for well more than half a century. But the tall, lean rancher-naturalist is less concerned with proving that ranches help conserve biological diversity, than with simply ensuring that ranching will survive in a changing world. He isn't sure it can. Like the grizzly bears that live on his family's Shoderee Ranch, north of Waterton, he's retreated before the tidal wave of development about as far as he can go. Glaister and many other ranchers are starting to know how it feels to be an endangered species.

Dave and Lucille Glaister raised their family west of Millarville, Alberta. Their ranch sprawled along the edge of the Bow-Crow Forest Reserve, in a foothills landscape rich in deer, elk, bear and moose. It was prime cattle-growing country, and a fine place to raise kids — perfect in all respects except one. It was only a half hour's drive from Calgary.

They don't live there any more. Their former ranch is now subdivided into small acreages, most of which house "rurban" commuters who work in the booming city, then retreat each night to half million dollar homes in the scenic foothills. Each acreage has its own roadway, lawn and buildings. Many feed horses on undersized, overgrazed pastures. Pet cats hunt in the underbrush and family dogs chase deer at night. Yard lights have banished the undisturbed darkness that used to greet the Glaisters when they rose before dawn.

Until recently, the Alberta foothills were among the last places where Canada's prairie ecosystem seemed likely to survive. Elsewhere, most has been lost to cultivation and urban development. The earliest, and greatest, losses were in western Ontario and Manitoba where less than 1% of the tall grass prairie survives uncultivated. The fescue grassland region — extending from western Manitoba in a fertile arch through Saskatoon and Edmonton south to Calgary — fared little better. The somewhat drier mixed grass region is Canada's wheat belt: miles and miles of rolling grain stubble stitched together with barbed wire fences. Ghost bison graze among granaries and grid roads.

Only those parts of the prairie too dry for cultivation or with too short a growing season survived the twentieth century's epidemic of landscape change — and those are where ranchers now face the next wave of land conversion.

Ranching country is scenic, wildlife-rich and relatively inexpensive for those seeking a recreational hideaway or a scenic setting for a commuter home. Instead of cultivating the grassland, subdivisions and acreages carve it into weedy little bits. Grizzlies aren't welcome in acreage country — some residents might appreciate them, but their neighbors don't. Wolves are a romantic idea until they run the family horse through the fence. Upland sandpipers, long-billed curlews and sharp-tailed grouse can't adapt to patchwork prairie patrolled by pet dogs and cats.

The Glaisters sold their ranch when the trickle of new acreages around them became a flood. They liked some of the new neighbors — but trespassers, stray pets and other petty problems continued to increase. As land prices increased, they could no longer afford to lease pasture or buy new land. Their taxes grew past the point where the economically marginal business of growing cattle could yield a reasonable income.

Larry Simpson puts the financial dilemma faced by development-besieged ranchers in perspective. "Land in the Alberta foothills was worth about $100 per acre in 1971," he says. "Today land sells for ten to eighteen times more. But cattle prices — well, back then you would have to sell maybe ten calves to buy a truck. Now it takes 40 or 50. So commodity prices have comparatively gone down while land prices have gone up."

Dave and Lucille, and their grown children, decided to get as far away from Calgary's fevered real estate market as possible when they sold the family ranch in 1991. Their search for a more remote refuge led them to the Shoderee, one of prairie Canada's last large ranches. The Shoderee sprawls along Pine Ridge, a long moraine carpeted with rough fescue grassland and aspen forest that connects westward with Waterton Lakes National Park's windy mountains.

At night, on the Shoderee, no lights show in any direction. By day, red-tailed hawks scream above the aspens, the sounds of geese and cranes carry from hidden sloughs, and the woods and willow tangles are a bedlam of birdsong. The family regularly see grizzly bears. From time to time they see wolves too.

"One morning I was having breakfast," says Glaister, who keeps a spotting scope mounted in the living room for watching wildlife, "and I saw fifteen whitetail bucks go out across the hay field. One after another. Fifteen of them."

The Glaisters love the wildness and diversity of their new home. They barely had time to settle in, however, before the juggernaut they had fled was at the door.

Quarter sections — normally the smallest un-subdivided unit of ranchland — adjacent to the Shoderee have recently sold for $1200 an acre. Smaller acreages have sold for $40,000 an acre. No rancher can hope to pay the carrying costs on that kind of money simply by raising cattle. As land prices increase, even established ranchers who own their land outright find themselves caught in a tax squeeze. Recently the Alberta government passed new legislation that forces municipalities to tax land based on its current market value. Some ranchers have seen their yearly tax bills triple or quadruple simply because of their location adjacent to one of the hottest recreational destinations anywhere: the Canadian Rockies.

Area ranchers are no longer surprised to return home after a long day to find a real estate broker's card tucked into their screen door. "Even the ones I've run off already do it," says one local rancher. "They just wait until they see me go out."

Larry Simpson says that the Nature Conservancy of Canada has begun to focus on the ranching country along the eastern slopes of the Alberta Rockies ". . . because all the conservation values are there, including predators. Sure, there are conflicts that occur from time to time, but the fact remains that those animals are there because the habitat exists. Landscapes can recover from most everything, but not from concrete."

Simpson represents an organization that calls itself the real estate arm of the conservation movement. His job is to invest donated money to get the greatest return in conservation of endangered nature. Spending other people's money is a big responsibility, so he does his homework. Real estate experts he has consulted predict that as many as 60% of the ranches in western North American will be sold in the next twenty years. An entire generation of ranchers is nearing retirement age; many have complicated estates to settle. If current real estate trends continue, a lot of their ranches will end up in the hands of speculators and developers.

Like Dave Glaister, Larry Simpson is tall and lean, but the resemblance stops there. Simpson has an intense, focused personality. He seems driven by urgency — like time is running out. Indeed, he says, it is. "The cultural heritage and natural heritage of western North America could potentially undergo a transformation in the next twenty years that will be as profound and long reaching as the loss of the buffalo. Different, yes: but no less significant."

Larry Simpson uses satellite images of Canada to make his case for what he calls Canada's one percent challenge. For all Canada's vast size, he points out, only one percent of the country is both arable and biologically intact. That one percent — mostly in the dry southern prairies or in a thin arc along the Alberta foothills — contains almost half of all Canada's endangered species. And that one percent continues to die the death of many cuts as gas pipelines slice through native prairie, towns and cities grow, and, with increasing regularity, ranchers give up the struggle and cash in by selling their land to developers.

The Nature Conservancy of Canada recently launched what Simpson calls the Waterton Front Project — an ambitious campaign to permanently protect at least eight major ranches adjacent to Waterton from subdivision. Already the Nature Conservancy has placed conservation easements on nine quarter sections and has other deals pending — but Simpson points out that the same pressures that beset Waterton are at play in the Crowsnest Pass, the Porcupine Hills, and the foothills west of Calgary and Red Deer. The challenge is as immense as it is urgent.

"If Canada fails to meet our 1% challenge — with our level of education and relative affluence compared to other nations — that suggests to me that the world must almost surely fail in conserving biological diversity."

Others share Simpson's sense of urgency. World Wildlife Fund Canada released its Prairie Conservation Action Plan in 1989, stating: "In only 100 years, the Canadian prairies — grasslands and parkland — have been so radically transformed by human activity that they have become one of the most endangered natural regions in Canada . . . Canadians need to ensure that native prairie, with its wild plants and animals, survives in the west and is conserved for its intrinsic values, from which this and future generations can benefit."

All this is true — but why worry about ranching? Cattle, after all, are not bison. Cattle can overgraze prairie, helping weeds invade and reducing food and cover for native wildlife. Cows are notorious for spending too much time in riparian areas where they trample and graze wildlife habitat and damage streambanks. Ranchers have rarely been noted for generous feelings toward large predators — in fact, it was agricultural "pest" control that erased grizzly bears and wolves from much of their North American range.

American conservation writer George Wuerthner goes so far as to argue that subdivisions are better than ranching. In the American west, private land is more limited in extent than in southern Canada. Once ranching is no longer viable there, he says, nearby public lands can start to recover from decades of cattle damage. His argument, however, has a fundamental flaw: the private lands are usually the most ecologically productive habitats — those along valley floors and streams that early homesteaders scooped up first.

Most of the range damage American conservationists complain about dates back to the late 1800s when eastern speculators poured millions of cattle into the open range. Especially in the arid and semi-arid grasslands west of the Rockies, where native vegetation had evolved in the absence of large herds of grazing animals, the damage was massive.

Canada, according to historian Barry Potyondi, never suffered the massive overstocking of open range that took place farther south. Overgrazing was only a local problem that appeared in the twentieth century as growing numbers of hopeful colonists fenced and cross-fenced the range, confining cattle into smaller and smaller tracts of grassland and reducing the economic margins within which ranchers had to operate.

Most of Canada's rangeland lies east of the Rockies where vegetation evolved under the influence of large herds of bison. Spared frontier overgrazing, Canada's grasslands actually benefit from cattle ranching which promotes vegetation diversity. The key is well-managed grazing — management that approximates what the native grassland was used to before the arrival of the domestic cow. After a century of ranching, most ranchers who are still in business have proven their ability to keep native ranges healthy.

Riparian damage is a different problem; many ranches still have so-called *sacrifice* areas down by the creek where cows spend too much time. In the past decade, however, a growing riparian restoration movement has spread across Alberta, southern B.C. and Saskatchewan. Rather than giving their herds year round access to creek bottoms, ranchers fence out riparian pastures and develop wells or dugouts to provide water to their herds when they are on upland areas. By grazing riparian areas only when soils and vegetation are most resistant to damage, participating ranchers restore the willow thickets, reedgrass swales and cottonwood forests that make prairie riparian areas some of the most productive and important habitats in prairie Canada.

Predators remain a thorny issue. The Glaisters have lost cattle to grizzlies. Nearby ranchers have lost stock to wolves. Those who view foothills grasslands primarily as cattle country rarely harbour warm feelings toward animals that can kill livestock. Even so, ranchers like the Glaisters value the presence of large predators, only calling in wildlife officers when they actually suffer livestock losses. The irony, of course, is that wolves and grizzly bears still range many parts of the Alberta foothills only because ranching — which keeps the landscape largely natural — ensures that they can find wild prey and, in the case of the bears, a diversity of plant foods. In southwestern Alberta, recently, some ranchers have begun working cooperatively with Alberta Environmental Protection to head off predator-livestock conflicts before they happen.

Most of the environmental criticisms aimed at ranching relate to management practises that can be and, increasingly, are being improved. Meantime, as long as ranching families like the Glaisters can keep the land intact and make a reasonable living at ranching, the last and best remains of prairie Canada's biological diversity will have a fighting chance.

"A well managed ranch operation," says Larry Simpson, "is a living, working model of a steady state economy. If the entire world could be managed and kept in as good condition as many ranches, then we would be in good environmental shape."

As well-heeled urbanites and developers drive up the real estate value of Canada's best surviving grassland ecosystems, ranchers like the Glaisters are losing their power to continue protecting the places they love. Larry Simpson is determined to ensure that they don't stand alone. The ecological — and social — stakes are simply too high.

'Hope on the Range' was first published in Nature Canada magazine in 1999.

Guarding the Land

by Donna Fleury

Increasing demand for urban and recreational development property, along with dramatic land price hikes, puts landowners who want to conserve and protect their landscapes in a tough position. "The combined consequence of everyone (selling) will be a loss of our natural and western heritage," says Larry Simpson, Alberta Director of the Nature Conservancy of Canada.

Simpson predicts "that virtually every site with high biological and aesthetic value within a three-hour drive of any major urban centre in the country, will either be lost to recreational development or be under substantial pressure within the next 20 years. I used to think people who said that were simply being alarmist, until I began looking at a map and the statistics," he says. "Unfortunately, it's happening."

Conservation easements are a relatively new land management tool that may help slow this urban sprawl. They were introduced to North America in the last decades and only legislated in Alberta in the fall of 1996. An amendment to the Alberta Environmental Protection and Enhancement Act now makes it possible for landowners in this province to protect the natural values of their land for conservation purposes in this way.

By statute, such an easement can be granted to protect, conserve and enhance the environment, including its biological diversity or natural, scenic or aesthetic values, explains Arlene Kwasniak, staff counsel with the Environmental Law Centre in Edmonton. It also provides for a number of land uses consistent with those purposes, and is usually placed on the title in perpetuity.

These easements are often used where landowners want to preserve the natural values of their land, but realize they'll have to transfer ownership sooner or later, says Kwasniak. They can be used as an estate planning tool to help families retain their land.

In southern Alberta, some conservation easements are placed on ranchland to preserve it as a prairie grassland. "The conservation easement is not designed to preserve agricultural land per se, it is there to preserve the natural or aesthetic values of the land," Kwasniak adds.

A conservation easement has to be registered against the title of the land, with the easement held by a qualified organization. The title itself remains with the landowner. "Because landowners are transferring an interest in their property, usually in perpetuity, it's important to fully appreciate what the decision means," explains Kwasniak.

For example, there are potential tax benefits. Recent amendments to the Income Tax Act can make the donation of a conservation easement a gift of capital property. "However, a donation of an easement is a disposition of property, so it's important to consult with a tax expert to determine any tax benefits," says Kwasniak.

Landowners must also consider other factors such as municipal property taxes. "Ranchers and farmers should make sure the conservation easement doesn't preclude any agricultural uses and ensure the land under easement is assessed at agricultural value not fair market value," explains Kwasniak. "We're working with both provincial and federal governments to change property and tax laws to make conservation easements more beneficial for landowners. However law reform takes a long time."

As of May 1999 there were a total of 36 conservation easements registered in Alberta, according to Brian Free of Alberta Environment. The easement holders include both conservation groups and municipalities, with the split about 50-50 to date. Conservation easements aren't a tool for everyone, Free notes, but the number so far indicates they were needed and people are using them.

Along with municipalities, several conservation groups are eligible to hold conservation easements in Alberta, including the Nature Conservancy of Canada, Ducks Unlimited Canada, and the Southern Alberta Land Trust Society (SALTS).

SALTS was formed and is managed by a group of ranchers in southwestern Alberta, north of Waterton Lakes National Park. Concerned about the loss of land to development and how this would affect ranching along the eastern slopes in the future, the group started looking for a community-based solution in the early 90s, explains Glenn Pauley, executive director in High River. After much research, SALTS decided to form a land trust, which offers a flexible community-based answer to some of its concerns. Land trusts, such as the Montana Land Alliance, are very common in the U.S.; however U.S. tax laws are much more favorable to landowners.

"One of the group's biggest issues is the question of how to pass on land which has had its value inflated by development pressures," explains Pauley. "Along with education, one of our biggest initiatives is to work with ranchers to develop practical inter-generational land transfers and estate planning," he adds. With the average age of ranchers increasing, a lot of land is expected to change hands in the next 10 to 15 years. A conservation easement is a flexible tool, allowing ranchers to set aside a portion or the whole ranch, or to reserve some portions under the easement to allow for a future residence for their children.

A common concern is whether conservation easements affect land values. "We've found, in some cases, that if an easement is placed on a property, the surrounding properties increase in value. Open spaces are becoming more valuable to people, and they are often willing to pay more for land that is guaranteed to remain as open space," Pauley said. "We currently have about 2000 acres under conservation easement, and expect that amount to double very quickly."

SALTS continues to work with landowners and other organizations to develop more attractive tax benefits for landowners.

The Nature Conservancy of Canada is also qualified to hold conservation easements. "We primarily focus on landscapes that have high aesthetic and biological values," explains NCC's Simpson. "In some cases, landowners approach us, or if it's a landscape we're focusing on, we may approach them. We work with landowners to review the various tax advantages, and in some cases we may offer to invest."

The NCC is working to improve tax incentives under Revenue Canada's tax code that would make easements more attractive to landowners. "Most landowners are land-rich and cash-poor, so current tax incentives are not a real advantage," says Simpson. Therefore, many landowners who choose to use a conservation easement do so because they believe its the right thing to do, not solely for tax reasons.

"For new land purchases, there are some advantages," says Simpson. For example, new owners living along the eastern slopes can reduce their after-tax costs of a property purchase with high natural values by as much as 25%. Simpson's final advice to land owners is, "If you have a beautiful property that you love and want to keep intact, even though you may need the money, then at least talk to one of the interested conservation organizations about your options before selling."

Ducks Unlimited Canada is another qualified conservation organization. "Our mission is waterfowl and wildlife habitat, so we would expect land to have a good wetland base in order for it to fall inside our mandate," says Les Wetter, an agrologist in Red Deer. "We primarily use conservation easements in situations where people want to donate wildlife habitat, but continue to maintain land ownership," he adds. DU also undertakes wetlands restoration and development projects on private land, without easements. It has a number of such projects in southern Alberta.

"Guarding the Land" was originally published in the September 1999 issue of Alberta Crops and Beef magazine.

Donna Fleury *is a freelance writer and professional agrologist, with over 17 years experience in agriculture. A copy writer and editor, she primarily writes feature articles and public relations materials for Canadian agricultural publications, ad agencies, and private and public organizations. Donna also specializes in the design and development of technical, educational and instructional materials. She lives west of Millarville, south of Calgary, Alberta. Donna participated in the 1997 and 1999 Writers Workshops.*

The Bear

Few can speak of the Waterton-Glacier National Park area without bears – especially grizzly bears – soon becoming the focus of the conversation. Since earliest times humans have shared this rich and productive landscape with both black bears and grizzlies. The bear taught aboriginal people lasting lessons about foods, medicines and survival. As the essays that follow show, we still have plenty to learn from, and about, the bear.

Our relationship with the grizzly, even more than with the black bear, is complex and challenging. In much of North America, there is no relationship: human settlers avoided the challenge of learning to live with grizzlies by eradicating them. Here in the Peace Park region, however, people take pride in their ability to coexist with an animal that too many people still fear.

John Russell's "Encounters with Bears" questions that fear. His sensitive and careful observations raise important questions about the degree to which our prejudices might blind us to the possibilities for a much more rewarding relationship between human and bear. Wayne Norstrom offers a more pragmatic, but no less relaxed, reason for enjoying life with bears. Both essays suggest that fear of bears is simply fear of the unknown; come to know bears better and fear gives way to curiosity, enjoyment and respect.

In spite of the possibilities for peaceful coexistence, we still have a long ways to go. Elaine Sedlack's "Ole Creek Grizzly" must somehow survive in a changing, increasingly-crowded national park environment. Bruce Masterman's grizzlies survive only so long as they can resist the temptation to dine on beef. Innovative ideas, scientific research and practical experience, however, offer hope that principled and patient humans can help bears avoid that temptation, as Candace Savage points out in "Grizzly Bear's Picnic."

Conservation of grizzly bears, which have been wiped out from most of their former range in the lower 48 states, is a compelling issue for those who love the Peace Park region. Many are startled and dismayed to learn that both the Alberta and B.C. governments still license sport hunters to kill the great bears each spring. But Don Meredith looks beneath the surface of this issue in "The Morality of the Grizzly Hunt" to explore the currents of biology, pragmatism and politics that keep the annual hunt a part of the grizzly's world.

Grizzly, Glacier National Park.   **Photo by Jim Mepham**

The Ole Creek Grizzly

by Elaine Sedlack

"Just up the trail a bit is the place where Pete had his run in with the grizzly," Art warns me as we climb into the saddle to continue our ride up Ole Creek. I remember that story. Pete was a packer for Bear Creek Ranch and had been packing in gear for a youth group that was working at Ole Lake last summer. On this forested part of the trail he came face to face with the grizzly, who was blocking the trail. With a string of pack horses behind him, Pete couldn't back up and there was no room to turn them around. He had to let the grizzly make the first move. While Pete sat on his horse watching anxiously, the grizzly attacked a log lying by the side of the trail, furiously ripping it apart. When he had finished displaying his anger at this intrusion into his territory, he relinquished the trail and disappeared into the forest, leaving a shaken Pete to continue with the pack string. It was a wonderful example of displaced aggression that Pete will never forget.

We continue our ride up Ole Creek with Dolly and me in the lead, followed closely by her foal Philly. Behind her is Art on Tico; then Karen the mule. The trail leads through the forest along the valley floor as it gradually ascends to Ole Lake. Grizzly sign is on the trail now — paw prints in the muddy spots and scat here and there. Maybe that is why Tico is suddenly interested in keeping up with Dolly. When we left Walton Ranger Station this morning we could hardly get him to move. Neither pushing him from the rear with Dolly nor riding way ahead stirred him into anything faster than about a one mile an hour walk. Since we had twenty-six miles to go, over Firebrand Pass and down to Lubec Ranger Station, we were exasperated. But now, as I urge Dolly into a trot, Tico stays right behind. Dolly puts her head down to sniff the bear scat and snorts her usual warning that a bear is around, but at my urging she continues trotting up the trail. I fully expect to round a bend in the trail and meet the grizzly. I'm sure Dolly knows this too, but she continues confidently up the trail. Attitude means a lot.

I have always had an affection for this grizzly who makes his home on Ole Creek. I first met him one evening in June shortly after we moved permanently to Walton Ranger Station. After a day of paper work and house work, Art and I took a ride up Ole Creek to check on trail conditions and break in the horses a little for the long summer ahead. It was a beautiful warm evening. The sun was still high in a bright blue sky. We rode quietly through the woods the half mile to Ole Creek. The forest smelled damp after recent June rains and everything was a bright fresh green. Ferns were unfurling their leaves for summer. The trillium had almost disappeared, although a few of the bright white, three-petaled flowers remained in the shadier places. The first signs of bear grass were appearing. In an especially wet area I spotted the delicate beauty of a calypso orchid.

Ole Creek, still in spring runoff, crashed wildly under the bridge as we carefully crossed. On the far side of the bridge the trail turned sharply to the right and ascended gently along Ole Creek, climbing high above the creek on the open hillside.

Three miles from the ranger station we spotted a large, dark colored bear on the hillside about 300 yards above the trail. It appeared to be too large for the typical black bear we have in the area, so we climbed the hillside on our horses for a closer look. The bear did not seem to be aware of us, or if he was, he chose to ignore us. He continued feeding and ambling up the hillside. Even his leisurely hill climbing was too fast. We couldn't close the distance between us.

Art finally left his horse with me, and grabbing his binoculars, took off on foot toward a small drainage the bear appeared to be headed for. I watched and waited nervously, hoping the bear had continued on its current path. After what seemed like a long time, Art returned and reported he'd had a good look at the bear through his binoculars. It was a very dark grizzly, probably weighing about 400 pounds. That was our first actual sighting of the Ole Creek grizzly.

The autumn before we had found the remains of a dead elk at an elk wallow on Ole Creek. There were grizzly tracks all around. We speculated that this was the same grizzly and wondered if Ole Creek was his home. We wondered if the elk had been wounded by hunters outside the park and then had retreated into the park where the grizzly found it, or if it had been injured in a battle with another bull elk during the fall mating season. In any case this grizzly had not been causing any problems and no hikers had reported sightings of it.

A week later Art had been exploring the area and found a dead elk on the side of Scalplock Mountain, about one mile from the ranger station. It had apparently died in an avalanche off Scalplock the winter before and had just melted out of the snow. When he went back a few days later to check on the carcass there were only a few bones left. Our big dark grizzly had been well fed.

Since he had come that close to the ranger station, we took precautions around the compound to make sure we did not accidentally attract him and cause his eventual demise through our own carelessness. We collected the garbage out of the bear proof garbage cans in the picnic area every evening because even the scent of garbage might have attracted him. We made sure the picnic area was clean. We also let the few hikers that ventured up Ole Creek know that the grizzly was living up there and they should be alert when hiking. Art posted bright orange "Grizzly Frequenting Area" signs at all the trail junctions. The grizzly had never caused any trouble and we didn't want to change that pattern of behavior.

* * *

Walton Ranger Station lies tucked away on the heavily forested west slope of the Rocky Mountains near the Continental Divide. At West Glacier, the entrance to Glacier National Park and the Going to The Sun Road,

Highway 2 picks up the Middlefork of the Flathead River and follows it along the southern boundary of the park. It reaches a forested plateau with Glacier National Park on the left across the river and Flathead National Forest with the Great Bear Wilderness on the right. Little settlements lie scattered here and there along the road. About 25 miles from West Glacier the highway crosses the Middlefork. Just across the bridge, nestled in the woods beside the river, lies Walton Ranger Station.

When we first moved to Walton in 1970 the ranger station complex consisted of a small two-bedroom log house with wood heat, a very small wood frame office located behind the house, a wood shed, gas house, and garage with a rescue cache. Further back in the woods was a bunk house, shower house, cook house complex in three separate buildings for the trail crew or emergency fire fighters, and an ugly, small trailer that was home for the seasonal fire guard. Behind that was a large log barn and corral.

U.S. Highway 2 ran right in front of the house up a steep 20 foot high bank, and the Middle Fork of the Flathead River ran along behind the garage; I could see it from the kitchen window. Behind the garage and along the river was a small picnic area, designated as such by an official engraved wooden sign saying "PICKNICK AREA". Off the picnic area was the trail head for the Ole Creek and Boundary Trails.

At the time there were very few hikers in this remote section of Glacier National Park. The trails are long routes through forested valleys and don't have the dramatic scenery of the more popular trails. They did offer peace and solitude.

Across the river and up the hill about a mile away was the railroad community of Essex. At the height of the Great Northern Railroad's existence, Essex had been a thriving concern, with school, church, grocery store, dance hall, round house, depot, bars, and the large Izaak Walton Inn. With the decline of the railroad, Essex had also declined and now consisted of a few houses lived in by a handful of railroad workers, a few summer cabins, the one-room school, the wood-heated church, and the Inn, which had changed hands many times and was showing its age.

Up the road another half mile was the Half Way House and post office, and five miles further west was Denny's Underpass Inn, a small road house where you always felt apologetic when you stopped because the proprietor acted like he wished you hadn't bothered.

There was no television reception at Essex, especially down in the low spot where the ranger station sat, and the radio only worked from dawn until dusk, which in winter meant eight to five. One winter the highway was closed 22 days in January and those same 22 days the phone didn't work. Most of the folks living there were resourceful and proud of living "on the hill."

Surround these little dots of civilization with three million acres of rugged mountain wilderness and you begin to have an idea of what the neighborhood was like.

Our arrival at Walton should have been a warning of things to come for we were snowed out by a grand November blizzard, and when we finally did get there, had to shovel our way to the door. There weren't many visitors those first few winters. Just surviving took a great deal of our time. There was always firewood to split, roofs to shovel, driveways to plow, wildlife to count, poachers to chase, ski trails to maintain, avalanches to watch out for, and road problems on the narrow, windy, slippery highway.

Our lives were run by the seasons and the weather. But the longer we stayed at Walton the busier it became. Cross-country skiing grew popular and in summer the trails became full of eager young hikers escaping the cities and suburbs. The river became crowded with floaters. Some of our old ski runs at Essex were now groomed trails and the old Izaak Walton Inn was revitalized into a cross-country ski center. The little railroad community had a new subdivision with a few summer homes. Denny's Underpass Inn became a warm, friendly hangout for folks from east and west of the divide.

* * *

As other areas of the park became crowded, people discovered the solitude of the Walton trails. Our peace was gone and so was the grizzly's. I particularly remember a day that became one of the worst days of my life. I was up at 4:30 in the morning to get Art off on the trail. The fire crew was also gone, leaving me alone at the ranger station. About 11:00

in the morning I was washing the breakfast dishes when I heard a car roar into the driveway and screech to a halt. Even before the knock on the door I knew this was trouble. But running footsteps and the urgent pounding on the door of the house confirmed my worst suspicions. There had been an accident on the narrow road through the park, involving a car and a young man on a motorcycle. Despite my best efforts and the help of a doctor who was passing by, the young man died.

It was 2:00 p.m. when I returned to the ranger station, hungry but too upset to eat. I wanted to sit in the corner and cry, but I didn't have time to brood before there was another knock on the door. This time it was a couple of young men who wanted to backpack and needed a permit. Since I was still the only one at the ranger station I took them over to the office, discussed their plans and trail options and warned them about bears. After I gave them their permits, I started back to the house when another hiker showed up. It continued like that until about 7:00 p.m. when I finally had a break. There sat the breakfast dishes still in the sink where I had left them that morning. I realized I hadn't eaten since 6:00 in the morning and I was hungry. I entertained thoughts of running down the road to Denny's because I was too tired to cook and didn't want to eat alone. But any thoughts of the day being over were only wishful thinking; there was another knock on the door.

This time it was a friend from Missoula who had climbed Mount St. Nicholas. On the hike out Dick had tried to take a short cut by fording the Middle Fork, but was greeted by an uncooperative landowner who lived across the river from the park. As Dick tried to ask permission to cross the property, the landowner pulled out a pistol and fired over Dick's head. Dick got the message and dragged his weary body back across the river, up the bank to the trail and back to the ranger station. He wanted to register a complaint.

It was now 10:00 p.m. and dusk was setting in. As I started to lock the office door I thought surely this must be the end of this day, but I was wrong. No sooner had the thought flashed through my mind, when I was practically accosted by a very excited man who came trotting off the trail, followed by a quieter teenage boy. The man had been out for a short walk behind Lubec when he met the teenager. The boy had planned to hike the entire 26 mile trail over Firebrand Pass and down Ole Creek to the ranger station by himself, though Art had warned him not to hike alone on Ole Creek because of the grizzly.

Though the bear hadn't caused any trouble, he was beginning to show signs of irritation at the increased human use of the area. He especially didn't like the "Grizzly Frequenting Area" signs Art had been putting up to warn hikers. Every time Art put up a sign the grizzly tore it down. Not only did he tear all the signs down on a regular basis, he also left claw marks or fur on the trees where the signs had been posted. It was his territory and he apparently wanted all other critters, including humans, to understand that.

Somehow the boy had managed to talk the man into hiking the whole 26 mile trail with him. For the man it had been one of the most exciting things that had ever happened to him. They had come face to face with the Ole Creek grizzly. It had been a peaceful encounter with the grizzly surrendering his trail to the hikers, but the man was so excited about it he could hardly talk. It was, he said, a day he would never forget. Amen to that I thought.

And then I thought about the great bear and how benevolent he could be. Did the bear understand that his fate was probably doomed unless more people like this man could have the same experience and remember it and cherish it for the rest of their lives?

Grizzlies do that to people. A chance encounter lasting only a minute or less is something you never forget. I thought it was wonderful the man had that opportunity and I hoped when he returned to his home in the city he would become an advocate for the bear, whose very existence is threatened by encroaching civilization and habitat destruction.

After that day both the grizzly and I seemed to be less tolerant of all the intrusions in our once peaceful lives. I dreaded days when I was left alone at the ranger station to deal with whatever problems arose and wondered why the park service didn't pay me or supply a back up person. The grizzly became increasingly annoyed at the surge in use of his area. It was after that when Pete had his run in with the grizzly.

The bear had frightened some backpackers at Ole Lake. The hikers dropped their packs to retreat and the bear discovered that these humans he resented could be a source of food. He started hanging around the campground at Ole Lake or making regular trips to it. Finally Art had to close the campground in hopes the grizzly would give up this quest and seek his normal food. Art kept a close watch on the bear and on conditions at the two campgrounds on Ole Creek.

* * *

That is one of the reasons for our trip up Ole Creek today. Art wants to see if there is any sign of the grizzly. It is September now and most of the hikers have returned to their homes and schools or jobs. We also plan to leave Tico with Tom, who is staying at the old Lubec Ranger Station for the fall to watch for poachers. While we are gone for 10 days Tom will use the horse to patrol. We continue trotting up the trail, alert now for the grizzly we know is in the area by the fresh scat and paw prints. Dolly too is alert but trots ahead confidently. We round a bend in the trail and just ahead 30 yards is our bear. Seeing no hesitation from us, he quickly runs off the trail and up the hillside about 25 yards where he finds a large rock and climbs up on top. I stop Dolly to watch the bear.

He stands on top of his rock, posed like a mountain goat, king of his domain, peering down at us. We stare, fascinated, at the bear. Dolly and Philly watch him intently, but show no fear. Soon I feel the need to leave the grizzly to his peaceful home and urge Dolly onward.

I wish the grizzly luck and a long peaceful autumn. I hope he finds a secure place away from hikers next summer; I worry about him. Too many encounters with people could result in his death or capture, a terrible fate for such a magnificent creature.

Encounters with Bears

by H. John Russell

During the course of a year or so I was privileged to have several encounters with grizzlies. Many were on or near our family ranch on the edge of Waterton Lakes National Park. The park includes only a small portion of the grizzly habitat in the area. Much more usable spring and summer habitat surrounds the park. I was with my partner, Valerie Haig-Brown, when I had the first encounter. We were following Cottonwood Creek in our natural hay meadow while checking an electric fence that keeps the cattle out of the fish habitat.

While ambling along, we suddenly became aware of a grizzly looking at us from across a beaver pond in the creek. He was an impressively large animal and beautifully marked with a massive blond forehead between dark brown ears and eyes that appeared small for the size of his head. His sides were grayish blond and his legs dark. He proceeded to feed on the willows beside the water, about 150 metres away. I presumed he was eating the abundant willow catkins. He may also have been picking off the fresh shoots on the tips of the branches.

As he walked around he would occasionally disappear into the landscape in spite of his size just by stepping behind a small willow clump.

We realized then he could have been there when we went by about twenty minutes earlier. He probably chose to let us see him rather than melt into the landscape as we returned from our work further upstream. This brings up interesting questions. Why would he show himself when it was not necessary? Do grizzlies like to socialize with people in spite of how we treat them? If we treated them better would they be even friendlier toward us than they are?

We sat down in the grass on our side of the creek as he very slowly moved from willow to willow, looking at us occasionally but otherwise going about his business as though we weren't there. Some would suggest we were rash to stay so close to such a dangerous animal. Were we endangering this animal's life, or our own, by staying and watching him? We both had pepper spray as we usually do when walking or working around the ranch. It might well be argued that bear spray, which has proven very effective in deterring attacking bears, was not meant to be used to increase our boldness with them. Just as wearing a seat belt should not make us drive aggressively, bear spray should not make us act boldly with bears. In a general sense, I would agree.

In my defense, however, I would respond that this is both the bear's and our home so we should learn to enjoy each other's company. I choose to live here because I like bears and like living in bear country. Probably a dozen bears live on the ranch when the Saskatoon berries are ripe. If I go running for the house every time I see a bear, I'm not going to get much done. I would rather take the attitude that it is a privilege to live with bears and it makes more sense to enjoy them than to fear them.

I also believe that bears get to know the people they share the land with and actually enjoy them in some way that I can't explain. I don't live on our land in fear of a bear attack any more than one would fear a head-on collision while driving. We take precautions, but don't stay at home because of the chance of a collision. When I see a bear I normally stop what I am doing and watch it for a while. They are such fascinating animals most people would like to do the same, if the bear is remote enough for them to feel safe. The only difference for me is that a bear can be closer and still I feel safe, simply because I live with them and see them more often than most people.

I'm not suggesting that familiarity causes carelessness, but rather a finely tuned calculation of risk, just as long-time drivers have judgment skills inexperienced drivers don't have. All mammals communicate through body language and some of it is common to all. The more one observes them the more one understands this language. The greater the understanding, the less threatened we feel around other animals. Cows kill people, too, so if you work with them you need to know their clearly expressed warnings of imminent aggression before it happens. I accept the risk of living with and associating with bears on a day to day basis. I would sooner take a crack at calming a disturbed bear than have to dodge an oncoming car in my lane.

Eventually the large male grizzly disappeared into the forest and we continued checking the fence. It had been a normal day with the extra spice of seeing a calm, almost contemplative, bear. I have little doubt he returned to the creekside soon after we left.

It was not until August that I had my next visit with a grizzly, this time a sub-adult. I had been up on a ridge above the ranch watching birds with a friend. We had just emerged onto the cleared park boundary fence when the bear came bounding over a knoll ahead of us, heading straight at us along the fence.

I was walking ahead of Larry. Knowing, from the bear's gait, that he was not attacking us, I stepped to the side a bit so Larry could see this spectacular sight. The bear quickly narrowed the distance from more than one hundred metres to less than fifty when it suddenly saw us, turned, and went away just as fast as it had been coming at us. The ease with which he did this speaks of the agility of grizzlies. When it got back to the knoll it stopped, turned, and reared to get a good look at us and then bounded off the fence line.

Larry ranches just far enough out on the prairie that he never sees grizzlies on his place and is therefore not as familiar with them. Even so, he was very calm. After the bear left I remarked that I thought he was relaxed for a guy who had just had a close encounter with a bear. He said he hadn't seen me going for my bear spray so he figured things were not too serious. In fact, I had forgotten the spray, so I didn't have any to go for! However, I doubt I would have been going for it, since the bear's body language was very relaxed, something like a dog casually loping along toward us, and not in attack mode. Less experienced travelers in bear country could easily have assumed this animal to be charging at them.

A little later, I was hiking again with a couple of friends not far from where Larry and I met the bear. We walked to a lake where trumpeter swans nest most years. We were sitting near the shore, enjoying the ducks and sky reflections, when a hundred metres across a bay we saw a female grizzly emerge from low bush, eating the bountiful saskatoons. At her side were two cubs of the year, one very silvery, the other dark brown.

They fed along the opposite shore past us perfectly calmly without showing any sign of knowing we were there, even though we were talking in normal tones. (I am quite sure that at least the mother must have known we were there, but since we never saw her look at us that could only be an assumption.) After they were about two hundred metres away she caught the scent of something upwind, which was quartering toward us at the time. Her response was interesting. She sniffed the wind, then ran nervously upwind, stopped and half reared while sniffing, then ran jerkily forward and more upwind. She and the cubs went quickly out of sight. Since we did not see them again or whatever animal was creating the scent, we never learned if it was prey or another bear that had evoked this interesting response.

These were the last grizzlies I saw on the ranch that year. However, the next year continued the good record. The winter had been mild. We usually do not see bears on the ranch until May, but on April 27 I was driving out along our road to the highway on the way to an evening meeting. I rounded a sharp bend and surprised a large grizzly bear as he ambled through shallow snow that was accumulating on the road. He lumbered off the road as I came to a stop near where he had been. He was quickly out of sight in the forest, leaving me with an image of a beautiful fat silver tip grizzly, probably a young male, almost fully grown.

A few days later Valerie and I went for an evening walk. Most of the snow that had fallen during the previous night had melted that day. As we started out, the remaining inch of snow was still wet and soft. As we went by a corner post that bears use like a rub tree, we realized that there were some very large grizzly tracks approaching the post. His tracks told the story of what had happened very recently since they were sharp in snow that had been melting rapidly an hour earlier. He had come down the path we were on and stopped to sniff the post and then turned around and rubbed his back, leaving some hair on the barbed wire wrapped around the post.

After rubbing, he proceeded up a fence line that quarters away from the path he had come down. We walked along looking at these huge tracks and the little things that had caught his interest enough to divert his track and probably caused a casual sniff, like a stump or an old scat. Soon we were beyond where his tracks had entered the pathway. We walked another half a kilometre and then encountered his tracks again. These tracks were even fresher. In the time since we first saw tracks at the rub post, the chill in the air had caused the snow to set up and develop a thin crust. This crust was now cracking around the edges of our own feet as we set them down and his tracks had the same feature, so we knew they were only minutes old.

We quieted down in hopes of not scaring him. We knew there was a clearing ahead on the trail he was now on and hoped to get a glimpse of him before he got to the other side. We walked along silently for about ninety metres and were approaching the clearing when Valerie whispered that she could see him. I turned. There he stood, on all fours, in the trees beside the trail looking at us. He was a dark brown grizzly with faint light brown tips on his hair. His face was huge and somewhat rearranged by the fights with other bears that he'd had in his life. Once he could tell we had spotted him, he lunged away into the forest and out of sight.

We continued to follow his tracks and found where, just about twenty metres from where we had stopped to look at him, he had been proceeding along the path when he probably heard our approach. He must have decided to see who or what was following him, done a U-turn into the bush, and moved back parallel to his path to wait for our arrival. I had been so intent on seeing him in the grassy opening ahead I had neglected to look on each side of the trail. Fortunately Valerie had been alert to that and we didn't miss seeing him, even if it was a brief sighting. He could have waited in much closer ambush to the trail and been more hidden in the undergrowth if he had wanted to attack, but didn't. (It is very unusual for grizzlies to become aggressive toward people. They normally make every effort to stay out of sight, but occasionally show themselves.)

About a month later, after all the leaves were on the trees and the weather was warm Valerie and I went up to the lake, the only permanent lake on the ranch, to see if the swans were incubating yet. To avoid any chance of disturbing them we went up on the mountainside above the lake. From there we could see one adult swan feeding by itself and a white patch on a floating island of cattail. This was an almost sure sign that incubation had started. It was a beautiful balmy afternoon and we sat and glassed the countryside. A few elk were feeding in an opening in the aspen forest across the lake. As we watched these, other elk emerged from the aspens onto the lakeshore itself. They drank and then proceeded to wade and swim across a bay. The rest soon followed them into another opening closer to us.

As we watched this casual scene the feeding swan started swimming toward the incubating swan's island. When it approached, the sitting swan rose and went into the water. After a subtle greeting the first swan climbed onto the island and settled down while its mate began washing and preening before going off to feed. We were happy to have this proof that incubation had begun. With a small population of just three or four nesting pairs in southern Alberta, there is something satisfying in knowing that a population is continuing to reproduce, especially when you've had a hand in keeping the habitat in a state that is attractive to these beautiful birds.

As the day went by, two bears came into a clearing where we had first seen the elk, slowly walking and feeding through aspens at the edge of a grassy opening. They were about the same size and appeared to be best buddies. At first I thought they were a mating pair, but they surprisingly turned out to be a grizzly bear and a black bear. The two worked their way around the meadow and then emerged onto the lakeshore to drink. Then the black walked into the water to swimming depth, turned and seemed to be inviting the grizzly to join it. Eventually the grizzly followed and they swam around for a while. Next they reared up and started playfully boxing each other and spraying water all over as they swatted and nipped.

After a short bout water play, they walked through the trees into the opening, and began to rear and play as they had in the water. Soon they ambled into the aspen forest and we didn't see them again until later, on our way home, when we saw them feeding together on the carcass of a cow that had died while calving and been hauled away from the calving pasture. This is the first record that I know of anybody seeing members of the two species being on such friendly terms. We saw no evidence that they were interested in mating. It seemed that they had just developed a friendship by feeding on the same carrion.

In early September I went into the Westcastle Valley forest reserve to look for huckleberries, with pepper spray on my belt and buckets in my backpack. I climbed up the side of a mountain that usually has good berries, but not finding any I climbed up higher than I normally do and somehow got a little off course and into a rather forested part of the slope. Near the top of a shoulder of the mountain I stepped out of thick bush into an alcove of a clearing on the ridge top and immediately saw fresh grizzly sign in the form of a trench about four or five inches deep and five feet long. It looked like the bear was after a rodent of some kind.

After examining the trench I was about to continue on when I spotted two good-sized grizzlies at least 70 metres in front of me. They had their heads down and hadn't noticed me. The breeze on the back of my neck told me they were about to find out about my close proximity through their noses. I put my binoculars on them to observe their response as they got my scent. Much to my surprise I realized there were four of them, one slightly larger: a mother with three very large cubs. They were all so close together I hadn't seen the other two. I watched as they grazed on something near the ground, expecting any second that they would get my wind and I would find out involuntarily how they liked such close human company. My normal-sized can of pepper spray had suddenly shrunk to an inadequate size!

After 20 seconds the wind had not carried my scent to them, which was very odd. The mother started walking in my direction, still oblivious of my presence. I debated speaking to her, to let her know I was there. I was reluctant to have her discover my presence if I was within her comfort zone (the critical distance or personal space that all animals, including people, have around them). Still unsure, I backed down and around a few small trees to give myself more time to decide my course of action. As I stood there the female started walking downhill parallel to me. This made up my mind. I didn't want her to get below me.

I decided to strike off downhill while I still knew where the bears were. I had been hesitating to backtrack because the forest I had just stepped out of was very dense with undergrowth, not good for visibility. Since we humans are tied to our eyes when it comes to survival I was reluctant to enter. My decision made by the bears' direction, I went down through the bush until I came to an open draw in the mountainside. After about an hour I was back at my vehicle where I could see the whole slope of the mountain. I sat down with my back against a log and glassed the whole slope but was unable to locate the bears.

As I waited to see if they would come into view I regretted having lost contact with them. If I had encountered them at a hundred or more metres I would have been more confident. Looking at it another way I was handed a tremendous opportunity to visit with them at very close range and had not trusted them to respond in a social way. An opportunity lost. Though I can say that, in a conventional sense, I handled the situation the best that I could have and walked away from a potentially dangerous situation unharmed and maybe without disturbing the bears, I felt I failed them in another way. Perhaps I should have had more confidence and given them the benefit of trust. That aside, berry time is an important season for the bears as they fatten for winter, a serious time to concentrate on putting on the pounds, so maybe it was best I had just left them to pursue that goal.

Grizzlies are beautiful and intriguing animals, partly because of their size and shape and partly because they are potentially so dangerous. It makes sense that, when a predator sees a weak animal like a human, it should attack. What I find intriguing is that they do so only extremely rarely. Cougars, wolves and bears are all big enough to overpower unarmed humans. I have encountered them all, in daylight and darkness, and never experienced any aggression from any of them even when they have been only feet away.

I am convinced from these experiences and others that bears are not as fierce as they are portrayed by many writers. If we honour and respect them, they can enrich our lives. Bears conditioned to human food are an entirely different story and can be dangerous and destructive. Keeping such foods away from them, frees us to trust bears and enjoy their company, when they choose to let us.

John Russell *was born and raised in the Waterton area. He is the author of* The Nature of Caribou *and a co-author of* Waterton and Northern Glacier Trails. *He currently lives where he grew up, on a ranch bordering Waterton Park, and has always had bears for neighbors. John has a BSc in Zoology and has studied caribou for 25 years, mostly in the sub-arctic. During that time, using photography, he developed an accurate method of counting caribou in large migratory herds. He has also helped produce two arctic wildlife films for television and has studied grizzly and black bear habitat in Alberta and British Columbia. John has participated in all three Writers Workshops.*

Grizzly Bears Picnic

by Candace Savage

In east-central Alaska (near the Yukon border), it rained moose for two months in the spring of 1985. Train-killed moose — twelve tonnes in all. The last the animals knew, they had been browsing along the tracks, unaware of their onrushing doom. Soon their remains were being ferried aloft by chopper and flung into the muskeg and hills around the Mosquito Fork river.

The air-drop was orchestrated by Rod Boertje and his colleagues from Alaska Fish and Game, in an attempt to figure out what, apart from oncoming freights, was causing problems for the local moose. Not that the animals were endangered or even in decline. In fact, since their numbers had bottomed out in the mid-1970s, the counts had been remarkably stable. Stable and low. And that, for biologists charged with creating opportunities for moose hunting, was a problem in itself. If this region could theoretically support up to 1200 moose on 1000 square kilometres, why had the animals spent a decade at densities of 60 or 100? Everything seemed in their favour: decent weather, abundant browse, restricted hunting, low wolf predation. Yet the population was stuck in the cellar. What was going on?

The very first season of research, 1984, provided a promising lead. Although the region supported few wolves, it turned out to have a thriving population of grizzlies, which subsisted mainly on a monkish regime of roots and berries. But during moose calving season, the bears indulged in an orgy of meat-eating. Of 33 newborn moose radio-collared that year, grizzlies ate seventeen.

And so it happened, in spring of the following year, that the researchers decided to rain moose meat into the calving grounds. The idea was simple: the carcasses would serve as bait for grizzlies, which could then be caught and radio-collared, so that their diet could be more closely monitored. Again, the results were unambiguous. Grizzlies were keeping the moose in a predator pit by feasting on calves during their vulnerable first weeks.

In reporting their research to the *Canadian Journal of Zoology*, Boertje and his group drew the only possible conclusion. To boost the moose in this system, you would have to remove predators. What else to do with a problem bear except kill it?

But was this really the only choice? As the study progressed, the biologists began to notice a strange blip in their graphs. Usually, when they checked the moose in early winter, they found just one cow in ten travelling with young. But in 1985, every second cow they saw was followed closely by a calf.

As Boertje and his colleagues pondered this unexpected good news, they began to wonder if the upturn might be a result of their own efforts. There was, after all, the small matter of 12,000 kilograms of meat that had fallen, like manna from heaven, into the paths of bears and wolves that spring. Could this supplementary feeding — much of it provided, by chance, when the moose were giving birth — have diverted grizzlies and other predators from the tender young calves?

Five years later, Boertje was able to put the idea to the test, this time freighting 26,000 kilograms of road-kill into his research block at peak calving time. That winter's cow/calf ratio was the highest in nine years and up to four times better than anywhere else in the region.

"Diversionary feeding" had worked.

Who would have thought? After generations of numbly killing predators, convinced there were no alternatives, it turned out that feeding them might produce the results biologists were seeking.

Last spring, wildlife managers in the cattle country of southwestern Alberta, near Waterton Lakes National Park, used a variation on this theme to help reduce grizzly predation during calving. Their strategy was to "redistribute" carcasses of road-killed deer, by collecting them from rangelands in the valleys and flying them up into the foothills. As the grizzlies roused from hibernation and ambled downslope in the spring, they encountered the smorgasbord of carcasses that had been laid out for them, well away from the temptations of the calving pastures. Only one cow was lost to a grizzly (down from double digit losses most years), and the bears went on their way with minimal interference.

"We were really going against the grain on this," admits biologist Richard Quinlan of Alberta Environment. "But so far it's all been positive."

Our traditional confrontation with predators is literally a dead end, a joyless, repetitive routine of violence that wastes thousands of lives each year. (In British Columbia alone, conservation officers shot 35 grizzlies and 1619 black bears as "problems" in 1998.) "Diversionary feeding" is no teddy bear's picnic in which things always end well. Yet it stands as a welcome reminder that an oddball new idea can turn our thinking on its head, revealing possibilities we had scarcely imagined.

This article first appeared in the May/June, 1999 issue of Canadian Geographic magazine, as part of a regular column entitled "Curious by Nature."

Candace Savage *is the author of more than 20 books on the natural world and women's history, including Wolves, Bird Brains, Mother Nature, Beauty Queens and Cowgirls. She attended school in Pincher Creek before going on to study at the University of Alberta. Her work has been honoured by both the American and Canadian Library Associations, the Canadian Science Writers Association and the Rachel Carson Institute. Candace participated in the 1997 Writers Workshop.*

Hiker at Stoney Indian Pass, Glacier National Park.   **Photo by John Russell**

Of Bears and Man

By Bruce Masterman

The ground had been opened up and turned over across a bathtub-sized area beside a trail leading down to a small creek. The excavation looked like the work of a miniature bulldozer.

Our small group of hikers celebrating this summer-like autumn day stopped to examine the excavation. A few cast nervous sidelong glances at the surrounding trees. We all knew a grizzly bear had dug the shallow hole with front paws equipped with long curved claws. But why the bear had done it wasn't immediately clear. Was it digging for ground squirrels, perhaps? Kevin Van Tighem, who has worked as a conservation biologist in Waterton Lakes National Park since 1993, provided the simple answer. This bear was gardening. It was eating and at the same time preparing the ground for next year.

Sometime in the previous days, the bear had been searching for sweet vetch, a perennial legume that creates and stores starch in its roots all winter. In late fall and early spring, starch-hungry bears seek it out for a little carbo-loading. But bears don't just eat the legumes. Their digging splits the remaining roots and cultivates the ground, which stimulates new growth. That guarantees a steady supply of starch-heavy meals when the bruins emerge the next spring after a long winter's rest.

Interpreting such signposts in the natural world of the 525-square-kilometre national park is Van Tighem's job and his personal passion. As a conservation biologist, he's charged with monitoring the health of the park's diverse wildlife, trees and plant life. That can be a challenging task in a park that is part prairie, part foothills and part mountains. "Waterton is the most ecologically diverse area of North America's Rocky Mountains," says Van Tighem, a native Calgarian who regularly sheds his bureaucratic skin to write opinion-laced books and magazine articles about nature and conservation. "It has half again as many plants as all the other Rocky Mountain Parks."

Waterton is home to many other large mammals: bighorn sheep, wolves, moose, coyotes, cougars, mule deer, elk — 300 in summer and up to 1,400 in winter — in addition to grizzlies and black bears. It is a bear that now has Van Tighem's attention as he leads the hike along a trackless ridge in Waterton's northeast corner. Again, it isn't the actual animal, but a reminder that it was here. He points out a rock the size of a soccer ball that obviously had been moved, what he calls a "migrating rock." A bear, likely a black, had turned it over and licked up all the ants and other bugs hiding underneath. Eventually, another bear will come along and repeat the process, maybe even moving the rock back to its original location.

The ability to notice bear diggings and migrating rocks is one of the skills demanded of Van Tighem and other park officials involved in managing the creatures themselves.

Van Tighem has now led his small group to a rocky ledge, where they stop to catch their breath, dig sandwiches out of day packs and bask in the natural beauty around them. The ridge affords a spectacular view of the Waterton townsite and azure-hued lakes to the south, foothills to the north, prairies to the east and jutting mountain peaks to the west. Happy chatter surrounds me as I raise my binoculars to scan the valley floor and the clearings on the distant ridge.

To me, an outing in the Rocky Mountains and foothills isn't really complete until I've seen a bear. A grizzly is the ultimate, but a black is more than adequate. I'm not sure what it is about bears. Perhaps it's their size, or power. But more likely it's what they represent: the raw majesty of wilderness, and confirmation that man's hand hasn't yet wrought change to the landscape that would yank the welcome mat out from under bears and other wildlife.

No matter how hard I look, however, no bruins appear. My glasses zero in on anything remotely bear-like; they all turn into stumps, rocks, shadows and mere figments of my imagination. As I search, my mind wanders back in time, to an incident that occurred in early summer 1987 across the international border in the southeast corner of neighbouring Glacier National Park.

* * *

I was hiking into Upper Two Medicine Lake, along with guide Randy Gayner and his friend, Bruce Boody, a landscape architect from Whitefish, Montana. Fly-fishing for brook trout was the official excuse for the trip; mainly, however, it was a chance to stretch legs and imagination in gorgeous country after a few days' confinement in a conference room at the annual meeting of the Outdoor Writers Association of America.

We had taken a five-kilometre boat ride up Two Medicine Lake to the trailhead for the upper lake. A short trail led to our destination. We were on full alert the entire time. Huge clumps of fresh bear droppings dotted the path at regular intervals. Black bear tracks imprinted in the mud were dwarfed by grizzly prints featuring formidable-sized claw marks. I recalled the words of Montana outdoor writer-photographer Bill McRae, who calls grizzly tracks "nature's cure for loneliness."

We were on the final approach to the lake when a couple of hikers passed us, going fast the other way. They looked like they'd just seen a ghost. "There's a grizzly up ahead, a big one," one said before scurrying away. I looked at Gayner and Boody. They exchanged knowing glances. "Might as well go see," Gayner said. We all agreed.

I admit, however, that my mind was on two recent incidents: a few weeks earlier, a photographer was attacked and killed while taking pictures of a sow grizzly and her cubs on Elk Mountain, just 20 kilometres south of our present location. The photographer had approached too close in his zeal to capture that oh-so-perfect image. A few years later, a major outdoor magazine published his final photographs. They clearly showed the sow becoming increasingly agitated as the photographer encroached on her turf, ignoring the warning signs had cost him his life. His widow chose to have the photos published as a caution to anyone travelling in grizzly country.

Just a few days prior to our hike into Upper Two Medicine, veteran Montana game warden Lou Kis had been mauled during a botched release of a grizzly bear. The bear had been suspected of killing cattle. Captured in a culvert trap, wardens were releasing the bear when the trap flipped off the back of the truck, taking Kis with it. He landed on top of the bear. The bear severely mauled the warden before he managed to kill it with the last bullet from his six-shot service revolver. I interviewed Kis the next day in his Kalispell hospital room. Heavily bandaged, with his family at bedside, he felt deep remorse that the bear died due to human error.

Now we were about to complete the trek into the lake knowing a grizzly was nearby. We made our way slowly along the densely-treed trail, then broke out into a broad clearing that revealed the lake's sapphire-blue waters. Although the dimples of rising trout dotted the lake's mirror-like surface, fishing would wait. We had to know if the grizzly was still around. We scanned the opening for any sign. Nothing, I thought, relieved yet disappointed.

Then I saw it. Standing statue-like on a rocky outcrop below a jagged set of peaks called Pumpelly Pillar, the bear was big, blonde and, at about 500 metres, too close for my comfort. It appeared to have been carved from the stone itself. As we watched, we discussed how long the grizzly would take to reach us if it wanted to. Not long enough, we concluded. "This is really as close as we want him to get," Gayner said in classic understatement.

The bear returned our stares for several minutes. Then it began to move slowly down the ridge towards the lake, and us. Powerful muscles rippling and shoulder hump rolling like a Brahma bull's, the bear lumbered over the rocks with the ease and agility of a mountain goat. As it came closer, its shaggy yellow coat showed splashes of chocolate-brown fur on its legs and underbelly. "Probably just wants to get a better look at us,"

Gayner told the hushed group. "We'll just stay put until we see where he wants to go. It's best to give him all the room he wants." Nobody argued.

Thankfully, the bear didn't head directly toward us. It nonchalantly quartered westward toward an aspen and pine forest. The distance between us was about 275 yards when the grizzly entered the trees and vanished. After watching several minutes without seeing any sign of the bear, we decided it was safe to start fishing. For hours, we caught and released dozens of trout on silver spoons, Montana nymphs and Humpy dry flies. But the grizzly never left our minds.

In mid-afternoon, Gayner stretched out for a nap at the edge of the forest just behind us. Boody went for a hike. The three of us remaining had the lake to ourselves. I idly cast a fly to the edge of a drop-off ledge, peacefully lost in empty thought. Suddenly, the sound of rustling leaves stopped me cold in mid-cast. Something was rushing through the trees behind me. My heart went into overdrive and I dropped my fly rod. Turning to face what I was sure was the blonde grizzly, I tried to conjure up a defence. Instantly, I felt my face turn crimson. Two red squirrels playfully chased each other in the dry undergrowth within a few feet of the still-dozing guide. Chuckling, I silently gave thanks nobody had witnessed my reaction. We never saw the bear again.

That evening, we walked out in the dark. We'd fished so late that we missed the last boat heading back up the lake to our vehicle. We encountered a black bear with three cocker spaniel-sized cubs and a lone black bear, but gave each enough space that no problems developed. The day had been a success, fishing and bruin-wise.

* * *

A few weeks later, the phone rang in the Fish and Wildlife office in Pincher Creek, just 48 kilometres north of Waterton Park. Rancher Lee Nelson reported a grizzly had stepped into a spring-loaded leg snare the night before on the Poll Haven community pasture, a poplar and lodgepole pine forest abutting Waterton to the west and Glacier Park to the southwest.

At the time, the pasture was a hotbed of controversy involving rancher complaints about livestock being killed by grizzlies they felt originated from Waterton and Glacier parks. Officials on both sides of the border take a keen interest in what happens to grizzlies in Poll Haven; each grizzly removed from the pasture — either relocated or killed — means one less bear in the parks' ecosystem, a major piece of the ecological puzzle removed forever.

Officer Jan Allen had set a leghold snare a few days earlier after Nelson found one of his cows with deep gashes in its flank, suggestive of bear claws. The cow's calf was missing. After Allen hung up the phone with Nelson, he contacted other officers who were part of his special bear response team.

Tension was thick inside the three green-and-white government trucks as they slowly snaked along a muddy trail, threading through thick stands of trees. Entering a small clearing, an awesome display of power greeted the cavalcade; it looked like a small tornado had struck. Underbrush and willows had been uprooted and tossed about in the trees at the far end of the clearing. Poplars several inches thick were snapped like toothpicks. Long, deep gashes marked thicker trees, many of which were gnawed halfway through.

The source of the devastation lay partially hidden in a shallow crater gouged out of the forest floor. A shaggy-coated, chocolate-brown grizzly of about 500 pounds watched us warily, exhausted from a long night spent struggling to free its right leg from the heavy steel cable anchored to a stout tree. The bear's eyes blazed defiantly. While the other officers trained their slug-loaded shotguns and high-powered rifles on the trussed grizzly, Allen prepared a tranquillizer gun. The bear was in a relatively easy-to-reach spot. Allen knew too well the feeling of having the hair on the back of his neck stand straight up while crawling through jungle-like vegetation to check a snare hidden deep in bush where a grizzly is suspected of being. The added uncertainty of not knowing whether a grizzly is indeed caught, and how securely, creates extra tension.

The grizzly stood. He suspiciously eyed the people 60 yards away. Index fingers tightened against triggers; nerves were drum-tight. Then the bear charged. Right now, without warning. All eyes were riveted on the cable, which suddenly appeared thin as thread. The rage-powered bear released an angry bellow as he stretched the cable to the limit. A later review of my motor-drive assisted photographs showed the initial series in perfect focus, followed by several of nothing more than an indistinguishable black blur. My nerves failed the test.

We all tensed, everyone thinking the same questions but having no time or ability to vocalize them. Would the cable hold, or had the bolts securing it to the tree somehow loosened? Had the bear chewed through the anchor tree overnight? The answers came mercifully fast as the cable snapped the bear backwards. Defeated, he retreated into the trees, a low growl rumbling like thunder across the clearing.

Backed up by his armed officers, Allen carefully moved in and fired the tranquillizer dart into the bear's rump. At the solid hit, the grizzly angrily whirled to face the source of the sudden sharp sting. Within minutes, the big bear was sprawled in sleep. It was a healthy male with strong teeth and long scimitar-like claws that could bring down any prey it chose. There was no obvious clue why he had chosen Grade A beef, except of course that it was there. The officers hoisted the bear into the steel culvert trap and unceremoniously towed him away to a new mountain home in west-central Alberta, where his future was far from secure.

Grizzlies still kill the odd cow on the Poll Haven and on other land flanking Waterton Park. Thankfully, on average, the numbers are down from the late 1980s. Some area landowners consider grizzlies a curse; others accept them as a fact of life, a corollary of living near the understated natural jewel that is the Waterton-Glacier International Peace Park.

* * *

From our lunch-stop perch atop a windswept ridge, we could see the rugged Poll Haven pasture stretched out to the southeast. What we couldn't see was a real-life drama involving yet another grizzly that was playing just a mile north of us. A provincial conservation officer was in the process of live-trapping and tranquillizing a 272-kilogram male bear that had been hanging around a granary on a neighbouring ranch.

A few days earlier, the farmer had been inside the granary shovelling pelletized cattle feed. He heard what he thought was a cow rubbing against the outside of the building. A moment later, a grizzly bear ripped open a wood panel and thrust its head inside. The rancher yelled, loudly, and whacked the bear on the head with a shovel, causing it to make a hasty departure.

That night, cattle got into the granary and gorged themselves on the high-protein pellets, scattering them across the area. The pellets also proved to be irresistible for more hungry bears trying to put on a layer of fat for winter. When the rancher and a couple of cattle buyers showed up the next day, two adult grizzlies also arrived on the scene. They stood up on their hind legs less than 90 metres away.

The trio of humans backed off and called for help. Within four days, Fish and Wildlife had trapped three adult grizzlies. They were relocated to the Castle River watershed several kilometres away. After officers had trapped the first three bears, they thought that was that. But on the day Van Tighem led the hike up the ridge overlooking the ranch, a final check of the culvert trap revealed one last bear, a big male. The officers fitted all four bears — two males, two females — with ear tags and transmitters that give off telemetry radio signals that trace their movements. The officers also erected an electric fence around the granary to discourage more visits from hungry opportunistic bruins.

Not many years ago, those bears would have received the same fate as the grizzly sentenced to banishment for killing Lee Nelson's cow and calf on Poll Haven. They would have been moved far away, to the Nordegg or Swan Hills areas of northern Alberta. In fact, within just two years in the mid-1990s, a total of 18 local grizzlies had been shot as problem bears, hunted or relocated.

All that changed in 1997 with introduction of a new provincial grizzly bear management strategy for the region, where an estimated 60 grizzlies live in a broad area encompassing the Oldman River basin drainage.

Richard Quinlan, an Alberta government wildlife biologist, says that moving grizzlies far out of their home ranges likely doomed many to death as they tried to become established in new, unfamiliar territories. Many probably died of starvation or were killed by local bears, which would have viewed the newcomers as threats. Even so, Quinlan says it's important for the government to respond decisively to landowners' bear complaints; otherwise, he notes, some bears might just end up dead. "There is a strong suggestion people would take the matter into their own hands."

Managing the region's grizzly bears is a multi-jurisdictional challenge. Grizzlies that frequent Waterton Park move freely between the Flathead River valley in southeastern British Columbia and northern Montana, Glacier Park and private land in Alberta east and north of Waterton. As part of the new management strategy being implemented by provincial and federal officials, efforts are made to reduce grizzly bear predation on livestock. These include convincing ranchers to keep cattle out of isolated pastures in early spring, when grizzlies are on the prowl and eager to eat after fasting all winter. Ranchers also are encouraged to remove dead cows and calves during calving season rather than leaving them for bears to find. The popular thinking is that once a grizzly finds carrion near live cattle, the temptation to kill its next meal might be hard to resist. A limited spring season grizzly bear hunt is also considered a small price to pay to keep peace with area ranchers and stop them from shooting grizzlies as a potential threat.

The province and national park also have a program in which highway maintenance crews pick up road-killed deer, elk and moose regularly. Wildlife officials store the carcasses in deep freezers all winter. In spring, they airlift them by helicopter to remote habitats not generally frequented by human visitors. The meat piles are like stroll-in restaurants for hungry bears and wolves, that might otherwise be tempted to satisfy their hunger with easy-to-kill livestock.

Van Tighem, who has seen too many Waterton bears killed or relocated over the years, applauds the new provincial bear strategy as a "progressive approach." Many ranchers, he adds, take pride in having grizzly bears on their property because it shows they're good land stewards with a sound land management approach, including the preservation of prime wildlife habitat.

The future of grizzly bears and other wildlife in Waterton is also brighter because some private land bordering the park is now protected. The Nature Conservancy of Canada has purchased several quarter sections which it leases back to local ranchers. It also holds conservation easements on other land. Easements protect important wildlife habitat by preventing future development that would change the land, putting the squeeze on wildlife that moves between the park and adjoining private property. The general feeling is that massive development outside the park would make life impossible for grizzlies, while pushing land prices so high, ranching would no longer be viable.

Lunch over, our group resumed its trek along the rocky spine of the ridge. An excited murmur swept through the group when Van Tighem stopped to point out a slough on private land at the base of the ridge far below. Three trumpeter swans, two snow-white adults and a gray juvenile, paddled peacefully on the water.

Only three pairs of these endangered swans nest in southwestern Alberta. The rest nest in the Edson area, Elk Island National Park and near Grande Prairie in northwestern Alberta. Van Tighem considers their presence here as another validation of efforts made to protect the landscape from development.

We descended the ridge in single file, prepared to return home without having seen a grizzly or black bear. Nobody seemed disappointed. It was enough to know the bears were there, somewhere, in the trees or foraging on open mountain slopes, safe from prying eyes. Several times during the hike I'd heard mysterious rustling sounds in the forest as we passed by. But I hadn't been worried; probably just red squirrels.

Or not.

A version of this story originally appeared in the Calgary Herald in 1999.

__Bruce Masterman__ is an award-winning outdoor writer-photographer whose work has appeared in the Calgary Herald, Outdoor Canada, Fishing News, Western Outdoors, Fly Fisherman, Western Sportsman, The Conservator and Trout Canada magazines. He is also the author of Heading Out: A Celebration of the Great Outdoors in Calgary and Southern Alberta, and has contributed to two earlier books: Fish and Tell and Go to Hell: Alberta's Flyfishing Wisdom, and Assault on the Rockies: Environmental Controversies in Alberta. Bruce has received 23 national outdoor writing and photography awards from the Outdoor Writers of Canada, and won the 1998 Alberta Order of the Bighorn award. He participated in the 1997 and 1999 Writers Workshops.

The Morality
of the Grizzly Hunt

by Don H. Meredith

If you ever wonder how important wildlife and wild places are to people, just mention the phrase endangered species and watch emotions take flight. As an information officer for Alberta Environment (AENV), I receive countless inquiries about threatened and endangered wildlife from school children and teachers throughout the province.

How can we allow a fellow species to become extinct? It's a hot topic in the school curriculum, one that can trigger a wide range of emotional responses in both children and adults.

Now, add to this legitimate concern the hunting of a high profile species that's perceived to be endangered, and you have a very hot issue indeed. Such is the case with grizzly bear hunting in Alberta and British Columbia.

Before I go much further, I want to make two things clear. I am not a bear hunter, either grizzly or black bear. Although I hunt big game, bears are just not on my list of desired game animals. I can understand why others hunt them, but I don't. Secondly, although I am an employee of the Government of Alberta, the opinions I express here are my own. However, I do believe my position with government and as a non-bear hunter does provide me with a unique view of the issue.

The Facts

The grizzly bear is not endangered in either Alberta or British Columbia. Yes, it is classified as endangered in the United States, outside of Alaska. But in British Columbia the population is very healthy indeed. Here in Alberta the species is on the Blue List of wildlife species at risk. Blue List species are those that may be at risk and require special management to ensure they do not become threatened or endangered. (Red List species are at risk, Yellow and Green List Species are not at risk.) But why is the grizzly bear on the Blue List?

Of the two bear species that inhabit Alberta (black and grizzly), the grizzly is the least tolerant of human habitation. Like the wolf, it was exterminated from large tracts of North America as human settlement expanded from east to west. Ranchers and farmers did not abide a predator that threatened their livelihoods and their lives. Now, the bear is restricted to a few of the remaining wilderness areas on the continent, mostly in Montana, western Canada and Alaska. These are areas where development is either just getting under way or wilderness areas and parks have been established to conserve these remaining wild places and the animals that live in them.

Here in Alberta, we are on the eastern edge of a modern grizzly bear range which runs in a strip roughly down the western third of the province, from the extreme northwest corner through the Peace River region and the Swan Hills, to the foothills and Rocky Mountains of central and southern Alberta. In the south particularly, the range is limited on the east by agriculture, industry and urban development. These limits are absolute. The bear will not expand east from where it is now.

In the north, however, the grizzly has been expanding its range in recent years, moving out of the Rocky Mountain foothills into the boreal forest. Annual population assessments conducted by AENV indicate the grizzly bear is slowly moving into areas it hasn't occupied since the early years of the 20th century.

In 1987, biologists estimated the provincial grizzly population outside the national parks to be between 520 and 575 bears. (These are not absolute figures because it is difficult to count most big game species, especially grizzly bears. But they are the best estimates we have based on scientific survey techniques, that include capture and marking studies, and relating the results to known grizzly habitat throughout the province.) By 1995, similar studies indicated as many as 750 bears occupied the province. Today, the estimate is closer to 800 bears outside the national parks. (The three mountain parks are home to 125 to 150 grizzlies.) This is steady progress towards AENV's provincial population objective of 1,000 animals — the theoretical number of grizzlies the province is capable of supporting.

Although Alberta is on the margin of grizzly bear range, the bears are doing well here. Some might argue too well.

Why are the bears increasing in numbers and expanding into new range in the north? The answer to this question lies in the close relationship we have with the grizzly, centering around the hunt. As with most relationships, it is a two-way street.

The Hunt

There is a long tradition of hunting grizzlies in this province. In the early years, much of the hunting was unrestricted. In 1927, the government sought to control the hunt by requiring grizzlies be hunted under licence. However, the bear population continued to decline in southern Alberta. In 1969, the government closed the season in the south to protect the population there. In 1971, it restricted grizzly hunting to the spring throughout the province, eliminating the killing of bears incidental to the hunting of other big game in the fall.

In 1982, the season was reopened in selected Wildlife Management Units (WMUs) in the south where grizzlies were again becoming a nuisance. However, the number of hunters in each WMU was controlled through the introduction of limited-entry draw hunts. These draws were expanded to all grizzly hunting by 1989.

The result of these restrictions has been that fewer grizzlies are killed and more bears survive to reproduce. As bear densities increase, more individuals disperse into new habitat to find enough food and escape from aggressive males. Fortunately for the dispersing bears in the north, there is habitat to occupy.

However, there is a cost for this success. As our human population increases and more people enter grizzly habitat to exploit resources or just enjoy wild landscapes, they encounter an increasing number of grizzlies. The grizzly bear is a large predator that needs a lot of space. Fortunately, it avoids encounters with people when it can. But with more people in the bush, more encounters are unavoidable. The number of reported incidents of grizzly bears causing problems to the public in the 1970s averaged 25 per year. From 1988 to 1990, that average increased to 117 per year; and by 1993 to 1995, 303 per year.

Likewise, the number of so-called *nuisance* grizzlies handled by AENV, (those requiring transplantation to remote areas or killing because of public safety concerns,) increased from about six a year in the mid 1980s to 26 a year in 1997. Many of the bear-human encounters that led to the removal of the bears were life threatening, some ending in maulings or death.

This give and take relationship with the grizzly is one reason why the government allows hunting of this Blue List species. AENV justifies the hunt for the following reasons:

1) There is a small annual surplus of male bears available to support the season. Because AENV requires that hunters not kill bears that are found in groups of two or more individuals, most bears killed in the spring are males. Males kill and eat grizzly cubs. By reducing the number of surplus males, the population has a better chance of growing.

2) Hunting reduces the number of problem bears by killing many of those that are least wary of humans.

3) A hunted bear is a wary bear, and less likely to cause problems with people.

4) Because each grizzly killed must be registered with AENV, the harvested bears provide important information about the bear population, such as distribution and age of individuals.

5) Grizzly bear hunters are people who learn much about the bears and, as a result, are strong advocates for programs that conserve the species in Alberta.

The limitations placed on the grizzly bear hunt have not deterred hunters. On average, about 1,200 residents apply each year for 160 licences. That means it takes an average of about seven years to obtain a licence in the draw, depending upon where you apply. (It takes longer in the south; less time in the north.) Nor does getting a licence ensure success in the field. On average 12 grizzlies are shot each year, with the harvest in some years being as low as five and in others as high as 20.

What's the Fuss About?

If the taking of 12 mostly male bears each year is not affecting the population growth of grizzlies, then what is? The real culprit threatening grizzly bears is human encroachment on grizzly habitat. If you want to keep this species from becoming endangered, then you'd better protect where it lives. In order to do that, you're going to have to convince people that unlimited economic growth and grizzly bears do not mix. You can't have one with the other. If you want the grizzlies and a strong economy, then you must fit both the bear and its habitat into the economy/ environment equation.

In the last few years we have done remarkably well with the grizzly bear. Despite significant growth in human population and the economy, the grizzly population has also grown and expanded. But the accompanying increase in number of problem bear incidents shows us that there is a limit to the number of grizzlies that will be tolerated.

If habitat destruction is the main threat to grizzly bears, then why do some environmentalists single out grizzly bear hunters? Aren't we all in this together — we who want to conserve this noble symbol of our wilderness? Grizzly bear hunters are easy targets for a frustrated environmental movement. They hunt a high profile species, more for its trophy value than its meat. Is it that by attacking the hunters, protesters can take public attention away from their own inability to make a difference on the habitat protection front.

But what the hunt protesters do not understand is that by attacking one of the bear's allies, they attack the bear. While we argue over the killing of 12 bears per year, others are making irrevocable decisions about grizzly habitat that will ultimately seal the fate of the animal.

Must we hold to our ideologies so strongly that we have to sacrifice a species to prove we are each right? Perhaps we would do more for the bear if we all agree that fighting among ourselves does not solve the problem. By putting aside our differences for the animal's sake, perhaps we can learn a little bit from each other about how important this animal is to the heart and soul of the province, and work together to keep it here.

To me, the grizzly is a symbol of the quality of wilderness we still have in Alberta — true wilderness where I am not in complete control of what might happen, where I must take calculated risks in order to truly enjoy it. Experiencing such wilderness forces me to come to grips with my own mortality, and shapes my view of the world and my place in it. If the possibility of seeing a grizzly was removed from that experience, I would lose an important part of who I am and why I live in Alberta.

Is the grizzly bear hunt moral? Questions of morality are personal issues, although governments legislate morals all the time. But if hunting an animal causes someone to know and understand that animal better, and contributes to its conservation, then who am I to question the morality of the hunter? Instead, perhaps I should try to better understand that hunter, and rejoice in the fact the grizzly bear population in this province is still healthy enough to support a limited hunt.

'The Morality of the Grizzly Hunt' was originally published in the April/May 1999 issue of Alberta Outdoorsmen.

Bear With Me

by Wayne Norstrom

The first time always sticks in your mind and it certainly did with me. I was just a kid, fishing Sundance Creek west of Edson for my first ever grayling. I was catching a few too. But it wasn't the first grayling that sticks in my mind, it was the first bear.

I knew it was going to happen before it did. As I fished along the creek, which was willow-choked and brushy, I noticed a small willow moving about. There was no wind and a single willow just doesn't start shaking on its own. My imagination told me what was coming, but it was still a surprise. Bear! He appeared up the bank within meters of me. Every bear attack story I had ever read ran through my mind. Stories I had heard around the kitchen table took on new life. I could be in trouble.

Everything I knew about wildlife told me he would run as soon as he recognized me. I gave him a bit of a yell. He just looked at me. I started banging my rod and tin-framed landing net together. He looked around and came a couple of steps closer. I backed up. He followed. I don't remember how fast I could back up then, but I do know that when I backed into a U-bend on the creek, I backed across it without any problem. The bear followed me all the way back to the car. I still recall his simple curiosity and beautiful brown pelage, but at the time I wasn't reflecting on color. I was just hoping to live.

After the fact, I learned there was a minimum security camp just up the creek from where I was fishing and the bear was a regular customer at the camp. He saw me as a food supplier. My agile young mind, however, was thinking of myself as a food source. My position on top of the food chain was open to debate. So it is with bears.

The next bear that gave me trouble was west of Peace River. I was going to fish Stoney Lake, but before I even got the rod out, a bear came and debated the ownership of my still-cooking lunch.

This bear was different. He was young and mean. He came up within feet of me, popping his jaws and generally putting on a show. It turned out the bear had been ruling the lake shore for several days prior to my arrival. But on meeting me, he made a serious error in judgement. It was mid-May and I had a bear tag in my pocket and a rifle in the truck. He is now a rug.

The list goes on. I seem to be a bear magnet. I've spent over 20 years living and working with bears and I like them. They're extremely intelligent, strong, quick beyond belief, and curious. Curiosity and gluttony seems to be what puts bears in contact with humans, including anglers.

I like sharing my fishing trips with bears. A grizzly track in the mud tells me that I'm in a wild place. A black bear feeding along a lake shore seems to give the day new brightness. Bears seldom share the fishing, only the countryside. There's a lot of room for me and the bears. However, there have been and will be exceptions.

During the summer of 1998, two incidents of anglers encountering bears occurred in southwest Alberta. One angler suffered severe injuries, while the other was killed. Events like this are uncommon, but they do worry a lot of people, especially those who fish the backcountry along the Continental Divide.

"Aren't you afraid of bears, Norstrom?" is a question I get asked regularly.

"No, there's way more risk from a car accident then there is from a bear" is my reply.

"Are there bears where you fish?"

"Yeah, lots."

"Why don't you fish someplace else?"

"I like the fishing in those high streams," I argue. "Bears don't bother people."

"What do you do about bears? Do you carry bear spray?"

"I don't do anything," I say. "I just go on fishing," is my standard answer and it's the truth.

When I walk into some of the wild streams, especially those in grizzly-rich southeastern British Columbia I watch very carefully so I don't surprise anything. I'm especially careful after the bow season opens for big game. Stepping on a dead elk that a grizzly has claimed could prove interesting. I watch for fresh tracks and I watch for ravens - for anything that would suggest a food source is nearby. Once I get to the river, I fish. Sure, I see an occasional bear when I'm actually fishing, but my concentration is on the water and everything else sort of fades out. I'll bet hard cash that a lot more wildlife sees me chugging along the creek than I ever see. Going back out to the truck I'm usually too tired to care about anything. I just sort of wobble out.

Bears are a wonderful part of the outdoor experience. Seeing a bear or his track is a bonus in an already good day. A bear doesn't sit on the bank and criticize my casting style (unlike my buddies,) and I don't reflect poorly on his eating habits. We get along.

And best of all? That big grizzly track in the mud along the river's edge stops a lot of anglers. There's always good fishing on the other side of that track.

Here's to more tracks along more streams, and more bear stories around the campfire.

"Bear with Me" was originally published in the January 2000 issue of Western Sportsman magazine.

Wild crocus (pasqueflower) in the snow.   **Photo by Jim Mepham**

Last Words

The Waterton-Glacier International Peace Park has always been, above all else, a place of inspiration. The stone remains of ancient dream beds on the summit ridges of mountains are proof of this. The many ways in which modern humans have honoured this landscape offer further testimony — national park, biosphere reserve, world heritage site. This is a place that speaks to what humans can be at their very best, as members of the land community. Wallace Stegner wrote of the need for westerners to create "a society to match our scenery." The Peace Park offers continuing hope that this might, in fact, be possible.

What might such a society look like? Who would be the people that comprise it? How can we outgrow our origins?

Don Gayton's "The Mandolin and the Microscope" might seem, on first appearance, to have little to do with this place on earth. In his plea for a remarriage of science and the arts, however, Gayton captures the ultimate vision of the Waterton-Glacier International Writers Workshop.

Through writing inspired by natural beauty and informed by an in-depth understanding of our shared history, living ecosystems, and the conundrums and challenges that arise out of our often-troubled relationship with the natural world, those who participate in this special gathering every other year hope to contribute to just that kind of reintegration.

The twentieth century was a time of profound disharmony and unprecedented scientific discovery. Even as our ambitions and technology led us into an increasingly abusive relationship with the ecosystems that sustain us, our scientific curiosity led us to a deeper and more comprehensive understanding of them. Now, faced with the daunting challenge of restoring the health of wild habitats and rediscovering ourselves as people who belong to North America, rather than people who simply exploit it, we have unimaginable scientific understanding available to draw from. We also have communities of people — like the ranchers and First Nations people who live adjacent to the Peace Park — whose traditional ecological knowledge offer additional insights.

The challenge is this: how can we make ecological science understandable, and traditional knowledge accessible, to a society of people who live, for the most part, isolated from the natural world and the consequences of their collective decisions?

And the answer, at least in part, has to be through the work of writers — those who can best use language to bridge the gulf between the microscope and the mandolin, and our common futures.

Knowledge is only part of what might create a new kind of North American. Our attitudes and values need to evolve as humans increasingly crowd and dominate the natural world. In a vast natural world containing few human beings, selfishness and insensitivity would be merely personal failings. In a shrinking world crowded with people, however, personal failings accumulate into far-reaching ecological and social dysfunctions. When a park warden or ranger finally finds herself forced to kill a habituated bear, that death is really the product of a thousand human selfishnesses. Maxine Carpenter reflects on the need to find our way past superficiality into a more sustaining and insightful relationship with wild creatures. Jim Mepham challenges our ethics of wildlife photography and questions our interactions with the animals we purport to admire.

Waterton Lakes National Park. Glacier National Park. Generations uncounted have visited these wind-blasted mountains, lakes and forests for inspiration and hope. Joined together now as an International Peace Park and World Heritage Site, this place continues to offer us hope that — if we study to understand ourselves in the context of the ecosystems in which we find our being, and to adjust our behaviours in ways that will keep us worthy of those places — we can collectively find reconciliation, healing and a kind of nativeness and belonging that past generations could scarcely even imagine.

Photographic Integrity

by Jim Mepham

Several years ago I was able to sneak out of my day job as a teacher and head to Churchill, Manitoba to watch the annual migration of polar bears from their denning grounds to the ice floes where they hunt ringed seals. Photographers from far and wide visit the town of Churchill because of how easy it is to view these bruins. Large concentrations of the bears gather near the shore of Hudson Bay, awaiting the first ice of the year and an early start on the seal hunt. The bears have become accustomed to large bus-like vehicles loaded with photographers. This controlled access seems to work and the number of bear-human confrontations has decreased since the tundra viewing areas have been regulated.

Churchill takes great measures to keep bears out of town and prevent them from inadvertently finding human foods and garbage. Garbage dumps are off-limits to bears. Those that wander into town are locked up in a bear 'jail' until the Bay ices up and they can be released.

One day during my stay our guide took us to a tundra motel, a temporary overnight accommodation near a bear congregating area. At first I thought it coincidence that so many bears remained close to these units. Then I observed a rare polar bear phenomenon - the bears were eating a rock. At least that's what it looked like.

The bears kept returning to this one large rock and licking it - it was like a bear blarney stone. Since I knew feeding the animals was illegal, I had no other explanation. Maybe the minerals in the rock gave off an odor like bacon? Maybe something good tasting had accidentally spilled on the rock?

Unfortunately, neither was the case. Somebody had deliberately spilled bait on the rock to attract the bears, to make it easier for photographers to capture them on film. The unnatural concentration of bears this caused would almost certainly lead to problem bears, and problem bears inevitably are moved or destroyed.

This same situation prevails with brown bears and grizzlies in parts of Montana. Encouraged by irresponsible photographers, bears become attracted first to human foods, then to humans, and wind up being destroyed, sometimes only after a human injury or death.

An article I once read suggested getting a whole bunch of people to march through the woods and scare animals toward the lenses of waiting photographers. Another story suggests spreading peanut butter on a branch to attract small animals to the camera, or removing a toad from its natural home in a river to a backyard pool for ease of photography.

Are these actions ethical? Who's looking out for the animals? Do the ends justify the means in a photographer's quest for the perfect wildlife image? As a professional wildlife photographer, I feel I have an obligation to protect the subjects in my work from stress and danger, stronger than my obligation to serve a publisher's needs. I believe that outdoor photographers, both professional and amateur, need a code of ethics to protect the natural subjects we film. It is not enough to focus only on our desire to make a living or enjoy a hobby.

I wonder too, how fair photographic fraud is to the people who buy the magazines in which our photographs appear. Is it honest to give readers the impression that an animal who really lives on a game farm or a zoo is natural or wild? Isn't this a form of cheating? All my photographs carry a sticker noting the pictures were taken in the wild, and the animals weren't a pet or on a game farm. Such a guarantee would be a good first step in keeping the *wild* in wildlife.

There has been a lot of bad press regarding the treatment and working conditions of the wild animals in Waterton - Glacier International Peace Park. This is to set the record straight. All of the animals in the parks are treated humanely and are provided with the necessities of life: three square meals, veterinary care, etc. They are not required to be visible or in the parks for any more than 8 hours a day, with some weekends. They don't have to be up before 6:00 a.m. and aren't expected to work in the dark (except Owls). Contrary to popular belief, they are not required to pose for photographs, though many will do so upon being asked nicely and given treats. All the animals retain copyright on their image and sound recordings. The animals accept no responsibility for damage to cameras and other equipment or for injury to humans or pets.

Bighorn ram, Glacier National Park.   **Photo by Jim Mepham**

Respecting Nature

by Maxine Carpenter

Is there some sensible ground between John Wayne and Walt Disney? The question addresses the search by thoughtful people for a balanced approach to the environment in general and wildlife in particular.

The attitude of the John Wayne contingent is simplicity itself. Wildlife is the enemy. The only good bear (wolf, fox, raccoon) is a dead one. When encountering a living being which has not been domesticated for use by humans, we must eliminate it, no matter what damage this does to the balance of nature and no matter how much time and energy must be squandered in redressing the negative consequences of the war on wild things. Recently I joined a group of writers and park wardens at Waterton Lakes National Park to meet a rancher who is engaged in a total war against grizzlies, a man who has found new meaning in the phrase 'a losing battle.' He not only aspires to raise cattle in the middle of grizzly country, an enterprise which is often done successfully, but he wishes to do it without taking the most basic of precautions. He symbolizes one of the most common of human attitudes toward the creatures who share the planet with us.

The other common attitude is the Disney stance. This says that living wild creatures are adorable fuzzy toys which can be approached with cameras and bags of potato chips. It's okay, in these peoples' minds, to stop the car, chase a bear or a moose and take a photo of Junior posing beside the animal, especially if the animal is a cute baby. The fact that the baby's mother is probably nearby doesn't register with the film makers until mom rushes to the defence of her young, an act which earns her the title of problem animal, and usually condemns her to death. Since wild wolves have been relocated from Canada to Yellowstone, unprepared and uninformed park visitors have appeared in droves, seeking to *experience* the wolves.

As any thoughtful person will concede, neither of these approaches to wild things has merit. The answer to our relationship with nature can be summed up in one word: respect.

Respect allows people to admire and value wild creatures and places without destroying them and without violating their essential wildness. It allows humans to coexist with their planet mates, to learn about them and to stand in awe of them. Most importantly, it lets other life forms continue to exist.

Who knows? If we can achieve an attitude of respect for other species, we may even learn to feel it for our own.

'Respecting Nature' was originally published in the Parksville-Qualicum Morning Sun in September 1999.

Maxine Carpenter often writes about nature, travel and wildlife, her lifelong preoccupations, for a number of Vancouver Island newspapers and magazines, including the Parksville-Qualicum Morning Sun, She has won several regional and one national award for her newspaper column, which often covers environmental and wildlife issues. She has written a guide to freshwater fishing on Vancouver Island, for use by provincial parks personnel and an article for BearWatch Journal. Maxine was a participant in the 1999 Writers Workshop.

The Microscope and the Mandolin
Reintegrating Art and Science

by Don Gayton

As lute-maker Calastro Parochia of Padua put the finishing touches on the first mandolin, Marcello Malphigi of nearby Bologna explored the potential of the newly-invented compound microscope. This was Italy in the 17th century, a time of Renaissance symmetry and intercourse. Luthiers, of course, conferred with their musicians, and instrument-makers with their scientists, but they also worked across disciplines. These folks lived in the same culture, and frequently across the street from one another. Although the record does not show, composers like Antonio Vivaldi might have gazed astonished at magnified fleas, and we know the great microscopist Robert Hooke studied painting and music.

If I may use the microscope and the mandolin as metaphors for science and art, then I can say truthfully that they were once thoroughly entwined, and not the clinically separate entities they are now. Ecosystem restoration — this young and Quixotic science of repairing damaged ecologies — seems an unlikely candidate to effect the reunion of art and science, but that is precisely what I wish to propose.

The mere attempt to write about such a union presents difficulties. Should I use self-aware and expository language, in the tradition of Robert

Hooke's 1665 book *Micrographia,* or should I wax lyrical and allegorical, as in Vivaldi's *Concerto in C Major for Mandolin and Strings*?

The potential union is further complicated by definitions. Science is easy to define; art is tricky. Webster defines it as "the conscious use of skill and creative imagination in the production of esthetic objects." "Esthetics" is in turn defined by "beauty," which in turn leads back to either "pleasuring the senses" or "exalting the mind and spirit." Human artifice is also required, with constructed representations of things, rather than those things themselves, being considered art. As a person with a lifelong obsession with natural landscapes, particularly grasslands, I take issue with that part of the definition. When I stand in the bluebunch ranges of the Chilcotin, high plains blue grama of Colorado, or the fescue-danthonia of Alberta's Eastern Slopes, my senses are pleasured directly, my mind and my spirit are exalted, and there is no human artifice in between. If natural elements are naturally placed, do they qualify as art?

My primary thesis is that science and art, which have been traditionally and clinically separate from one another for close to 300 years, have now reached the stage of consenting adulthood. In other words, they can now cohabit, and fear neither spousal abuse, codependency or spiraling sinkholes of interdisciplinary corruption. Born and raised in the same Renaissance neighborhood, and with common roots reaching far back into human history, the mandolin will now have nothing to do with the microscope. We are slowly waking up to the vast dislocation this separation has caused, yet no one has any idea how to bring art and science back together.

Ecosystem restoration is a unique new activity, signifying a number of historic turning points. That groups of people come together to attempt the rehabilitation of ruined pieces of pond or desert or grassland acknowledges that earth's resources have limits, that the biblical model of human domination of nature is flawed, and that a new and lasting relationship between humans and nature can be worked out. Because those profound turning points are implicit in the activity, I know in my guts that ecosystem restorationists are the chosen ones to effect the reunion of art and science, to arrange a safe and informal meeting ground, a kind of box social for these two eligible but socially inept adults. They can discreetly trick science and art into getting to know each other. Like unattached friends, art and science will respond much better to informal events *(a bunch of us are going out to pull weeds and need your help,)* than to formal proposals *(why don't you join a singles' club?)*. My guess is that once science and art get to know each other, the two will fall into bed and start ripping each other's clothes off with a lustiness and abandon that will truly shock us all.

To be historically accurate, I should revise this single consenting adults metaphor to one of a married couple who have endured a lengthy, 300-year trial separation, who want to get back together, but is each too proud to ask. So ecosystem restorationists need to act as matchmaker, reconciler and marriage counselor to the microscope and the mandolin.

I do need to be forthright and honest here, and admit that we're not talking, right now anyway, about a marriage of equals. Science has got all the marbles, and has all the weight of cost-benefit, rationality, legisled requirements, standard deviation, and canonical analysis to bring as a dowry. In spite of all these sparkling riches, though, there is worry in the microscope family. All is not sweetness and light in the house of science.

Look at all the phenomenal energy and acuity science has trained on nature. We can record the neural twitches of a moth's antenna by exposing it to vanishingly small quantities of semiochemical molecules. We can fractionate the contents of a single plant cell into a dozen different categories. But has all our magnificent scientific achievement resulted in a corresponding growth in our willingness to care about landscapes, and ecosystems? About the salt marsh or the tule elk or the leopard frog? No, it has not, or very bloody little, considering the time and resources that science consumes. Scientists and managers continued to put dagger after dagger into the heart of the Columbia, the greatest salmon-bearing river in the world, long after they knew their hydroelectric dams were killing it. There is an underlying scientific fear of passion, of commitment exceeding the bounds of rational process, and a shying-away from the sacred. We perform instead a kind of blinkered, cybernetic management, carefully doling out equitable portions to competing resource users, but never consulting the ecological doomsday clock.

Art can contribute to the growth of caring about the landscape, and it can help science learn how to care. We live in an era when the majority of us do not have the casual childhood experience of forming bonds with natural landscapes, and this is where art can step in, to provide analogues of that experience.

Let's ask ourselves the question, why restore ecosystems? Not how do we restore them, or what to restore to, but why? Why do we fight to preserve wilderness areas, to what end? What is the overarching metaphor? What makes people bust their asses with grant proposals, weed wrenches and vegetation transects, all for no economic gain? Science can't answer that question, but art can, and to take this a step farther, art must. Art, esthetics and non-rational activity are a prerequisite for ecosystem restoration. They are the means by which we learn to care enough, to bond to natural landscapes, to believe in them, to commit to learning their processes, their secrets and their maladies. Science without art is mere Onanistic exercise, but art without science is also negative, a conscious turning away from huge fields of human endeavor.

I have very few practical suggestions on how to bring about this re-marriage of the microscope and the mandolin. All I know is that it must first happen at the level of the lonely and ostracized individual artist or scientist who, on his or her own, attempts some pathetic and highly irresponsible crossover project. Once that first crossover work is done, this person can then perhaps move forward into some quixotic and ridiculous collaboration with an equally disturbed counterpart from across the great art/science divide. Then dozens, no hundreds of these fusion events must occur before this marriage has any hope of happening at the social, educational and institutional level.

I feel a desperate need to give something back to these natural landscapes that have awed me with their painful beauty, humbled me with their massive complexity, and have permanently claimed chunks of my soul. An outdoor remarriage of the microscope and the mandolin, on restoration ground, would be a wonderful gift.

Don Gayton *is a range ecologist and the author of two award-winning books,* Landscapes of the Interior: A Re-exploration of Nature and the Human Spirit, *and* The Wheatgrass Mechanism: Science and Imagination in the Western Canadian Landscape. *He has had articles published in such magazines as* Harrowsmith, Canadian Geographic *and* Equinox, *and has written, published and presented many papers. He currently works in ecological restoration for the British Columbia Ministry of Forests at Nelson, B.C. Don was a participant at the 1997 and 1999 Writers Workshops*